ion Services

Forensic Practice

Series Editors: Dr Adrian Needs, University of Portsmouth, and Professor Graham Towl, HM Prison Service and National Probation Service/University of Birmingham and University of Portsmouth

The books in this series take a research-based applied psychological approach to a wide range of topics in forensic psychology, and are aimed at a range of forensic practitioners working in a variety of settings. They will be of use to all those working within the criminal process, whether academics or practitioners.

Published

Psychology in Prisons
Edited by Graham Towl

Applying Psychology to Forensic Practice
Edited by Adrian Needs and Graham Towl

Psychology in Probation Services
Edited by David Crighton and Graham Towl

Psychology in Probation Services

Edited by

David Crighton and Graham Towl

BPS Blackwell

BLACKWELL PUBLISHING
350 Main Street, Malden, MA 02148-5020, USA
108 Cowley Road, Oxford OX4 1JF, UK
550 Swanston Street, Carlton, Victoria 3053, Australia

The right of David Crighton and Graham Towl to be identified as the Authors
of the Editorial Material in this Work has been asserted in accordance with
the UK Copyright, Designs, and Patents Act 1988.

First published 2005 by Blackwell Publishing Ltd

Library of Congress Cataloging-in-Publication Data

Psychology in probation services / edited by David Crighton and Graham Towl.
   p.   cm. – (Forensic practice)
   'A BPS Blackwell book.'
   Includes bibliographical references and index.
   ISBN 1-4051-2469-5 (pbk.: alk. paper)
   1. Prisoners–Mental health services–Great Britain.   2. Mentally ill offenders–
Mental health services–Great Britain.   3. Criminals–Mental health services–Great
Britain.   4. Probation–Great Britain.   5. Forensic psychology–Great Britain.
I. Crighton, David A., 1964–   II. Towl, Graham J.   III. Series.
RC451.4.P68P745   2005
364.6'3'019–dc22

                                                           2004009015

A catalogue record for this title is available from the British Library.

Set in 10/12.5pt Photina
by Graphicraft Limited, Hong Kong
Printed and bound in the United Kingdom
by MPG Books Ltd, Bodmin Cornwall

The publisher's policy is to use permanent paper from mills that operate a sustainable
forestry policy, and which has been manufactured from pulp processed using acid-free
and elementary chlorine-free practices. Furthermore, the publisher ensures that the
text paper and cover board used have met acceptable environmental accreditation
standards.

For further information on
Blackwell Publishing, visit our website:
www.blackwellpublishing.com

Contents

Foreword

Professor Herschel Prins, Universities of Loughborough and Birmingham

In responding to the Editors' very gratifying request to produce a Foreword to this substantial and highly informative collection of contributions I was led to reflect briefly on one or two of the more significant changes that seemed to me to have occurred in the criminal justice and mental health care systems in the past fifty years. Fifty plus years represent the time I have spent working in the systems. When I began my career (then, as a probation officer) in criminal justice way back in 1952, the now often forgotten Criminal Justice Act of 1948 had not long been implemented. Some of its provisions were, in fact quite groundbreaking. For example, the abolition of corporal punishment as a penal sanction, the introduction of a revised form of preventive detention (PD) – subsequently to go through numerous revisions (extended sentences of one kind or another), the new (and comparatively short-lived), sentence of Corrective Training (CT), and a more forward-looking sentence of Borstal Training. Of particular interest to today's forensic psychiatric practitioners was the introduction of a formal power to make treatment for minor mental conditions a condition of a probation order. Parole was introduced in its early guise in 1967; Crown Courts replaced the ancient courts of Quarter Session and Assize in 1971. Determination of responsibility for crime (or, to be more precise, erosion of it), received impetus with the introduction of the Homicide Act of 1957. Those who espoused its introduction with some zeal could not, perhaps, have foreseen the complex situations that would arise involving the differing perspectives of law, psychiatry and psychology. These issues involving mental disorders received further attention in the Mental Health Act of 1959 which did away with longstanding lunacy legislation, the 1959 Act being replaced by the Acts of 1983 and 1995. Currently we are faced with the possibility of a further enactment – one that has aroused much controversy and concern. In the last two decades we have witnessed not only a steady rise in the prison population and a large number of inquiries into both institutional and community mental health care, but a bewildering array (deluge would perhaps be a better word) of sentencing legislation. Some of this has been ill thought through and has led to frustration and anxiety on the part of sentencers, both professional and 'lay'. As Macduff says in another context in Macbeth: 'Confusion now has made his masterpiece' (Act 2, Sc. 3, 1.59). I could continue in this vein and my choice of examples has, perforce, been highly selective and some may consider idiosyncratic. So be it. When I worked in probation the service was small and essentially local. Some of its practitioners both at grassroots and management levels were 'loners' in their practice. Standards were patchy but, for the most part, indicative of dedication, the latter being encouraged and enhanced by the effort of a small band of Home Office Probation Inspectors. The availability of psychiatric and psychological assistance was, for the most part, slender; one had to seek out a well-disposed and interested local general psychiatrist or educational psychologist for help with difficult cases. The professions of forensic psychology and psychiatry were in their infancy. It is highly satisfying to record that they have now attained their 'majorities'. It would, however be erroneous to assume that the discipline of psychology played no part, for example, in the education and training of probation officers. (Psychiatry had been involved for many years.) The former specialist Home Office ('Rainer House') probation training course drew on the work of both child and social psychologists and the trainers drew students' attention to such pioneering works as Cyril Burt's *The Young Delinquent.*

Probation work has gone through many 'sea changes' and is now a complex endeavour in terms of both its organization and its practice. This is well attested to in the various contributions in this volume. Psychologists have helped the service to focus its work more sharply, particularly on 'what works', and provided facilitation and support to its remit for public protection and the need for well-thought-out risk assessment and management. As this book demonstrates, psychology now has an integral as distinct from an adjunctive part to play in this arena aided by the linking of penal and community services in a more clearly delineated fashion through the implementation of the National Offender Management Service (NOMS). It would be a mistake to think that the idea of a combined correctional service is entirely new. (When I served in the Probation Inspectorate in the mid-1960s such an idea was being mooted even then!) The contributions in this book fill out in clear but modest fashion the various ways in which psychology can further the work of the service as part of the ever-changing criminal justice and forensic mental health enterprises. Above all, the contributors demonstrate ably that there are no 'quick fixes' – a point that should be noted and digested by politicians of all parties. In the final analysis the core concern has to be the management and control of the individual offender. As the Editors rightly emphasise 'Psychology is about people, their mental life and behaviour' (p. 00[19 ms]).

Editors' Preface

This collection of chapters is intended to capture some of the range of work under development and delivered by the emergent applied psychology services in probation.

The collection begins with a chapter by Graham Towl and David Crighton who give an overview of the development of services in probation over recent years. They also provide food for thought with regard to future possible developments.

In Chapter 2 David Crighton outlines the context of the National Probation Service (NPS) links and work with the courts. He goes on to describe the developing area of psychologists work with the courts. David concludes with a number of helpful observations about the potential role of psychologists. Sharon Mayer, in Chapter 3, brings a fresh perspective to the forensic context of probation work by sharing her ideas on the potential and current contributions of counselling psychologists in probation services. The role of counselling psychologists has perhaps been underplayed in Criminal Justice in the past, this is corrected with some useful insights into the range of therapeutic practice that counselling psychologists can bring to bear on the work.

Andrew Bates has spent much of his professional life working with sex offenders and describes such work (Chapter 4) in a community setting, giving an account of some of the benefits of partnership, multi-agency and multi-disciplinary perspectives. Chapter 5 is on risk assessment. Some key concepts in the logic of risk assessment and management processes are explicated including a discussion of the current vogue for structural risk assessment tests. Sara Casado and Amy Beck, in Chapter 6, describe some of their involvement in work to address suicide and intentional self-injury when working as practitioners in the NPS. They describe the importance of multi-agency approaches, cognitive behavioural approaches and staff training and support.

Chapter 7, by Anne Williams, gives an overview of groupwork-based interventions aimed at reducing the risk of reoffending of participants. Coverage includes a range of policy and practice issues. Derval Ambrose, in Chapter 8, gives a more detailed account of 'cognitive skills' groupwork including an intervention for addressing substance abuse. She emphasizes the importance of evidence-based practice and gives a measured review of evaluation data.

Next, in Chapter 9, Tania Tancred covers the important and rapidly developing area of Multi-agency Public Protection Arrangements (MAPPA). It is evident that this is likely to be a potentially high area of growth in the prospective work of forensic psychologists contributing to the general domain of risk management and public protection. Chapter 10 is on domestic violence work with male offenders. The authors, Jane Lindsay, Dermot Brady and Debbie McQueirns give an overview of the context of such work and describe the structure of interventions to address this important area of practice. They complete their chapter with reflections on possible future contributions from applied psychological services. Debbie McQueirns describes the 'lifer system' in Chapter 11 with a clear focus on the role of the NPS with life sentence offenders. She finishes her chapter with an exhortation to include psychologists in advice and decision-making at each stage of the life sentence that she describes.

The final chapter in this collection sets out to contextualize the work of applied psychologists working in probation services in terms of effective partnership working. This echoes the strategic framework document for applied psychological services in prisons and probation (HM Prison Service and National Probation Service, 2003a), which emphasizes the importance of a greater diversity of applied psychologists and the need for prison and probation staff to work in closer partnership.

Applied psychological services in probation on a national basis are in their comparatively early stages of development. This collection of chapters is intended as a contribution to provide a record of existing service developments but also ideas and potential innovations for the future.

David Crighton and Graham Towl

Series Editors' Preface

The first volume in this series (Towl, 2003a) presented a collection of largely descriptive chapters, which outlined the work of psychologists in prisons. The present volume adopts a similar approach to areas of involvement by psychologists within the new and developing context of the National Probation Service, an organization that only began to employ psychologists directly in 2001.

The chapters give a picture of recent, current and potential areas of contribution. The book is not a manual for psychologists working in probation settings. Nor is it intended to provide in any comprehensive sense a critical evaluation of practice, theory or research, although some chapters contain elements of this. It does, however, provide a wealth of contextual and procedural information, much of which centres upon multi-disciplinary and multi-agency working in relation to offenders in the community and the courts. This should be of value both to new and aspiring practitioners and to individuals who have gained their professional experience in other areas of the criminal justice system.

An important thread of continuity with the first volume is apparent in the variety of work that is described. There is also a strong resonance with the second volume in the series (Needs & Towl, 2004), which gives accounts of applications of psychology across a range of forensic contexts and concerns. A particular theme of that book is that psychology, as practised in the settings concerned with criminal and civil justice should draw upon the insights, findings and methods of a wide range of traditions within psychology: from organizational to cognitive, from social to developmental. The present volume takes this further. Whereas the first two books had much to say about 'forensic psychology', the present one contextualizes the specialism as an area of applied psychology.

This was prefigured in the final chapter of the second volume (Towl, 2004) and has become a cornerstone of policy for recruitment of psychologists in HM Prison Service and the National Probation Service (HM Prison Service and National Probation Service, 2003a). Several chapters in the present volume refer to the very positive development of a much more eclectic range of psychological specialisms and services being delivered by individuals with a background in, for example, counselling or health psychology. The first chapter provides the rationale for this approach. Overall, the description and exemplification of this approach to the provision of an applied psychological service is possibly one of the book's major points of interest.

There have been precedents, or at least congruous developments, elsewhere. These include the increasing employment since the 1990s of counselling, health and, in some cases, forensic psychologists into areas that were formerly the preserve of clinical psychologists. In addition, the British Psychological Society project on Occupational Standards in Applied Psychology identified large commonalities in the competencies exercised by psychologists from different fields. Unsurprisingly, though, it was recognized that specialisms had differences in aspects of their knowledge base and in their familiarity with certain contexts.

The success of the policy of importing members of other specialisms into 'forensic' areas will depend upon their delivery of good quality psychological services that are relevant to the needs of the organization. Interestingly, success in this endeavour might renew interest in the possibility of a generic training in applied psychology at postgraduate level, followed by specialization, followed by a greater degree of lateral transfer than is common at present. The essential unity of applied psychology may be affirmed.

To the extent that maximizing the contributions of applied psychologists from a variety of fields constitutes a radical approach, there is perhaps something appropriate in pioneering this approach in an area that has until recently been relatively unexplored territory. This book is an important first step in mapping this territory and charting explorations to date.

Adrian Needs and Graham Towl

Revolving Doors

No authors' royalties are payable for this text. These all go to Revolving Doors, a charity that does valued work in supporting offenders and former offenders in the community.

Revolving Doors Agency is an independent charity set up in 1993 to demonstrate new ways of working with people with mental health and multiple needs in contact with the criminal justice system. It runs experimental link worker schemes, which go into police stations, prisons and courts to support those people who fall through the net of mainstream services.

Link workers aim to help this vulnerable and sometimes chaotic group achieve a greater degree of stability in the community by improving their access to crucial services such as GPs, housing and social care. They make use of assertive outreach techniques and provide casework support as a whole team to those with the most complex needs. Joint working with mainstream agencies is key to the approach and includes being based with a local team. Staff backgrounds include social work, nursing, occupational therapy and supported housing, making a range of skills available to clients who need to navigate complex social, health and benefits systems.

Prison provides an opportunity to engage vulnerable people when they most need it, with the aim of establishing a supportive relationship prior to release. Referrals are taken of people returning to the local community after short sentence or remand. Those identified at police stations are also supported throughout their time in prison and afterwards. The key is to bridge the gap between community and criminal justice services, for example link workers provide training for prison officers to increase their awareness of mental health needs and of ways to gain access to services in the community.

The agency uses the learning from the schemes to assist other organizations seeking to set up or develop similar projects at the interface of mental health and criminal justice.

More information on: www.revolving-doors.co.uk
E: admin@revolving-doors.co.uk
T: 020 7242 9222

Contributors

Derval Ambrose – National Probation Service, London area
Andrew Bates – National Probation Service, Thames Valley area
Amy Beck – National Probation Service, Surrey area
Dermot Brady – National Probation Service, London area
Sara Casado – National Probation Service, Sussex area
David Crighton – Deputy Head of Psychology (Prisons and Probation) and Visiting Professor of Forensic Psychology, London Metropolitan University
Trudy Leeson – National Probation Service, Derbyshire area
Jane Lindsay – University of Portsmouth
Debbie McQueirns – National Probation Service, London area
Sharon Mayer – Devon Partnership NHS Trust, formerly National Probation Service, Devon and Cornwall area
Tanya Tancred – National Probation Service, Kent area
Graham Towl – Head of Psychology (Prisons and Probation) and Visiting Professor of Forensic Psychology, University of Birmingham and University of Portsmouth
Anne Williams – HM Prison Service and National Probation Service, West Midlands area, formerly NPS Wales

Acknowledgements

As editors we are particularly grateful to Mark Harris of Victim Support for reading and commenting on the draft of this textbook. The text has significantly benefited as a result of the process. We are also grateful to Mary Smith, seconded to the North East Probation Consortium, for her helpful comments on an earlier draft of this text. Any errors that remain are of course attributable to the editors and authors.

As editors we would like to acknowledge the encouragement and support from the production team at BPS Blackwell and, in particular Sarah Bird, for her enthusiasm for this publication.

Finally we would like to thank colleagues in applied psychology. Their thoughts and comments over the years have shaped our thinking on the ways in which applied psychology might more efficiently deliver effective work across the National Offender Management Service.

Chapter One

Applied Psychological Services in the National Probation Service for England and Wales

Graham Towl and David Crighton

Introduction

Very recently a new approach to bringing together the work of the prison service and the probation service has been announced (Home Office, 2003a). The Government response to the report has stressed the importance of the further development of an integrated 'offender centred' management service across prisons and probation. Thus from June 2004 it is intended that there will be a new National Offender Management Service (NOMS) with responsibility for reducing reconvictions and punishing offenders (Home Office, 2004). In view of these announcements of some key structural changes it will remain unclear for a time precisely what the new organizational arrangements will mean for probation staff. The announced changes referred to above sit well with the strategic framework for applied psychological services in prisons and probation (HM Prison Service and National Probation Service, 2003a). An underpinning theme of the framework is the ongoing development of a closer partnership working across prisons and probation.

Overall our view is that the likelihood will be that more applied psychological staff will be needed to work in probation services. This is partly because of a likely renewed focus on risk management – where applied psychologists can make some significant contributions (see Chapers 5 and 9). It is also because there is a significant and arguably undue skew in terms of psychological staffing in the direction of HM Prison Service who employ around 800 psychological staff compared to fewer than 40 nationally in the National Probation Service.

This is an exciting time in the development of correctional services: opportunities abound for applied psychological contributions to further improving service delivery.

Background

The National Probation Service was formally launched in April 2001. It was at this point that the first joint recruitment of trainee forensic psychologists occurred in partnership with HM Prison Service. Twelve months earlier the first joint head of psychological services for prisons and probation had been recruited in preparation for the joint service developments.

Historically probation services across England and Wales had tended to access applied psychological services through health providers and the private sector. Thus no career infrastructure existed for 'in-house' psychological services. Currently there is a 'mixed economy' for such service provision, with a growing infrastructure for 'in-house' services. However, the precise future development of services is by no means a foregone conclusion. Psychologists working in this newly developed area will need to demonstrate their cost effectiveness and ability to deliver good quality services that meet the needs of community-based services.

Other chapters in this book give the most up to date picture of some key emerging areas of applied psychological practice in probation settings. In this chapter the strategic framework for psychological services across prisons and probation is outlined. An overview of some of the work in probation services is also given. Finally, there is a focus on future possibilities in terms of service developments in the light of recent organizational changes.

A Strategic Framework for Psychological Services

In early 2003 the Strategic Framework for Psychological Services in prisons and probation (HM Prison Service and National Probation Service, 2003a) was distributed. Underpinning the framework document were three key themes associated with good quality service provision and professional policy and practice. First, what has become known in political parlance as the 'modernization agenda', which refers to the reforming of public services. Second, there is a clear and renewed focus on ensuring that psychologists receive appropriate training, supervision and Continuing Professional Development (CPD). Third, the need to link the work of applied psychologists from whatever specialism to the strategic and corporate plans for both organizations. The framework provides a clear direction for operational managers in probation services and psychologist colleagues to navigate the change process to enhance service delivery. The approach is consistent with recommended best practices in delivering change in public services successfully (CMPS, 2002).

Area psychologists

The strategic framework begins with an account of the initial professional policy and practice issues, which began to be more effectively addressed during 2000 and 2001. One pivotal organizational change in improving service delivery at all levels was the setting up of a national structure of 'area psychologists' in HM Prison Service. The area psychologists played (and continue to play) a critical role in ensuring the implementation of the three-pronged agenda underpinning the strategic framework both within prisons and also as a national network of senior contacts for probation services. In Wales the area psychologist post was a jointly funded appointment across probation and prisons.

Applied psychologists: improving professional diversity

Traditionally applied psychologists in prisons have tended to be predominantly in the forensic specialism. This is beginning to change with the growth in numbers of counselling psychologists particularly in women's prisons. There is also the beginning of the development of a health psychology service, for example in the London area. Occupational psychologists in HM Prison Service although geographically dispersed have made some significant contributions to the work of the organization, for example in the challenging area of staff recruitment. The increased diversity in professional backgrounds and perspectives bodes well for the future for both HM Prison Service and the National Probation Service.

Staff diversity

On the subject of staff diversity this is a very challenging area where the psychology profession has not achieved as much as it perhaps should have. To begin to address this there is a developing two-tracked system to the training of psychologists. The most common track is from the higher education sector directly into psychological assistant posts in prisons with a promotion route to what is termed the trainee psychologist grade. Such candidates already have the Graduate Basis for Registration (GBR) with the British Psychological Society (BPS) and may join the trainee psychologist grades directly. The psychology graduate population is not particularly diverse, with a significant skew towards affluent young white women.

Those universities with a stronger track record on diversity issues (such as social class, ethnicity, disability and gender) are increasingly being targeted by area psychologists when considering invitations to speak to undergraduates about prospective careers in applied psychology in probation and prisons. Nationally about 80 per cent of psychology undergraduates are women and this is reflected in the gender breakdown of applicants for posts in probation services and in the prison service.

Another starting point for those wishing to qualify as applied psychologists in whatever specialism (clinical, counselling, educational, forensic, health or occupational), is as a candidate with 5 GCSEs working as a psychological assistant.[1] At this level of educational attainment there is likely to be a greater diversity of backgrounds amongst candidates. Increasingly there are opportunities for undertaking the educational attainment necessary for the Graduate Basis for Registration with the British Psychological Society (BPS) funded whilst working as a psychological assistant. Although psychological assistants are not routinely employed by the probation service at the present time there is scope for their further development whether as direct employees or as secondees.

The area of diversity has been relatively neglected within applied psychology, in contrast to developments within the National Probation Service (NPS) where diversity has increasingly been put at the heart of organizational functioning (Home Office, 2003a). This issue is discussed in greater detail below. Clearly psychologists can learn much from colleagues in the NPS with a much greater understanding of the policy and practice issues associated with diversity.

Standards and Accountability

Those employed as qualified psychologists (i.e. Chartered with the British Psychological Society),[2] are professionally accountable for their work and that of their supervisees. Chartered psychologists are expected to adhere to guidance in relation to their professional practice issued and disseminated through the auspices of the BPS. Also, the Applied Psychology Group for psychological services in probation and prisons issues periodic professional guidance. One of the key organizational arguments in favour of using qualified psychologists in that it is useful as part of corporate risk management. It does not mean that the organization has no responsibility with regard to the conduct of its professional staff. However, such accountabilities are significantly offset by the accountability of the individual qualified practitioners across a range of professional fields. Crucially, by using qualified staff there can be greater assurance that quality services are being delivered.

The benefits for qualified psychological staff are in interesting, well-paid, stimulating and varied job roles with excellent benefits.

Flexibility

In effectively starting afresh in the development and delivery of applied psychological services in probation, some of the inflexibilities in the culture common amongst forensic psychologists in prisons are not there in the same way. Thus, for example, trainee forensic psychologists in probation services often deliver services in the evenings. This cuts against the tradition in prisons whereby the working week has been chiefly seen in terms of '9 till 5' Monday-to-Friday service delivery. Such historic inflexibilities are common in the public sector. This does not though diminish the need to address such unhelpful restricted practices. The design of services needs to include more fully a consideration of the needs of a range of stakeholders, including the recipients of services whether at an organizational level or in direct work with individuals. In HM Prison Service there are some signs of change with a 24-hour year-round service provided in terms of specialist advice in the management of serious incidents in prisons. However, psychologists in probation services appear, on the whole, to be further ahead with such flexibilities. It is important that this service strength is developed. Developing this point, providing the right services in a timely manner is crucial if psychologists want to make the fullest possible positive impact on the work of probation services.

Fundamental to the notion of 'flexibility' is the need for the organization to be more flexible in accommodating the needs of staff. As noted above, the employee profile of trainee forensic psychologists tends to be that as a group they are young white women from wealthier socio-economic groups. Qualified psychologists are much the same in demographic make-up; however, unsurprisingly they tend to be a little less young! Many such staff place a premium on being able to work flexible hours, including where appropriate the capacity to undertake some work from home. There needs to be a matching process of the needs of the organization and the needs of psychological staff. However, ultimately the needs of the organization in terms of the demands upon it to deliver key public services must come first. Despite this there can be significant room for much more flexible working hours and practices and significant gains from doing this.

Expanding Choice

The opening up of posts for a broader range of applied psychology practitioners is essential in expanding the choices open to probation services in terms of how some of the key elements of their business objectives may be achieved. It is important that the NPS does not repeat the mistake made in HM Prison Service of an overreliance on forensic psychologists at the expense of other applied psychology specialisms. This could be particularly important when looking at services for mentally disordered offenders where clinical, counselling, forensic and health psychologists may each potentially have an important role to play. Indeed in the area of alcohol and drugs misuse those applied psychologists arguably best placed to provide services may be those in the health psychology field. There is also no a priori reason why services may not be provided by a higher number of psychological assistants essentially using this as a more cost effective initial (especially for the academic and research elements of qualification) training grade. Psychological services in prisons have tended to be relatively slow to take such opportunities. However, the prize for probation services in doing so is that they may benefit from greater diversity, improved retention of staff and ultimately more rounded practitioners.

From the perspective of qualified psychologists most will benefit from having some trainees that they are professionally responsible for. Also many will thrive if there is a broader range of work to undertake. This is important for trainees too. Often qualified psychologists are best used with the strategic planning, quality control and training aspects of specific interventions. For example, this would be the case where psychological staff are used in connection with the multi-disciplinary groupwork-based interventions. This reflects a change of role for such psychologists in relation to such interventions where, over recent years, in prisons they had become involved with arguably too much of such direct work at the expense of other contributions and roles, which are more directly linked to their areas of core skills and expertise.

Principles for Effective Service Delivery

Applied psychological services need to be provided in a professional and ethical manner, taking account of stakeholder needs. There needs to be a clear link with the work towards the delivery of the 'business needs' of probation services. As indicated above it is particularly important that a range of applied psychology specialisms are considered before advertising and appointing for specific posts. Finally such services need to be provided on an economic and effective basis.

What Do Applied Psychologists Have to Offer?

The applied psychology specialisms have a range of knowledge, experience and skills. Much of the knowledge base is common across the specialisms. Indeed there are probably greater areas of commonality in approach across specialisms than differences. Psychology is about people, their mental life and behaviour. The accurate and ethical application of such knowledge is what applied psychology is about. As indicated above, the various specialisms have differing emphases; however, there is much overlap between them. The BPS as the professional body for psychologists in the UK provides detailed information on applied psychology via its web site (see bps.org.uk). The chapters in this book will serve to illustrate some of the key and emerging areas of applied psychological practice in probation services. This brings us on to the next substantive section of the chapter, which will give an overview of some of the key and emerging areas of applied psychological practice in probation services. This is not a detailed review of all the work that is being undertaken by psychologists but rather a set of signposts covering current and possible future practice. It is worth reiterating that the developments in the application of psychological practice are relatively new and changing, and it seems probable that this will be an iterative process of development over the coming years.

Overview of the emerging work of applied psychologists in probation services

One of the growth areas of applied psychology practice has been in contributions to the courts in particular and to the legal process more widely. Applied psychologists have increasingly been called upon to give expert testimony in both criminal and civil courts. Research by psychologists has also told us more about the effects of the court process on participants including children and vulnerable adults.

As noted in the text the probation service has a long-established relationship with the courts, having begun life essentially as a service to the courts. Although the role of probation has long since expanded to deliver a much wider role in the criminal justice system, work in the courts remains a fundamental aspect of probation practice. Recent legislative changes have also added stress to the public protection role.

The range of non-custodial sentencing options available to the courts has also expanded in recent years and applied psychologists have an important role in supporting this process. The probation service has a long history of developing and implementing groupwork with offenders and, with the advent of the NPS this has been built on by the development of groupwork interventions aimed at reducing the risk of reoffending (HM Prison Service, 2003a). Many of these are based on 'pathfinder projects' that developed examples of existing best practice in NPS areas, and these are increasingly being 'rolled out' nationally. Examples here include the development of three group-based interventions with sexual offenders (developed by Northumbria, Thames Valley and West Midlands areas). Similarly consistent approaches to a number of other areas of offending, such as domestic violence, other violent offending, drink driving and others, have been developed.

Such interventions are in their early days and will undoubtedly develop and change over time. They are also part of a wider model of case work assessment and intervention with offenders, specifically focused on the reduction of risk of reoffending. Psychologists have a lengthy history of research into the area of risk assessment and management, and are well placed to contribute in developing this area of professional practice across disciplines and indeed across agencies.

The shift towards a public protection role has also brought with it for the NPS a need to manage 'high-risk' offenders in a systematic manner. This has resulted in the development of a multi-agency and multi-disciplinary approach in the form of Multi-agency Public Protection Arrangements (MAPPA), which provides for a framework of area-based Multi-agency Public Protection Panels (MAPPPs) (Home Office, 2003b). These enable the development of broad-based assessment and intervention strategies aimed at risk management. Psychologists, generally contracted in from National Health Service (NHS) services, have often been involved in this area. The advent of an in-house psychology service for the NPS has created the opportunity to ensure more consistent levels of input from applied psychologists and also to enhance and develop cross-agency working with NHS colleagues.

Future developments

The criminal justice system has seen a period of very rapid change and, in looking to the future, this seems likely to continue. The Government clearly aims to have a criminal justice system that both inspires confidence and is responsive to public need (Home Office, 2003b, 2003c). In order to achieve this it seems clear that the different parts of the criminal justice system need to work better together. Indeed the Auld Report (Department for Constitutional Affairs, 2002) concluded that the criminal justice system is not a system at all in any meaningful sense. Further evidence for this proposition is evident in the Carter Report (Home Office, 2003c). This theme is also reflected in the Government's response to the Carter Report (Home Office, 2004). The administration of what might be broadly termed justice is the remit of a number of Government departments and local and national agencies.

Priorities for the future seem likely to remain similar to those of current concern, although the coordination and delivery arrangements look set to change fundamentally. Crime reduction and the protection of the public from crime, and also from the fear of crime, are likely to remain central to the agenda of criminal justice agencies. Similarly the 'justice gap', by which is meant the attrition of offenders from each stage of the process, from investigation, charging, prosecution and conviction, seems likely to remain a key concern. With the recent announcement of the formation of a National Offender Management Service it looks likely that some key aspects of criminal justice management are about to be subject to significant 're-engineering'.

Concerns to ensure better working across the criminal justice system are also likely to play a key role in future developments. Early steps have been taken in this respect, for example with the establishment of what have been termed the 'grade 1 trilateral' meetings between Government departments central to the administration of justice and corrections.

Applied psychologists across all of the main criminal justice agencies are well placed to contribute to an agenda of greater public protection. However, the distribution of psychological services has been largely one of historical accident. In the past probation services tend to have been relatively poorly provided in comparison to prisons, which have a longer history of 'in-house' services. Similarly, community forensic services within the NHS tend to have been rare and under-resourced, in turn impacting on the ability of the NPS to draw on psychological expertise.

The Carter report (Home Office, 2003c) has set the likely direction for correctional services and the wider criminal justice system. The recommendations of the Carter report highlight a number of strategic aims that build on earlier reviews of the criminal justice system. These include:

- A need for greater integration of correctional services between probation and prisons in the form of a 'National Offender Management Service' (NOMS)

- A more 'seamless' approach to managing the risks posed by offenders in community and custodial settings and for more 'cross-cutting' work between departments and agencies
- A need to focus resources in a cost-effective manner and remove duplication of work by Government departments and agencies
- A need for correctional services to have public protection at the heart of their work
- A need to design services around the individual needs of the offender

The full potential of applied psychology has yet to be realized in offender management services. The recent publication of 'Driving Delivery' as a national strategy for developing partnership working in applied psychology is helpful in that it provides a clear framework for operational managers to look at what can be provided (HM Prison Service and National Probation Service, 2003a). The strategic framework for psychological services in both NPS and the prison service also serves as a guide to the potential contributions applied psychology has to make to the improvement and quality of service provided by such organizations. The strategic framework sits well with the Carter report. Two key underlying themes of both occur. First, the 'modernization agenda' cuts across both documents. Second the need for greater and richer partnership working in criminal justice.

The development of a strategic framework has also had benefits for applied psychology practitioners in providing a focus for service development and delivery linked to national objectives, within an appropriate professional training and development framework. An understanding of how each psychology specialism could contribute to the work of the NPS is essential for applied psychologists of whatever specialism.

Forensic psychology is the most widely recognized specialism in NPS and forensic psychologists are able to undertake a range of work. This would include the provision of individual assessment and intervention work, which could be for criminal and civil courts as well as other judicial bodies, such as the Parole Board and mental health review tribunals. Forensic psychologists are also able to work both individually and provide groupwork in a range of forensic settings and can have an active consultancy role with the NPS, police and prison services.

The focus of occupational psychologists is primarily concerned with the functioning of people at work. They are also involved in how people respond to and benefit from training, as well as looking more closely at how groups or individuals interact in the workplace. There are many ways in which occupational psychologists can support aims of the services, and the prison service already has a number of psychologists working in areas such as recruitment, training and the occupational health of staff.

Clinical psychologists have a history of working in partnership within the NPS. The aim of clinical psychology is to reduce psychological distress and promote psychological well-being (British Psychological Society, 2000a 2000b). Clinical psychologists are generally situated in multi-disciplinary teams in the NHS and are well placed to advise on issues such as serious mental illness, depression and anxiety, addictive behaviours, family and personal relationships, neurological disorders and adjusting to physical illness. The major application of clinical psychology within NPS would be the potential support it could offer to NPS employees in undertaking challenging work with offenders, as well as the training of staff in dealing with varied issues such as learning disabilities and intentional self-injury. There is also clear scope for trainee clinical psychologists to undertake placements with NPS teams within the context of primary and secondary healthcare placements (Crighton, 2003a). Overall there is potentially much more that the clinical specialism has to offer services like the NPS.

There is considerable overlap between the work of clinical and counselling psychologists although the latter specialism in terms of British Psychological Society recognition is somewhat younger than clinical psychology. Counselling psychologists are trained in both individual and groupwork skills that can assist offenders in resettlement and healthcare interventions. This specialism applies psychology across a range of diverse human problems by taking a holistic stance. They are also able to examine further issues that have been brought into the wider context, and underlying factors of what has given rise to them. The ability to offer counselling psychology services as part of resettlement with the NPS would potentially greatly assist work with life-sentence prisoners released on licence. This can ensure that any problems faced upon release could be explored. This could be particularly useful with new relationships that offenders may form upon release. It could also ensure that any existing issues that the offender has addressed whilst in custody are followed up. The potential contributions of counselling psychologists also extend to direct assessment and intervention work with employees of the NPS.

A new specialism, which is rapidly evolving, is health psychology. Health psychologists use the application and practice of psychological methods of working into studying the behaviour that is relevant to illness, health and healthcare. The areas of work where health psychology might be most beneficial to the NPS would be potential input into working with addictive behaviours such as substance abuse, and rehabilitation of offenders. This could be from both a research and practical perspective. The health of NPS employees is also an area of work; for example why and when employees seek professional advice in relation to their own health, and how this influences sickness levels. Research into the prevention of undue stress amongst employees may also be an important developmental area of work. Given the likely specialist nature of such work, developments may be at regional level, or indeed cross-regional level, with services such as health psychology contracted in to meet needs across a number of services, or across different parts of NOMS.

Educational psychologists have the potential to advise the NPS on learning and development of (young) offenders and assist in developing interventions with those who may have learning difficulties and are therefore unsuitable for groupwork. They are primarily concerned with the learning and development of children, often acting as consultants to schools. They are also able to advise operational managers upon education provision and resources as well as the practical management of challenging behaviour, with both child and young offenders. With the Employment Training and Education (ETE) service offered by the NPS, there is potential for educational psychologists to develop a role, perhaps on a contractual basis working with offenders undertaking ETE as part of their community order. They might also be used to advise operational managers upon the development of such services.

The potential advantage of having a broad range of applied psychologists such as those discussed above is potentially great to NOMS. The range of skills and expertise that can be offered and developed within these organizations has the potential to build upon their existing quality and services provided to offenders on behalf of the public as a whole.

Conclusions

Correctional services are a key part of the criminal justice system and seem likely to be increasingly central to efforts to protect the public from crime and the fear of crime. Work in the community is likely to be one of the key areas here. There is increasing evidence that broad-based interventions, addressing issues such as housing, educational and employment deficits and behavioural difficulties as part of community sentences may be effective (also providing good value for money) in reducing criminal behaviour (Social Exclusion Unit, 2002).

In order to deliver effective working across NOMS there needs to be an increasingly multi-disciplinary and multi-agency approach and the development of this is reflected throughout the contributions to this text. Applied psychologists from the full range of specialisms are well placed to contribute to these exciting and challenging developments.

NOTES

1   Recently moves have been made to allow candidates to sit an entrance examination as an alternative to traditional educational qualifications, which may disadvantage those who have already been disadvantaged by earlier educational experiences. This requirement has already been modified to allow 'equivalent' qualifications.
2   It seems likely that statutory registration of psychologists across the UK will become law in the near future, when the responsibility for qualification will pass from the BPS to the Health Professions Council (HPC) and crucially, be on a statutory basis.

Chapter Two

Work in the Courts

David Crighton

The roots of the modern offender management service in the community stem from work in the courts, in the form of the police court missionaries. Historically, therefore, probation officers were officers of the court. For many years this has not been true, but the historical legacy has continued in the form of a 'special relationship' between probation and the courts (Hills, 2002).

The Criminal Justice and Court Services Act 2000 (CJCS Act) represented a watershed in the way that the probation service worked with the courts. First, the act established a National Probation Service (NPS) to replace the network of locally governed services that had evolved. The act also served to bring probation into line with other criminal justice agencies that contribute to the work of the courts, using an area structure based on the police service area boundaries. Area probation boards were created to oversee the work of local services and, whilst these continued to involve members of the judiciary and magistrates, representation was considerably broadened and based on approval by the Home Secretary (Home Office, 2003b). The area boards replaced Probation Committees that had governance responsibilities and had been largely dominated by representatives from the courts. These committees had shown significant variation in performance.

The CJCS Act also marked a clear shift for the probation service away from that of what was seen as a social work agency to a law enforcement agency (Home Office, 2002a, 2002b, 2002c). As Hills (2002) observes, this is undoubtedly an oversimplification of what went before and indeed also of the current role of probation, but a shift in emphasis has been clear.

Role of the National Probation Service (NPS) in Court

It is generally accepted that the NPS provides a key service to the courts. Hills (2002) describes it thus: 'From the courts perspective, the probation service is present in court to provide information about community disposals and about defendants, and to assist in the process of remand and sentencing.'

The exact nature of the role of the NPS in court is however less widely agreed. Hence, whilst it is widely accepted that a service is provided to the court, it is not widely agreed that this involves probation officers sitting in court (Samuels, 1996).

A thematic review of court work by HM Inspectorate of Probation (HM Inspectorate of Probation, 1997) casts valuable light on the work of Court Duty Officers (CDOs). It found that just over 25 per cent of CDOs' time was spent 'being available' for the court or collecting results. In turn around 7 per cent of their time was spent in direct contact with offenders and only 1 per cent with the general public. This represented a marked change from historic practice where probation officers had often taken on a more general welfare role.

The NPS has always had accountability to the courts for those under supervision. More recently though there have been moves towards the courts being more specific about the nature of the supervision provided. An example of this would be the development of Drug Treatment and Testing Orders (DTTOs), which specify in detail much of the work to be undertaken in supervising offenders.

The 1997 Thematic Review also highlighted areas of concern in relation to past practices. Courts were often frustrated by an inability to obtain timely information or to contact reporting officers and, should the need arise, having them attend court. Previously courts would expect to hear evidence from a probation officer who had prepared a report, or where an offender under supervision had reoffended. This practice waned during the 1980s and 1990s to the extent that it now comparatively rarely happens. Another change has been the development of a high administrative load on CDOs, often involving routine tasks such as checking court lists. In turn this has led to a number of probation service areas developing the role of probation service officers and others to cover aspects of the court role (Hills, 2002).

The changes in the role of the NPS and its relationship with the courts is likely to result in marked changes in court work in coming years. A precondition of effective practice will be the development of more effective two-way communication. NPS practitioners will need to communicate effectively with the courts information about ways in which offenders can be assessed and managed, in ways that may ultimately reduce crime. Similarly and related to this point the NPS will need to communicate effectively the services available. Court-based staff and those providing information to the courts will therefore need a good understanding of community sentences and also of the evidence base supporting particular interventions and combinations of interventions (HM Inspectorate of Probation, 1997; Towl, 2000, 2004; Hills, 2002). At a strategic level across criminal justice services and agencies the links between the National Offender Management Service (NOMS) and the courts, through the Sentencing Guidelines Council, will be crucial if the promise of NOMS is to be realized.

The flip side of these changes is that the courts can more effectively support the work of service providers of community sentencing options and research-based interventions. At a practical level courts may be able to make pre-sentence report appointments and community sentence first appointments in court, thus reinforcing the importance of these to offenders and improving attendance rates. In addition local Criminal Justice Boards have been established with a view to facilitating better co-operative working across agencies and, indeed, seeking to eliminate points of friction (Home Office, 2002b).

Hills (2002) also argues in favour of the development of effective working 'protocols' between courts and the NPS areas as a means of facilitating such working across the criminal justice system and also with other agencies such as health and social services. Such 'protocols' have the scope to be further extended to cover effective multi-agency working between other criminal justice agencies as well as health, social services and housing (Svanberg et al., 1996).

What Does the NPS Do in Court?

The role of NPS staff in court can be broken down into three main areas. First, staff have a role in advising on bail applications. Secondly, there is a role in providing reports for the courts. Thirdly, there is what might be termed an advisory and liaison role. All of this feeds into the broader remit of the NPS to collect and channel information about offenders to begin effective work with them (Hills, 2002).

Bail

All probation service areas are required to provide a bail information service, which is included within the role. This will involve direct contact with offenders to provide advice on bail and also to validate information contained in bail proposals. It will also often involve liaison with other agencies, for example in the case of mentally disordered offenders bailed for psychological or medical assessment. Some areas also run what might be termed 'second chance' bail advice based in prisons and designed to catch offenders suitable for bail who have slipped through the net and into custody, when in fact they would have been eligible for bail.

Bail information services were originally developed to keep offenders out of custody by taking a pro-bail stance, uniquely providing information that might support a bail application. As the probation service came to focus more on risk issues in the mid 1990s the role shifted to one of providing neutral information, either for bail, or against it, if risk indicators were noted. It may also be worth noting that since such work did not bring in what might be termed 'core business' for the probation service, in the form of offenders to supervise, it was often accorded a relatively low priority in the face of limited resources. This contrasts somewhat with the situation in youth courts where bail support schemes exist and are, in general, seen as a high priority.

Effective bail services require a good knowledge of community accommodation options for offenders. They also require effective multi-agency and multi-disciplinary work. For example, bail arrangements for psychological or medical reports will require good working relationships with 'in-house' psychologists as well as health-and-social-services-based psychologists providing services in the area.

Reports

The NPS is generally involved in providing two major types of reports: Specific Sentence Reports (SSRs) and Pre Sentence Reports (PSRs).

Specific Sentence Reports

These are brief reports provided by the NPS, which address an offender's suitability for a Community Punishment Order (CPO) or a short Community Rehabilitation Order (CRO) (Hill, 2002). In law these short reports are pre-sentence reports intended to provide the court with a swift response to a specific question and obviate the need in such cases for the time and delay involved in providing a more detailed PSR.

The growing use of SSRs has not been universally welcomed. There are significant concerns that they steer the courts away from reaching a fully informed view, based on a broad and in-depth assessment of the offender.

In this respect it can be argued that the effectiveness of the risk assessment method used by the NPS will be crucial. The method chosen is titled
the Offender Group Reconviction Scale (OGRS) (Taylor, 1999). This is an
empirically based system, which provides broad 'risk bands' for offenders. In
future it seems likely that these groups will tend to be subject to more detailed
PSRs, whereas lower-risk groups may not. Some caution is warranted here,
though. As with other empirically based systems OGRS depends heavily on
past reported offending behaviour. As such it is likely to be poor at detecting
those in the early stages of high-risk offending and is particularly poor at
addressing the needs of lightly convicted offenders facing sentences for very
serious offences.

Pre Sentence Reports

These were formerly called Social Inquiry Reports (SIRs) but were retitled
PSRs to reflect the shift in role of the NPS. Arranging for the preparation of
such reports has long been a part of the CDO's role. In addition they would
generally also be responsible for presenting such reports to the court, and
where possible offer clarification or supplementary information.

A PSR is defined in s.162 of the Powers of the Criminal Courts (Sentencing)
Act 2000 (PCC(S) Act) as a report in writing that is submitted by a probation
officer, social worker or member of a youth offending team. The report is
written with a view to assisting the court to reach the most suitable means of
dealing with the offender. The format for PSRs is designated by the Home
Secretary.

Under s.81(1) of the PCC(S) Act, when the court is forming an opinion on a
custodial sentence under s.79(2) or s.80(2) of the act it has a duty to obtain a
PSR. However, this does not apply where the offender is over 18 years and, in
the opinion of the court the circumstances of the case make a PSR unnecessary;
for example, where the sentence is clear and a PSR would make no difference.
It is worth noting that not obtaining a PSR does not invalidate a sentence in
such cases, but that in any appeal the court must consider the failure to
obtain a PSR and obtain such a report, except where the court also feels it is
unnecessary.

For those under 18 the court must obtain a PSR under s.81(3) PCC(S) Act
unless the offence is triable only on indictment and the court feels a PSR is
unnecessary, or alternatively where a recent report already exists.

Similarly some sentences place a responsibility on the court to obtain a PSR
unless they feel it is unnecessary. These would include cases where the court
plans to impose a Community Rehabilitation Order (CRO) with certain additional requirements under schedule 2 of the PCC(S) Act, a Drug Treatment

and Testing Order (DTTO),[1] or a supervision order with additional requirements. It remains the case that only exceptionally would a court make a CRO without hearing from a probation worker.

In providing such reports the NPS reporting officer, social worker or youth offending team member will draw upon a range of information such as previous knowledge of the offender, previous interventions and responses to these. Reporting officers may also recommend completion of medical, psychological or psychiatric reports. These may be requested as additional reports to cover areas that cannot be adequately addressed in the PSR. There is however no single model of how area services do this.

The development of 'in-house' applied psychology services presents the NPS with an opportunity to improve services to the court in this respect. In the past, psychological reports have primarily been requested from local NHS primary care and secondary care services. In areas without specialist court liaison or forensic services this has often resulted in considerable delay and reports that may have limited relevance to the court. In-house psychology services, working effectively with health and social services colleagues, present a clear opportunity to address such issues.

Contents and presentation of PSRs

Some of the main criticisms of SIRs was a lack of consistency in content and a lack of relevance to the needs of the courts (HM Inspectorate of Probation, 1997). Even before the introduction of PSRs it was clear that the format and content needed to be changed.

In the green paper 'Punishment and Supervision in the Community' (Home Office, 1999) it was set out that PSRs should have a clear focus on public protection and reducing criminal behaviour. In order to achieve this the green paper suggested requirements to address background factors as well as an assessment of the offenders' willingness to stop offending, an assessment of sentencing options and an assessment of risk to the public. As a result, the Home Office developed National Standards for the Probation Service (Home Office, 2002d), which began to prescribe what a report had to contain. Equally it was made clear that sentencing remained a matter for the courts and that PSRs should provide options but not recommend appropriate sentences. The current format for PSRs is designated nationally and is subject to national standards applicable to the production of such reports.

Under s.162(1) the PCC(S) Act defines PSRs as written reports to the court, ending the practice of probation officers giving oral reports to the court. A copy of the report must be given to offenders, or their legal representative or, in the case of unrepresented juveniles to the offender's parent or legal guardian. Under s.156 (3) the act also makes clear that it is bad practice to read the whole of the report in open court, since PSR reports may contain personal information. The defence can however quote parts of the report and indeed often do so in mitigation.

Whilst reports to court would generally be presented by the CDO the defence can if they wish call reporting officers and examine them on the contents of the PSR. Reporting officers may also choose to attend court. As with other types of report to court particular care needs to be taken when referring to admissions to facts of the offence that have not been formally accepted in court. R. v. Cunnah [1996] 1 Cr. App. R(S) 393 addressed this issue. In this case the PSR made reference to a full admission to the offences as alleged by the victims, but a plea of guilty had been accepted by the prosecution on a more limited basis. The judge however proceeded to sentence on the basis of the version of events contained in the PSR. There had been no discussion of this with counsel and, on appeal, the sentence was reduced to one in line with the basis on which the guilty plea had been made and accepted.

However, in the case of R. v. Salisbury Magistrates' Court ex parte Gray (TLR 1 July 1999) the court of appeal affirmed the duty on PSR writers to investigate the nature of the defendants offending, and where that presented new information which made the offence more serious the court was entitled to determine the case on the basis of that information; because the PSR is automatically served on both parties the right to change its contents is inherent. This could take place by means of a 'Newton hearing' (where guilt is not at issue but there is a trial of the facts surrounding the case) something the court of appeal considered should have taken place in the case of Cunnah.

Other court reports

As noted above the other main group of reports requested by the courts are medical reports, which tend to include reports made by health professionals, such as applied psychologists.

Full coverage of this area is not within the scope of this chapter. However, such reports can address a wide range of physical and mental health issues and offenders can be bailed with a condition that they attend for completion of such reports. Offenders can also be assessed by a primary care medical practitioner in a prison healthcare centre. In addition offenders may be subject to assessments under the provisions of the Mental Health Act 1983 (Jones, 2003).

Copies of such reports must be given to the offender's legal representative. In cases where offenders are not represented they must be given, as a minimum, the 'gist' of the report.

In addition to medical and related reports the court can also request reports on youths, following remand to local authority care. Such reports tend to be produced by Youth Offending teams (YOTs) and NHS practitioners. Reports on school attendance and behaviour can also be requested for young people.

The Potential Role of Psychologists

As with other NPS staff much of what psychologists have to offer the courts takes place outside the judicial forum and concerns the development and communication of more effective interventions with offenders. Psychologists therefore have a significant potential contribution in the evaluation of existing community sentence interventions. Psychologists also have the potential to contribute significantly to the development of new interventions with offenders. It seems clear that current interventions with offenders are far from optimal. We still know comparatively little about what interventions effectively reduce reoffending and why, and it would be inaccurate to give any other impression to the courts. Likewise it would be a negation of public duty not to look for interventions that might reduce crime.

Applied psychologists may also have a significant contribution to make to risk assessment and management. It has been decided to implement a structured risk assessment system termed the Offender Assessment System (OASys), which is, in turn, largely based on the Level of Service Inventory – Revised (LSI – R) (Loza & Simourd, 1994; Andrews & Bonta, 1995). Oasys provides a major step forward in comparison to unstructured approaches to assessing and managing risk. However, OASys is unlikely to meet the needs fully for precise and detailed assessments with high-risk offenders (see chapter 5).

The single largest area of work for psychologists in supporting the work of the NPS in the courts though is likely to be the provision of psychological reports. In this respect psychologists have the potential to deliver a valuable service by providing timely reports to the courts on 'high-risk' offenders.

The role of psychologists in providing reports for the courts has developed to some extent with the implementation of a joint psychology service for probation and prison services. The posting of a number of experienced forensic psychologists and the growth in training places based in the community have led to greater use of in-house psychologists to undertake specialist areas of risk assessment and mental health assessments. This seems to be an area likely to develop further with the increasing focus on effectively assessing and managing risk for the NOMS.

NOTE

1   As the name suggests this is a new form of court order that requires offenders to
    undertake drug testing and drug treatment under the supervision of the NPS.
    Such work is generally carried out in partnership with specialist NHS or voluntary
    service partners.

Chapter Three

Counselling Psychologists and Mental Health Work in Probation Services

Sharon Mayer

Mental health has attracted much political attention in recent years, so much so that it has been identified as one of the four key priority areas across National Health Service (NHS) reform (Department of Health, 1999a, 2000a 2000b). The Government's White Paper *Modernising Mental Health Services* (Department of Health 1998) and the National Service Framework for Mental Health (Department of Health 1999a) prioritize the development and accessibility of comprehensive and robust services for any individual experiencing mental health difficulties.

Diversity is a common theme emphasized within these policy documents. This is highlighted, both in terms of the uncompromising importance placed on anti-discriminatory practice and the recognized desirability to achieve a wide-ranging skill mix of mental health practitioners and inter-agency collaboration.

It has been estimated that one in four people will experience some form of mental health problem in their lives with 70 per cent subsequently being discriminated against in some way. By raising the profile of mental health issues it is hoped that any form of prejudice or discrimination against people suffering from mental health problems will become as unacceptable as racism or sexism in today's society (Department of Health, 2001).

It is widely accepted that there is much scope for the improvement of mental health services across agencies, which includes the National Probation Service (NPS). The importance of psychological therapies ranks highly in terms of proposed treatment strategies, and the skills and knowledge base of applied psychologists from whatever specialism, working in all areas of mental health, are recognized in terms of enhancing workforce-planning initiatives.

Mentally Disordered Offenders

Mental disorder in England and Wales is defined under the terms of the 1983 Mental Health Act. Four broad categories that constitute the definition are 'mental illness, arrested or incomplete development of mind, psychopathic disorder and any other disorder or disability of mind' (Mental Health Act 1983).

The proportion of offenders passing through the courts that have some form of mental disorder or mental health difficulty is disproportionately higher than that in the general population (Gunn, Maden & Swinton, 1991). Government proposals to reshape mental health provision have, perhaps unsurprisingly, been particularly well received within the criminal justice system.

It has long since been accepted that 'mentally disordered offenders' present a number of challenges for effective professional practice. The publication of the Reed report (Department of Health, 1992) documented a strategy to address some of the challenges and provide guidelines for the delivery of services by various Government agencies, including probation services. Harris (1999), who discusses the issue of organizational responsibility in relation to mentally disordered offenders, points out that this spans social services, health, probation and prison services. Problems of inconsistent clinical diagnosis and resource limitations have traditionally led to demands being made on such professionals that have been difficult to meet.

The probation service acknowledges that specialist mental health work lies outside its range of generic professional competencies. Grant (1999) reflects on the potential involvement of psychological or psychiatric services to improve performance in relation to the rehabilitation and public protection agendas of the NPS: 'No agency has a monopoly on expertise, and probation officers are not infrequently invited to operate forms of clinical therapy in respect of which their training is less than comprehensive' (Grant, 1999).

Referrals for mental health assessments and treatment intervention have historically been made to outside agencies such as community mental health teams (CMHTs), local forensic outreach services, secure units or high-security psychiatric hospitals. Provision across the 42 individual probation areas has varied quite considerably with clinical psychologists, psychiatrists and Community Psychiatric Nurses (CPNs) being the most common providers of services. Whilst probation staff who have utilized these resources have valued them, there has been a lack of accessibility and consistency of provision across the NPS.

What Can Applied Psychologists Offer?

Forensic psychologists are now impacting significantly on the working practices of the National Probation Service particularly in terms of their contribution to risk management and public protection procedures and offending-behaviour-focused interventions. There are clear indications that the NPS is beginning to draw appropriately on a range of aspects of forensic psychology in order to maximize the resource potential that they now have available to them with individual psychologist's skills and experience being matched to organizational needs (Wilmott, 2002a).

In terms of broadening the scope for 'joined-up' working practices across NOMS, the emphasis here is not purely on repeating the prison experience in the probation setting but rather utilizing this to create a responsive infrastructure in keeping with organizational philosophy, purpose and policy.

The HM Prison Service and National Probation Service document, in presenting a strategic framework for psychological services in prisons and probation helpfully draws attention to the emerging scope and desirability for psychologists from other applied specialisms to become more highly involved in the joined-up working practice of both the HM Prison Service (HMPS) and NPS. 'The use of a mix of applied psychology specialisms has the potential to add to the breadth and depth of each specialism through shared learning and better quality of service' (HM Prison Service and National Probation Service, 2003a).

With this in mind, it can be argued that in relation to mental health issues, counselling psychologists have an important potential role to play in the NPS service delivery, which would complement the role that forensic psychologists are now shaping.

Proposed Changes in the 1983 Mental Health Act

The Government's White paper on changes to mental health legislation broadens the definition of 'mental disorder' to 'any disability or disorder of mind or brain, whether permanent or temporary, which results in an impairment of disturbance of mental functioning' (Department of Health, 2000c).

In essence this means that those diagnosed as having 'personality disorders' who are also offenders can be subject to compulsion and treatment just as those with mental illnesses can be – subject to certain conditions (Craissati, 2003). Compulsion being exercised via care plans is designed to benefit the patient or to manage (risk) behaviours associated with mental disorder, which can be implemented in the community rather than hospitals. Explicit within these proposals are the increased responsibilities of 'consultant psychologists' in relation to the diagnosis of mental disorders and subsequent directives to make compulsory treatment decisions.

In the wake of such proposed reform of the 1983 Mental Health Act this may be a particularly poignant time for the NPS to be considering partnership arrangements with applied psychologists.

> The broad definition of mental disorder, the abolition of the so-called 'treatability test' in relation to psychopathic disorder and the provisions enabling compulsory treatment in the community – will highlight the need for community and in-patient services. (National Institute for Mental Health England, 2003)

Multi-disciplinary and multi-agency workforce planning is a recognized prerequisite for their effective implementation.

What Can Counselling Psychologists Offer in Relation to Mental Health Provision?

Counselling psychology takes its place alongside other psychology specialisms within mainstream professional practice, balancing an appreciation of the salience of scientific enquiry and the significance of traditional psychotherapeutic traditions (see Leiper, 2002). 'It continues to develop models of practice and research which marry the scientific demand for rigorous empirical enquiry with a firm value base grounded in the primacy of the counselling/ psychotherapeutic relationship . . .' (British Psychological Society, 2001).

Counselling psychologists study the underlying psychological principles of, and need to demonstrate competence in, a range of therapeutic approaches across a variety of client groups effecting competent integrative psychotherapeutic practice. They work collaboratively with individuals and groups to empower lifestyle change and personal development (see Bor & Watts, 1999).

Counselling psychologists work in a wide range of settings across agencies in the public, voluntary and private sector. Many work in the NHS, contributing to the delivery of mental health services in GP surgeries, community mental health teams, in specialist psychiatric or personality disorder services. The Department of Health's evidence-based clinical practice guidelines includes counselling psychologists as one of the major providers of psychological therapies.

Within mental health services, high levels of discrimination and harassment have been identified as an area of major concern to policy-makers and professionals in this field. It is recognized in the standard working practices of counselling psychologists that they seek 'to recognise social contexts and discrimination and to work always in ways which empower rather than control and towards high standards of anti-discriminatory practice appropriate to the pluralistic nature of today's society . . .' (British Psychological Society, 2001).

The National Service Framework for Mental Health specifically includes criminal justice agencies in its recommendations for inter-agency workforce planning to address present shortages and future needs of mental health services (Department of Health, 1999b). The potential use of counselling psychologists to implement these recommendations creates the prospect of flexible and extensive therapeutic interventions being made available within the NPS for offenders who present with mental health difficulties.

Possible Therapeutic Approaches Counselling Psychologists Could Offer

It is likely that most counselling psychologists will be proficient in the application of a cognitive behavioural approach to therapy as indeed are forensic psychologists. However, it is the additional training in further therapeutic approaches that enables counselling psychologists to offer a more extensive and responsive range of alternative therapeutic interventions in relation to mental health issues.

Forensic psychotherapy

A popular multi-disciplinary therapeutic approach, which has been shown to impact positively on the assessment and treatment of personality-disordered offenders, is forensic psychotherapy. This approach has at its core the application of a psychodynamic perspective in the pursuit of an understanding of the potential role offenders' unconscious mechanisms may play in relation to their criminal behaviour (Welldon, 1994). In doing so, forensic psychotherapy promotes an increased capacity for offenders to contain their emotions and thereby avoid repeated incidents of impulsive criminal behaviour. Emphasis is not singularly placed on the offender's presentation and motivation for treatment, but consideration is also given to the level of social and interpersonal support available to the offenders as well as their own personal resources to facilitate effective treatment intervention.

Whilst clear emphasis is being placed on the desirability of multi-agency and multi-disciplinary working, such shared care arrangements can often result in tensions between the various individuals involved. One of the benefits of using an approach based on psychodynamic theory in relation to work with personality-disordered offenders, is that this facilitates a deeper appreciation of the impact this work can have on staff by analysing the manifestation of counter-transference reactions and inter-staff splitting (Norton & McGauley 2000). Counselling psychologists with skills and experience in this area of therapy could therefore be a great asset both in terms of working with offenders with mental health difficulties and NPS staff.

Systemic therapy

Mentally disordered offenders may be socially excluded and have poor social and family networks or they may live with or have a lot of contact with family members or identified carers. Systemic therapy looks at the individual as part of a wider system, for example the mentally disordered offender as one member of a family, and considers the influence of social and relational contexts. It is based on the premise that the individuals' behaviour will be influenced and maintained by the way other individuals and systems interact with them.

Involving families or carers in systemic therapy has been found to be greatly beneficial, particularly in relation to reduced relapse rates or admissions to hospital (Mari & Streiner, 1996). Carers themselves are often undersupported and this approach can also be used to address this issue. Family members can learn how to interact more therapeutically on an everyday basis and the mentally disordered offender can learn to identify more with the family unit or family system, which results in the modification of behaviour by all parties (Greene & Uganizza, 1995).

Brief therapy

Brief therapy can have a variety of theoretical orientations, including cognitive-behavioural, psychodynamic and systemic, all sharing the fact that the length of the therapy is purposely kept brief. Practical considerations such as the limited availability of specialist therapists, time frames and financial constraints have popularized the appeal of brief therapies in the field of mental health.

Solution-focused brief therapy is a particularly versatile approach that can be used with individuals or work with couples, families or wider systems, and has been found effective for individuals suffering from mental health difficulties. It is a method designed to explicitly focus on people's competencies and strengths rather than deficits and weaknesses .

Cognitive Analytical Therapy (CAT)

Cognitive Analytical Therapy is a time-limited therapeutic approach combining psychodynamic and cognitive perspectives. It was originally developed for use in the NHS mental health services in response to the growing call for effective and brief psychological interventions for people suffering from all forms of mental health problems and for alternative interventions for those who were presenting as more difficult to help (Ryle, 1990, 1997).

Pollard and Potter (1999) consider this approach particularly relevant to work with 'hard to help' offenders. For example, those who have experienced childhood traumas are diagnosed as having a personality disorder (PD), display violent tendencies, engage in drug abuse, self-injury or decline help. They acknowledge that angry, threatening and 'manipulative' clients can leave probation staff feeling uncomfortable, frustrated, helpless and de-skilled in their professional practice. They suggest that CAT can provide a framework to enable difficult issues to be addressed whilst simultaneously reducing the likelihood of provoking a feeling of rejection in the offender and negative reactions in the worker (Pollock, 1997).

Dialectical Behavioural Therapy (DBT)

Dialectical Behaviour Therapy (DBT) is a therapeutic approach that is commonly used in the treatment of those diagnosed as having a 'borderline personality disorder'. It combines cognitive and behavioural therapy and engenders an attitude of acceptance of the individual as they are 'in the moment'. Therapists validate this acceptance as the beginnings of change in the individual and proceed to teach 'new and balanced' ways of thinking, feeling and behaving. Many people diagnosed with 'borderline personality disorder' engage in self-injurious behaviour and this approach has reported positive success rates in the reduction of this behaviour (Linehan et al., 1991).

Specific issues related to women's experience of mental health problems are also a high priority in the Government's commitment to addressing discrimination and inequality in mental health service provision. This approach is felt to be especially well suited to work with women. An increase in 'coping beliefs' and a reduction in self-injurious behaviour, suicidal ideation, depression and dissociative experiences were reported in women mentally disordered offenders having undergone DBT in a secure psychiatric hospital (Low, 1998).

Multi-modal therapy

The disproportionately high number of ethnic minority offenders in the psychi-atric system in England and Wales has prompted the need for culturally appropriate interventions. Multi-modal therapy is considered to be a particu-larly fitting and effective counselling approach for people of minority ethnic backgrounds (Ridley, 1995). This therapeutic approach focuses on the personal experiences and perceptions of the individual and applies an idiographic approach aiming to 'fit the therapy to the client'. In contrast to the majority of traditional therapeutic approaches, it considers interpersonal, sensory and biological dimensions alongside imagery, cognitive, behavioural and affective components in an attempt to ameliorate bias to find a therapeutic style that reflects a sensitivity and relevance to the individual's culture and belief system (Lazarus 1989; Palmer, 2000).

Group therapy

Therapy groups, as opposed to individual therapy, are often employed in forensic and mental health services. Using an interpersonal process-orientated approach to group therapy, the focus is placed on how the group members interact in the 'here and now' as they make their own contributions to the group therapy process and receive multiple feedback from others (Yalom, 1995). This approach has been found to be particularly effective in the treat-ment of individuals diagnosed as having 'borderline personality disorders' where levels of social isolation, egotism and deviant behaviour have been seen to decrease (Greene & Uganizza, 1995).

Counselling Psychologists' Contributions to Service Delivery

A variety of potential therapeutic approaches that counselling psychologists could offer NPS have been outlined above. Whilst all these approaches have the potential to impact on mental health services across agencies, there are specific areas of service delivery within the NPS where it is suggested that their application and evaluation could be most beneficial.

Mental health assessments in relation to
Pre Sentence Reports

The first point at which most offenders come into contact with the probation service is when the court requests a Pre Sentence Report (PSR). In accordance with the Powers of the Criminal Courts (Sentencing) Act 2000 (PCC(S) Act) the probation service is required to provide the courts with a PSR to inform the sentencing procedure. Such reports may refer to any concerns relating to the offender's mental health.

It is at the PSR interview stage that probation officers often identify possible mental health difficulties in offenders – particularly now that the comprehensive Offender Assessment System (OASys) risk assessment (Home Office, 2001) is being introduced across the NPS. For example, there may be indications that individuals are experiencing symptoms of anxiety or depression, they may report a history of incidents of self-injurious behaviour or other examples of maladaptive cognitive and behavioural mechanisms, they may have been given a psychiatric diagnosis or are being prescribed psychotropic medication, or they may present extraordinary or bizarre behaviour.

Consequently the probation officer may seek to obtain clarification as to whether the individual can be categorized as fitting the description of having a mental disorder, in terms of the 1983 Mental Health Act when considering making sentencing recommendations in their report. Specific sentencing options available to the court when considering how to sentence an offender who is or appears to be mentally disordered include Community Rehabilitation Orders (CROs) with psychiatric requirements, hospital orders, interim hospital orders, guardianship orders or an absolute or conditional discharge if it is felt that the individual would be unable to benefit from any other order.

The salience of providing an appropriate mental health assessment procedure is reflected in the literature relating to issues of diversity. Black and other minority ethnic communities, for example, have reported a lack of cultural sensitivity in this process and access to appropriate assessment, treatment and care has been inhibited by racial discrimination. This has been found to be particularly so for refugees and asylum seekers. Multi-disciplinary assessments undertaken in partnership have been evidenced as enhancing the quality of these initial assessments (Department of Health 1999b).

The prevalence of mental health difficulties in offenders is of concern to the probation service for several reasons. Achieving the balance between accurately addressing mental health needs, offending behaviour and public protection issues is paramount in such cases. An unidentified mental disorder can potentially impede the rehabilitation focus of the various community orders an offender may be placed on. Many individuals who experience mental health problems find it difficult to engage with services, or else are highly resource intensive and a minority present as a risk of harm to themselves and/or others.

Counselling psychologists are well placed to provide mental health assessments to add to the robust social and crime related focus of the PSR prepared by probation officers. Sentencing options, which include proposals of the desirability for specific therapeutic interventions, treatment approaches or management strategies could be provided to the court in order to ensure that full consideration is given to an offender's mental health needs. This would assist the NPS in ensuring the individual needs of the offender are balanced against those of addressing offending behaviour and protection of the public.

There is however a practical difficulty here in that, under current law, such mental health disposals require a report by a registered medical practitioner. Where options for psychological interventions are being considered this presently results in a difficulty in that the assessment process does not start with a psychologist. In line with this, courts are generally unwilling to hear from, or to pay for, court reports by psychologists in this context. This has acted as a block to the further development of the role of psychologists.

Court Diversion Schemes for Mentally Disordered Offenders

It is axiomatic that if an offender suffers from a mental disorder, then their condition could be exacerbated by having to spend an enforced period of time in custody. Nevertheless, remands in custody for psychiatric or social reasons as opposed to concerns over public safety or the seriousness of the offence has lamentably been common practice with the courts (Department of Health and Home Office, 1992). This is despite the fact that the Home Office Circular 66/ 90 made it explicit that this should not happen, stating instead that mentally disordered offenders should receive the care of health and social services. The circular outlined effective 'court diversion' schemes that were operating in certain areas of the country, and it was recognized that suitable altern- atives for mentally disordered offenders needed to be put in place on a grand scale in England and Wales.

The interdepartmental Reed report (Department of Health, 1992) made recommendations for a nationwide standard practice of providing court assessment and diversion schemes as an initiative to avoid such instances. The report asked Justices' Clerks to engage in developing mental health assessment schemes based at magistrates' courts in consultation with local services and agencies.

A comprehensive review of several such schemes that have operated in England and Wales over the past decade was undertaken. Such schemes have varied in terms of the composition of mental health workers associated with them, ranging from single professionals such as Community Psychiatric Nurses (CPNs) or psychiatrists to multi-agency teams, some of which employ psy- chologists (Blumenthal and Wessely, 1992; Cavadino, 1999).

There is clear scope to extend participation to include the involvement of counselling psychologists in court diversion schemes. The Reed report acknowledged the need for additional staffing in agencies dealing with mentally disordered offenders and it may be that the probation service could seek to capitalize on this by employing the skills and experience of these applied psychologists in this way. This could include accompanying probation staff in attendance at court – carrying out brief initial assessments of offenders, providing verbal or written reports for hearings, or liaison with other agencies such as health, social services or the police. It could also extend to intervention work with mentally disordered offenders.

Their involvement could also include contributing to local multi-agency groups set up to co-ordinate the planning and development of services for mentally disordered offenders in their area. Where such mentally disordered offenders groups operate, they meet regularly to plan diversion arrangements at different stages of the criminal justice process as well as potential care and treatment options and monitoring procedures.

Home Office 'Approved Premises' and Mentally Disordered Offenders

Finding appropriate accommodation for mentally disordered offenders when they have been diverted or discharged from custody is also an issue of major concern for the NPS.[1] Mentally disordered offenders can often be subject to social exclusion and what has been termed the 'revolving door syndrome': being caught in a cycle of reoffending and perpetual recidivism if there is insufficient care in the community to break this cycle (Mills, 2002). There has been a call for such individuals to be cared for either within the NHS or else via alternative specialist services such as dedicated hostels (Gunn, Maden & Swinton, 1991; NACRO, 1995).

As part of an overarching multi-agency approach to the health and welfare of mentally disordered offenders, the Government urged Chief Probation Officers to work with other agencies to ensure availability of accommodation alternatives to prison custody pre and post conviction, to ensure that prison custody does not continue to be used in default of more appropriate accommodation, to advise on other possible options other than imprisonment and other courses of action where prosecution is not in the public interest (Home Office and Department of Health, 1995). It was felt that the development and improvement of multi-agency bail support arrangements for mentally disordered offenders, including the NPS, would inspire more confidence in the courts to remand defendants on bail rather than in custody for preparation of psychiatric reports (Cavadino, 1999).

One 'Approved Premises' in the West Midlands area was founded specifically to act as a residential accommodation resource for 'court diversion' schemes, originally in the form of a bail hostel. The aims of the hostel are to balance the socio-medical care of mentally disordered people with the need to protect the public from the criminal behaviour of individuals and to provide a safe environment in which mental health assessments can be carried out over a meaningful time frame rather than in a single session. This service has developed alongside well-established 'court diversion' and 'diversion at point of arrest' schemes in the area, a strong multi-agency mental health forum and partnership with a neighbouring specialist forensic psychiatric service for mentally disordered offenders who have committed very serious offences and/ or pose exceptional risk to the public (Brown & Geelan, 1998).

The target group of offenders is those who have a mental disorder as defined by the terms of the Mental Health Act 1983, and an up-to-date psychiatric assessment is carried out before a decision is made regarding admission to the hostel. In practice it is those who do not have a mental disorder sufficiently acute to render them in need of hospital treatment on a psychiatric unit that are deemed suitable for the hostel. This multi-agency resource 'provides a community placement for those within the criminal justice system who would ordinarily be psychiatric out-patients, and reduces the number of mentally disordered defendants and offenders needlessly remanded into custody' (Brown & Geelan, 1998).

Applied psychologists working in NHS forensic services in Kent have probation as their main partner for mental health project development, providing specialist accommodation with screening assessments, monitoring and evaluation of service delivery, training and consultation (Craissati, 2003). In probation areas where such specialist 'Approved Premises' are operating, counselling psychologists could provide the NPS with a similar in-house resource. However, as they are yet to be commonplace across the NPS the scope to improve existing residential capacity to deal with mentally disordered offenders has been identified as an alternative mode of service development (Cavadino, 1999).

There is a potential role for counselling psychologists to impact on the way such residential settings function, developing them, for example, on a therapeutic community (TC) model, where therapeutic groupwork and individual therapy could be run alongside offence-focused, educational and recreational activities. Counselling psychologists may also be drawn on to take part in decision-making with regard to the appropriateness of mentally disordered offenders being accommodated at such 'Approved Premises', particularly since balancing the mental health needs of an offender with issues of public protection feature highly in planned reform of the Mental Health Act 1983 and the Criminal Justice and Court Services Act 2000.

Multi-agency Public Protection Arrangements (MAPPA)

The Criminal Justice and Court Services Act 2000 saw the introduction of Multi-agency Public Protection Arrangements (MAPPA) as a vehicle to co-ordinate a shared strategy for the assessment and management of 'high-risk' offenders. As part of MAPPA, multi-agency panels convene to discuss supervision and management strategies, and to decide upon the level of risk of harm such offenders pose to the public or to themselves. Some forensic psychologists already working in the NPS are standing members on these panels, as are some clinical psychologists working in forensic community settings.

Whilst it is by no means necessarily the case that mentally disordered offenders pose a greater risk of offending than those who do not have a mental disorder, they are likely to be highly represented in the group of offenders who are subject to 'risk alerts'. As yet the role of mental health professionals is considered to be slow to develop:

> but should include liaison, consultation, and advise on the assessment and management of personality disordered offenders for criminal justice agencies via the MAPPP [and] provide assessments for the Courts, links with prison mental health care services, and preliminary examination. . . . treatment and assertive management of such offenders. (Crassaiti, 2003)

The scope for counselling psychologists to develop such a role is readily evident.

Probation areas may also want to consider the potentially wearing and stressful effect that this area of service delivery may have on their staff. Probation staff work constantly with a broad range of highly demanding clients, which includes high-risk violent or sexual offenders, mentally disordered offenders and victims. In this context staff support is a very important area and one that, it could be suggested, has often been neglected in the past. Counselling psychologists have a clear potential role here in supporting probation staff in undertaking such challenging work.

This might include the provision of appropriate debriefing and counselling services for staff engaged in working with such offenders, which provide a specialist support mechanism. In addition counselling psychologists could bring specific organizational intervention skills to improve the support mechanisms available.

Joined-up working practices

As has been indicated earlier in this chapter an obvious part of the counselling psychologist's role in the NPS could involve networking with other mental health workers in their local probation area. This might include psychologists, psychiatrists and CPNs working in community settings, secure units or prisons. This has the potential to cement multi-agency links across the correctional services and realize solid 'joined-up' working practices between mental health professionals. This holds the possibility to co-ordinate research, training and development initiatives, and facilitates the development of best practice across the area.

Resettlement of mentally disordered offenders

A significant proportion of high-risk offenders subject to the MAPPA will inevitably be prisoners approaching the end of their sentence. The inadequate resettlement of mentally disordered offenders is likely to result in their return to custody. Despite prison-based probation departments participating in the sentence planning and throughcare procedures in prisons (pursuing a 'seamless sentence' approach to their role), mentally disordered offenders have often in the past been subject to inadequate transitional arrangement in terms of their resettlement from custody into the community. Consequently this has left scope for a comprehensive review of the resettlement of offenders into the community (Southern, 1999). Developing effective joined-up working practices with mental health workers in prisons is therefore an important networking opportunity for counselling psychologists. Counselling psychologists undertaking this role may bring specialist knowledge of mental health issues to the process. In addition those employed by probation and prison services may bring detailed knowledge of the provision of psychological assessments and interventions undertaken in custody and in the community.

Care programme approach and mental health 'in-reach'

The care programme approach (CPA) involves the collaboration between the health authorities and social services in the pursuit of a multi-disciplinary assessment for health and social care needs and a subsequently designed co-ordinated and monitored care plan to meet these needs. The 1995 NACRO Mental Health advisory committee policy paper makes it clear that CPA should apply to all mentally disordered offenders, including those who enter into or are released from prison (NACRO, 1995).

The joint Department of Health and Home Office strategy document for developing and modernizing mental health services in prisons reiterates that mental health needs should be included in throughcare arrangements (Department of Health and Home Office, 2001).

The development of mental health 'in-reach' services and the transfer of funding and responsibility for prison healthcare services from the Home Office to the NHS have increased the scope for other applied psychology specialists working alongside forensic psychologists in prisons. This creates an opportunity that could both increase the potential for joined-up custodial and community mental healthcare services and enhance the profile and professional development opportunities of applied psychologists working within the remit of the National Offender Management Service (NOMS).

Joined-up working between applied psychologists in forensic settings

Examples can already be found of the flexibility applied psychologists can have in this field. Forensic psychologists, all with experience of working in prisons, exclusively staff the applied psychology unit in an NHS medium secure unit in North-East Yorkshire. Psychological interventions with offenders retain a largely cognitive behavioural focus. However, supervision may be facilitated from a variety of other models such as cognitive-analytic and psychodynamic, as well as cognitive behavioural approaches. Emphasis on clinical and mental health issues may lead to the sometimes inaccurate assumption that people detained under the Mental Health Act have offended solely as a result of their mental disorder, and that controlling their mental disorder will also control their offending (Bell, 2001).

Whilst forensic psychologists' consideration of risk assessment and management with offenders is likely to remain central to much of their work, there are potential gains from greater utilization of other applied psychology specialisms in forensic contexts. In addition there are potential gains from broadening the skills base of existing applied psychologists, for example by training forensic psychologists in a counselling-psychology perspective, and vice versa. This seems likely to generate synergistic gains for the probation service as well as for individual practitioners.

Counselling Psychologists in Probation and Prisons

There are already exciting developments in prisons in relation to the involvement of counselling psychologists working alongside forensic psychologists. Counselling psychologists are now directly employed by HM Prison Service to provide therapeutic interventions designed to address the mental health needs of women offenders in several establishments. This service continues to expand and is being seen to impact organizational needs positively (Cain, 1997). In response to this, a formulated structure of Chartered, trainee and student counselling psychologists is beginning to emerge within the prison service. The potential for this to become a routine training route for counselling psychologists is now approaching realization. To date there is little empirical evidence of positive impact. However, there is qualitative evidence with, for example, the greater involvement of psychologists in working with acutely suicidal prisoners, and in the greater provision of specialist support to other staff undertaking such challenging and stressful work.

In men's prisons a small but significant number of forensic psychologists with training in counselling psychology are also being invited to help address the mental health needs of prisoners in their establishments. Specifically this has been in relation to mental health 'in-reach' alongside the development of counselling services. Recognition of the benefits this holds for the prisoner, the organization and the psychologist paves the way for the very real prospect of the applied psychologist being supported to achieve Chartered status in both specialisms.

A prospective role for counselling psychologists to impact on NPS service delivery in relation to mental health has been identified and outlined above. If this is realized, then further scope for research, evaluation and training activities can follow in a similar way to how they have in prisons.

The potential also exists to emulate their emerging training route for counselling psychologists by offering student placements. Counselling psychology courses do not generally organize placements on behalf of their trainees, which means that counselling psychologists in training have considerable scope and flexibility in the selection of the placement experiences they choose. Whilst a large proportion of these will inevitably still be found in traditional NHS mental health settings a wide variety of alternative placement opportunities can be pursued within other agencies, and the voluntary and private sectors. Indeed it has been argued:

> Provided that students receive high calibre supervision, no placement should be ruled out . . . [and that] The clinical placement experience forms one of the cornerstones of the professional training. . . . supported by their personal psychotherapy, their clinical supervision, course work and by a general immersion in the mental health field (as indicated by attendance at lectures, meetings and conferences, and by extensive reading) – then these placements will help fortify the student for a challenging, rewarding, and ultimately helpful career in the mental health field. (Kahr, 1999)

The employment of Chartered counselling psychologists in the NPS would enable trainees (and volunteers) to receive the appropriate standard of supervision in their developing practice; as well as meeting important organizational needs.

NOTE

1   'Approved Premises' were established by the Criminal Justice and Court Services Act 2000 to replace Probation and Bail Hostels. The remit of 'Approved Premises' is also defined by this Act (National Probation Service, 2002).

Chapter Four

Assessment and Treatment of Sexual Offenders

Andrew Bates

Introduction

In the late 1980s various factors led to a greater public awareness of sexual abuse in the UK. These included the 1986 BBC *Childline* programme and its associated confidential phone-line, set up to offer counselling and advice to victims of child (sexual) abuse. Certain high-profile criminal trials focusing on rape cases and alleged widespread child abuse within communities in the UK (Butler-Sloss, 1988) generated significant media coverage and public controversy. There was the suggestion that issues of sexual abuse had not been acknowledged or dealt with appropriately in the past, and the recognition of the need for a more thorough approach to sex offender treatment began to develop. These political and cultural dynamics coincided with an increasing body of psychological practice and research evidence from North America (Marshall & Barbaree, 1988) that provided a greater theoretical understanding of, and the capacity to more effectively intervene with, those who committed sexual offences. A combination of all of these factors led criminal justice agencies such as HM Prison Service and the probation service to set up groupwork interventions for sex offenders using a more systematic, evidence-based approach than had been attempted in the past.

Early Involvement of Psychologists

Interventions with sexual offenders in the community is an area of probation practice that has involved both forensic and clinical psychologists for some considerable time. In some cases this even pre-dated the establishment of HM Prison Service Sex Offender Treatment Programme (SOTP), an initiative largely driven by forensic psychologists that began in 1991 (Grubin & Thornton, 1994). Barker and Morgan (1993) conducted a review of the practice of sex offender interventions within the UK probation services and, of the 55 services surveyed in England and Wales, 42 stated that they were running some kind of intervention for sex offenders while a further 7 said that they intended to in the near future. Barker and Morgan's survey showed up certain weaknesses in this area of probation practice, however, as 68 per cent of the interventions reviewed had only been running for five years or less. It was also considered that these interventions tended to rely upon the commitment and enthusiasm of individual practitioners and only a very small number were found to have any formal policy on how they were resourced, managed and supported. These deficits in practice have been largely addressed over the last ten years, not least by the increased involvement of forensic psychologists.

Many of the interventions identified, including those operating in Berkshire, Buckinghamshire and South-East London (Craissati, 1998) drew on specialist advice and consultancy from clinical psychologists working in local outpatient services attached to NHS medium secure units. In particular, this input from specialist applied psychologists, often working outside their formal Health Authority remit, tended to focus upon providing pre-treatment assessments of sex offenders, often utilizing psychometric tests such as the Multi-Phasic Sex Inventory (Nichols & Molinder, 1984). These psychologists would also be involved in consulting with probation staff after treatment sessions and in this respect providing clinical supervision for the work.

The Intervention Process and Objectives

Intervention work with sex offenders in the UK at this time, and since, was largely cognitive-behavioural in terms of theoretical approach as a result of the findings of the North American evidence-base (Marques et al., 1994; Marshall & Pithers, 1994). This was fortuitous from the point of view of the training of staff and application of new interventions as the techniques involved could be relatively easily taught, as opposed to, for example, the more obscure and specialized approaches of psychodynamic therapies. Perhaps it is not surprising that psychologically oriented treatments have been more demonstrably effective as psychologists tend to have particular skills in terms of gathering and analysing evidence about practice outcomes. In contrast some other therapeutic approaches have had less of a focus on evaluation.

The cognitive-behavioural approach is focused on the direct needs of not only the offender, but also society itself. The foremost aim is for the offender to improve his[1] quality of life and also that of any potential victim by not behaving in a destructive and highly anti-social way in the future, rather than by improving his general psychological well-being.

The intervention process focuses on reducing the expected high level of denial about the thoughts, feelings and behaviours that led up to their offending, with a view to the offender understanding and taking responsibility for what he did and thus becoming better able to deal with any urge to behave in a similar way in the future. Sexual offending is often perceived as an especially shameful criminal activity, lacking the supportive subcultural beliefs and attitudes that may be present for other types of offences. Anybody, faced with behaviour that is regarded as highly unacceptable is likely to deny or at least minimize what has been done in order to reduce his sense of guilt and shame. Cognitive behavioural sex offender interventions work on the basis that offenders acted as they did because they were sexually aroused and motivated to do so. Various psychological processes and deficits might lie behind this motivation, most commonly strong feelings of anger, powerlessness and a lack of control in life, which may have led to a need for offenders to offend in a manner that had become sexualized.

However, the crucial point is that they offended sexually because they wanted to do so and were able to overcome the many internal and external inhibitions in order for their motivating thoughts to be acted out. It follows that they might behave in the same way again under certain adverse circumstances.

Cognitive-behavioural interventions use exercises in which offending behaviour and associated thoughts and sexual fantasies are examined in detail using different models of human behaviour; for example, the four-preconditions model (Finkelhor, 1984) and the cycle of offending model (Wolf, 1984; Beckett, 1994). In this respect offenders become more used to discussing their behaviour and admitting associated fantasies both in terms of their extent and the degree of pleasure and significance that they in fact held prior to the sexual offence and subsequently. Offenders are required to examine the various rationalizations that they used to behave in this way, despite knowing it is wrong. These might include convincing themselves that such behaviour would not really harm the victim, that what they did 'just happened' or that they were powerless to stop themselves. As in other cognitive treatment settings such beliefs, which are often at best only partially true and will usually deny significant aspects of the behaviour and its consequences. Such beliefs are constructively challenged. The intention here is to point out inconsistencies in the offenders' beliefs and make holding on to them less feasible, so that they become obliged to accept the reality of what they did, why they did it and what damaging consequences for themselves and others it had.

If offenders reach this point (which they may not, as human defensiveness can be very resistant to seeing an objective truth and taking a painful responsibility for one's own behaviour) the further aspects of the intervention are pursued in group interventions. Central to these are the need to adopt tactics to manage and cope with future occasions when temptation to offend might reoccur. In this respect sex offender interventions include a focus on 'relapse prevention' similar to that developed in working with substance misusers (DiClemente, 1993). Within such models it is made clear to sex offenders that no intervention will 'cure' them but rather they will need to manage their own future behaviour as well as actively seek help when they become aware of an urge to reoffend. Such situations might be emotional (e.g. low mood, feelings of anger or powerlessness) or physical (e.g. proximity to a potential victim), but recognizing and developing practical ways of dealing with them is a vital part of the treatment process.

Early Research and Evaluation

In 1994 a piece of research was published by a group of psychologists, the Sex Offender Treatment and Evaluation (STEP) report (Beckett et al., 1994) This research was commissioned by the Home Office and evaluated six community-based treatment groupwork interventions as well as a privately run residential intervention for sex offenders that had been operating in the Midlands since the late 1980s. The research looked at the progress of 52 child abusers, focusing on psychometric measures that assessed various aspects of the offenders' attitudes and beliefs that were connected to sex offending behaviours. In this respect the scope of the research was limited, as it did not involve any behavioural follow-up of the 'treated' men, did not address the progress of men who had offended sexually against adults and overall had only a relatively small sample size. However, over the coming years behavioural follow-up of this sample became possible and the work was clearly an important step to providing systematic evaluation of this area of work.

Psychometric tests

The measures used by the STEP team formed the basis of the psychometric package now used nationally by the National Probation Service (NPS) to assess sex offenders. The purpose of these measures is to determine the offender's specific intervention needs and level of psychological 'deviancy' (i.e. differences in terms of relevant attitudes and beliefs from a non-offending sample) and to provide a baseline profile against which reported change can be measured in the future (i.e. evaluation of intervention effectiveness). The measures could be broadly divided into three categories (Beckett, 1998):

1. *Offence-specific*. These included attitudes that directly related to committing acts of sexual abuse (e.g. denial of offence planning and deviant sexual fantasy, sexualized views of children, justification for sexual abuse of children, deficits in victim empathy and relapse prevention knowledge and skills). All of these ways of thinking were the targets for discussion, challenge and change in treatment interventions run in the community.

2. *Socio-affective*. These measures focused on aspects of personality that were generally identified with, though not directly predictive of, sex offending behaviour. These included self esteem, emotional loneliness, assertiveness, locus of control (the degree to which one feels in control of one's own fate and circumstances) and general capacity for empathy. These areas were not originally specifically addressed in the groupwork interventions run in the community through both lack of time and facilities but also a general pervading belief that focusing on broader 'personality' deficits in offenders might just act to provide sophisticated rationalizations to continue with sexual offending. Subsequent research and the development of sex offender groupwork interventions in both prison and the community (Beech, 1998) has shown that these broader aspects of an offenders' functioning are significant in terms of predicting future levels of risk and do require addressing.

3. *Validity scales*. These scales are a key part of this psychometric evaluation process, given the limitations of self-report by subjects who might have a very strong vested interest in not presenting themselves in a sexually deviant light. These measures indicate whether a subject might be responding to assessment in a 'socially desirable' manner using impression-management and self-deception (Paulhus, 1998) to avoid being fully honest about tendencies and behaviours. High scores on these scales and others imbedded elsewhere in the psychometric assessment package effectively invalidate the scores achieved by a subject. These measures are very important in not seeing psychometric assessment as an infallible process but as something that can be faked. If such faking is detected, then results need to be considered accordingly.

Research findings and recommendations

The findings of the STEP research were to prove very significant in the development of community-based sex offender intervention over the next 10 years and in particular in the role of psychology within that process. In summary, the research identified that men with more 'deviant' psychometric scores required and benefited more from longer interventions. In addressing victim empathy deficits and developing relapse prevention awareness the interventions under review were showing less effectiveness than in other areas of intervention focus. Using the Group Environment Scale (Moos, 1994), the findings also showed that the most successful groupwork appeared to be that which was well organized and highly cohesive with group leaders who acted in constructive and empowering ways rather than being overcontrolling and confrontational. The research recommended that additional groupwork sessions were required to address the range of personality problems displayed by the more 'deviant' offenders and also to focus on deficits in victim empathy and relapse prevention. In addition to this the research observed that there was very little provision for fantasy modification work to be undertaken with offenders. There was a recommendation that psychologists should be more involved in community-based interventions in order to offer this kind of treatment that had previously been practised one to one by psychologists in institutional settings. It also stated that psychologists before intervention should systematically assess offenders in order to best identify the nature and extent of intervention work required.

Formal Development of the Forensic Psychologist's Role

As a result of the various developments in research and practice throughout the UK in the first half of the 1990s, a unique multi-agency community sex offender treatment programme employing a full-time forensic psychologist was established in 1995 (Beckett, 1998). Covering the three counties of Oxfordshire, Buckinghamshire and Berkshire it was called the Thames Valley Project (TVP). The project was funded by a variety of agencies that had a stake in the interventions with sex offenders, including the probation service, local health authorities and children and families social services departments. A business plan was drawn up by senior managers from these services, which stated how the need to combat sexual abuse was not confined to just one agency (e.g. the probation service). The health authority was involved because clinical psychologists and psychiatrists were increasingly being used to provide assessment and intervention work with sex offenders via the courts and other routes such as referral from primary healthcare settings. In addition to this the victims of sexual abuse would often require long-term input from health and social services. For social services there was also a need for risk assessment and management of offenders with a history of sexual offending in order for them to be safely allowed back into family situations, giving social services an additional stake in such interventions.

The Thames Valley Project featured an intensive intervention programme (run full-time over two working weeks) using cognitive behavioural approaches as described earlier and was resourced with a full-time staff to run six groups of eight men per year. An important feature of the Thames Valley Project was the presence of a full-time Chartered forensic psychologist with expertise in working with sex offenders. In keeping with the recommendations of the STEP report the psychologist, as well as acting as a group facilitator, was to provide individual fantasy modification intervention in certain cases and pre- and post-psychometric assessments of offenders for the purposes of pre-group assessment and the ongoing evaluation of the intervention. Later on in the life of TVP, an additional intervention module was created, which focused on 'life skills'. This addressed certain general personality deficits observed in more entrenched sex offenders, and inclusion on this extended option, as in HM Prison Service SOTP, was dictated by the presence of a deviant psychometric profile as well as other indicators including evidence of 'faking good' (e.g. impression management or self-deception) at assessment, any offence against an adult, or particular situational factors known as 'contextual risk', such as an offender living in a household where a child is present.

Role of Psychological Services in Working with Other Agencies

The TVP community sex offender programme proved to be an extremely fertile environment from which psychological approaches could be conveyed to other practitioners with interests in the contentious and high-profile area of working with sex offenders. Very quickly the specialist expertise within the Thames Valley Project team was much in demand, leading to a great deal of positive inter-agency work. This included, for instance, providing specialist input, including risk assessments, into child protection case conferences held by social services focusing on the needs of children living in households with men who had been through the TVP intervention. Further professional links were made in community mental-health teams and training placements at TVP were set up for Community Psychiatric Nurses (working with people with learning disabilities), specialist registrars in forensic psychiatry and clinical psychologists. These placements usually involved shadowing the forensic psychologist in general work and also when running a two-week intensive 'core' groupwork intervention.

Other cases where agencies consulted with TVP led to further training for staff from a local agency working with people with cerebral palsy, one of whom had been exposing himself to children. Further training was provided for local housing agencies whose staff would be required to work with sex offenders as part of their case-work. In addition, private psychiatric hospitals consulted with the project psychologist about their own proposals for assessment and treatment for those of their patients with a history of sexual offending. The 1997 Sex Offender Register led to the involvement of Thames Valley Police with the TVP. The team were able to advise on the best ways of risk assessing offenders held upon the register through processes such as the Structured Anchored Clinical Judgement (Thornton, 2002), the STEP psychometric measures and clinical assessment in certain cases. The Thames Valley Police eventually utilized the project's services in this respect so much that they began to provide ongoing annual funding, and referrals for offenders cautioned for a sexual offence have been made by the police, resulting in treatment carried out on a voluntary basis for offenders without the mandate of a court order.

Developments in Research and Evaluation

1. *Psychometric impact of treatment on relevant attitudes*. An evaluation of treatment gains according to psychometric test results before and after treatment was made during the early years of the project's existence. This was crucial in terms of ensuring funding from parent agencies, and evidence was required that the project was achieving its objectives. Yearly results consistently indicated that offenders would shift to a statistically significant degree post-treatment in the desired direction on the 'offence specific' variables, although not on the 'socio-affective' variables. This failing was one of the research findings that lay behind the development of the extended 'life skills' block. Future research will inform whether this additional module has an impact upon more general personality deficits in this group of offenders.

2. *'Partner's Group'*. Such was the need for TVP involvement in the area of child protection work (with social services) that a group for the partners of offenders who had been treated on the TVP programme was established. The purpose of this group was to provide a greater understanding of their partner's offending behaviour so that they could assist in monitoring them in the future and also make a more informed decision about whether or not they wanted to remain in the relationship. The psychologist's role in this part of the TVP was mainly to evaluate the group, although identifying appropriate

psychometric tests for this unusual purpose has remained something of a challenge and requires further development. Early indications from this research show that partners of sex offenders who remain in the relationship often do not develop real insight into their partner's behaviour. This contrasts with partners who leave the relationship, in which case the increase of understanding and awareness of issues of future risk was markedly higher.

3. *Working with the Police Service.* Research in police practice was also conducted under TVP auspices by three forensic psychologists for the Family Protection Unit of the Thames Valley Police. This focused on the particular challenges of interviewing suspects in sexual offences against children and devising an approach for this task using the police-practised PEACE (plan and prepare, engage and explain, account clarify & challenge, closure, evaluate) model of interviewing.

4. *Longer-term follow-up studies.* In conjunction with the Home Office long-term evaluation section a reconviction study was carried out of 183 sex offenders treated by TVP between 1995 and 1999 (Falshaw, Friendship & Bates, 2003). Subjects were monitored for an average of just under four years and details about post-intervention behaviour were drawn from three sources: two national police databases, which indicated any formal sexual reconviction and the files kept on each sex offender registered with TVP. This latter source enabled a more detailed process of evaluation, known in the literature as a 'recidivism study' (Friendship & Thornton, 2001), to be carried out, beyond the normal boundaries of the simple reconviction study. A total of 10 subjects (5% of the total) were reconvicted for at least one further sexual offence. Another 19 men (10% of the total) either had allegations made against them or committed an act that may have involved, or been the preparation for, further sexual offending. The pre-treatment psychometric test results of those who were recidivists were compared with those of the men who were not. On a measure of emotional loneliness the men who were recidivists scored higher than the men who were not. This difference was statistically significant.

The Process of Accreditation and National Roll-out

In 2001 community-based sex offender intervention underwent perhaps the most significant development since its origins in the late 1980s when the interventions developed by three probation areas were subsequently nationally accredited. All had a long-standing history in their geographical areas of Northumbria, West Midlands and Thames Valley (Fisher & Beech, 1999). Each had also undergone development and refinement, until they met the criteria required by a panel of independent professionals and academics in working with sex offenders. Thus they were deemed suitable for formal replication across the whole of England and Wales. The different qualities of each intervention were matched to the needs of probation areas (mainly geographical issues such as whether intervention delivery was required for a predominantly rural or urban area). In keeping with the previously accredited sex offender interventions, this process required the production of practice, theory and evaluation manuals, which detailed the intervention process and the research and evidence-base upon which it is based.

Each groupwork intervention required a groupwork 'programme manager' responsible for co-ordinating staffing issues and the overall general management as well as a 'treatment manager', responsible for managing the more clinical aspects of the intervention such as allocating offenders to groups and supervising staff by means of video monitoring. This development and formalization of practice coincided with the introduction of forensic psychologists into the National Probation Service (Towl, 2000, 2002, 2004) and in some cases forensic psychologists took up roles of programme and/ or treatment manager for probation-run interventions. Responsibility for overall national co-ordination of practice, training and research passed to the newly established National Probation Directorate based in London, which also employed psychologists with responsibility for psychometric assessment and evaluation of interventions.

Future Developments of Psychology: Research and Practice

Various new community-based initiatives in the field of sex offender work also provide opportunities for the development of practice and research by psychologists. The 'Circles of Support and Accountability' initiative (Wilson, 2003) has been imported from Canada as a pilot project into the UK. This innovative approach involves the recruitment and training of volunteers from the community to form into groups with a 'core-member' who is a sex offender at high-risk of reoffending, normally on licence following release from prison. The 'circle' acts as a support and guidance network for the offender, offering friendship and the chance to address issues of isolation and emotional loneliness that have been shown to correspond with reoffending by sex offenders. The Thames Valley area of the National Probation Service has a forensic psychologist involved with a two-prong evaluation of this approach. The evaluation uses psychometric tests to assess sex offenders' 'socio-affective' personality variables over time as they continue to live in the community with the support of their 'circle'. It will also feature elements of qualitative research by means of focus group discussion with circle members themselves about their motives for and experience of the project, identifying best practice and recommendations for development. Although in its infancy, this is one of many community-based initiatives that have, so far, welcomed psychological input.

Another such initiative is the Multi-agency Public Protection Arrangements (MAPPA), established nationally in 2001. These arrangements and the system of Multi-agency Public Protection Panels (MAPPPs) derived from them (as described in chapter 9) allow police, probation and other community agencies such as health, social services and housing authorities to discuss issues that arise from 'high-risk' and 'dangerous' offenders at large in the community. As one of the criteria for inclusion on the MAPPP discussion is being a registered sex offender, psychologists working in this area will have a direct link into this process. There is much opportunity here for psychologists to provide specialist risk assessments and management approaches for particularly dangerous or violent sex offenders.

A further recent development in community-based sex offender work has been the challenge of how to deal with the cautions and convictions of many offenders for possession of indecent images downloaded from the Internet. Although possession of child pornography has long been a criminal offence, in the past such material was generally difficult and expensive to access. Recent technological developments have meant that such material is now much more easily, privately and cheaply available via the Internet. The passing to the police of the credit card details of people who had paid for such obscene material from websites in the USA resulted in a very large number of convictions, many of which have attracted community sentences. This new aspect of deviant sexual activity is one that requires further research in order to ascertain the risk of repeated or even escalated sexually deviant activity and what kind of treatment is appropriate for such an offender. It is likely that there is significant scope for ongoing psychological research into all of these questions.

Conclusions

The full-time employment of a number of forensic psychologists by the National Probation Service since 2001 gives rise to more opportunities for the application and development of psychological practice in the community than ever before. The thrust of probation work in recent years has been case management of offenders and the treatment of offending behaviours. Further opportunities are arising for forensic psychologists working with sex offenders within this context. These may include facilitating groupwork interventions and then progressing to management of such services. Psychologists will continue to have a role in the application and oversight of psychometric tests, which have now become a core aspect of the intervention both in terms of assessment of offenders' treatment needs and providing data for short-term evaluations. Further research opportunities exist, in particular with reconviction and recidivism studies and co-work with the police, especially by means of access if possible to the extensive surveillance notes that are kept by the police on known offenders, allowing for detailed follow-up of sex offenders' behaviour after conviction and not simply the blunt instrument of reconviction data.

In addition to this the role of the psychologist is vital in providing specialist assessments that assist in the allocation of treatment places, in particular the use of tests such as the WAIS-III which is used to identify if an offender's IQ is below 80 and therefore not suitable for the existing groupwork interventions. Forensic psychologists in probation are also now becoming trained and practised in the use of a range of other assessment tools, including the Psychopathy Checklist – Revised (Hare, 1991; Hare & Hart, 1993). It has been argued that scores above 25 on this scale also indicate a possible lack of suitability for current groupwork interventions. One problem that arises from the advances in research that indicate the lack of effectiveness of existing interventions for certain offenders is the ongoing need for the development of other approaches for those who are excluded. Over time, psychologists in the probation service, as in the prison service, may well lead the way in the development of increasingly specialized interventions designed to reduce the level of risk presented by sexual offenders to society.

NOTE

1   Although women are convicted of sexual offences they are a small but nevertheless significant minority compared to male perpetrators. For the purpose of this chapter sex offenders are referred to as male on the basis that men make up the vast majority of such offenders.

Chapter Five

Risk Assessment

David Crighton

Introduction

In this chapter the process of assessing and managing risk within probation service settings is considered. Initially a definition of risk assessment and risk management is offered. This is followed by a review of the main concepts involved in these processes. The current approaches being favoured in probation services have increasingly involved the use of what may loosely be termed structured risk assessment 'tools'. In delivering an overall assessment of risk the probation and prison services have jointly adopted a system called the Offender Assessment System (OASys) (Home Office, 2001). This is a system that builds largely on the approach used in the Level of Service Inventory – Revised (LSI – R) (Andrews & Bonta, 1995). OASys is designed to meet a number of broad aims across correctional services in the form of allocating offenders to broad 'risk bands' and focusing case management on areas of risk. The probation service has sought, increasingly, to use more precise measures of risk for particular groups of offenders; for example those perceived as high-risk sexual or violent offenders.

A fashionable example of this is the Psychopathy Checklist – Revised (PCL – R) (Hare, 2003), which is reviewed as an exemplar in more detail below in terms of some of its strengths and weaknesses. The chapter concludes with a view of the future development of the role of psychologists in probation in developing and enhancing risk assessment work.

Risk assessment is a concept that cuts across much of the work of practitioners in the forensic field. It is also an area that has seen a recent growth in terms of research, within the area of forensic practice and also outside it (Monahan & Steadman, 1994; Towl & Crighton, 1997; Crighton, 1999; Prins, 1999).

Major Concepts in Risk Assessment and Management

A number of fundamental concepts underpin this area of work and this section addresses some of these. Perhaps the most difficult term in relation to risk assessment has been that of 'dangerousness'. The Chambers English Dictionary (1996) defines this as 'Something that may cause harm or injury. A state or situation in which harm may come to a person or thing.'

It is not a new observation that this term has been predominantly of use to lawyers and legislators, rather than to forensic practitioners. In a groundbreaking paper (Scott, 1977) attention was drawn to some of the difficulties associated with risk assessment and such concerns have proved to be well founded. In particular it was noted that 'dangerousness' is a complex concept that can be used in a variety of ways. For example, it is sometimes used to refer to a particular hazard. At other times it may be used to indicate that there is a significant probability of a hazardous event occurring. Such differing uses of the term may in turn produce confusion (Scott, 1977; Monahan, 1992; Prins, 1999). This observation has been referred to repeatedly in recent years because it remains germane to our understanding of the potentially fraught and challenging area of risk assessment.

Recently, some researchers have sought to break down this complex construct into its components and distinguish between risk, defined as the likelihood of an event's occurring, and danger defined as the degree of damage or harm that may follow an event happening (Prins, 1995, 1999).

The notion of dangerousness is a pervasive theme in criminal law and is a fundamental concern for applied psychologists (of whatever specialism) working in probation settings. For example, the term 'dangerous' is enshrined in a range of legislative frameworks addressing the management of offenders such as the Mental Health Act 1983 and the Criminal Justice Act 1991. It also seems likely that the new Mental Health Act will retain the term for its perceived utility in court settings. The challenge for forensic practitioners here is that the use, and indeed misuse, of this concept has potential to contribute to erroneous classification of offenders. Effective practice requires practitioners to assess and manage risks within the criminal justice system and to convey their findings in ways that are meaningful within that system. The criminal justice system is primarily geared to defining individuals dichotomously as 'dangerous' or 'not dangerous'. In reality, risks will always be probabilistic judgements (Towl and Crighton, 1996; 1997) and applied psychologists have a clear professional responsibility and accountability to keep this in mind when advising others on risk assessment and management.

Prediction

The notion that risks are probabilistic judgements leads neatly to the question of prediction, defined by Chamber's Dictionary (1996) as 'To say in advance. To foretell.'

Criminological studies on prediction are characterized by the identification of a range of variables such as age (Monahan, 1981) or the offence type (Copas, 1982) that are thought to be predictive of, for example, further offending. The actual predictive power of these variables, in isolation or combination, can then be tested using essentially correlational research designs. An example here might be using age, number of previous offences and previous violent convictions to predict reconvictions for violence within two years of the prediction. This research has been reviewed in detail elsewhere (Loeber & Farrington, 2001).

Researchers in this area have noted that the complexities of any human social behaviour makes it logically implausible that such predictors will ever be 100 per cent accurate. A more useful test of such prediction studies is to check the degree of accuracy of the estimated probability of the relationship between the measured variables and outcome and compare these with chance (Towl & Crighton, 1996). For example, an individual's height is likely much of the time to be an effective predictor of his or her weight. It is likely to yield a better than chance performance of predicting weight. However, the relationship between height and weight is not a simple linear relationship. There are very tall, thin individuals and short, stocky individuals who will not fit this simple empirical model.

Central to prediction studies is the use of precisely defined terms. These include 'predictor' and 'criterion' variables and 'base rates' (Monahan, 1981). Predictor variables are those variables that may be used to predict an event at a specified level of probability and the criterion variable is the defined outcome (Towl & Crighton, 1997). For example, a conviction for a violent offence within two years might constitute a criterion variable, whilst the number of previous violent convictions between the ages of 12 and 14 years might constitute a predictor variable. This may seem self-evident but, in reality, the use of terms such as 'dangerousness' tend to conflate a range of criterion variables. The careful use of defined terms allows practitioners to avoid this basic logical error.

Base rates are also an essential concept in the process of assessing risks and refer to the relative frequency with which a specified event occurs (Plous, 2002). This frequency needs to be considered in the process because it strongly affects the challenge posed to practitioners. An example might be suicide, which is a low-frequency event that is seen more frequently amongst offenders than amongst the general population. Even so, it remains a very low-frequency event. If suicide were occurring in 0.1 per cent of offenders, it would strictly speaking be possible to devise a risk assessment tool that was accurate 99.9 per cent of the time. The test would simply need to say that every offender was not 'at risk'. Such a 'tool' would be of limited value though to practitioners whose task here is in fact to identify the 0.1 per cent of offenders who will, in the absence of an intervention to reduce risk, complete suicide. In summary, overall low-frequency events will tend to be more difficult to predict effectively than high-frequency events (Monahan, 1997; Reason, 1997; Loeber & Farrington, 2001).[1]

The Use of Psychological Tests and Assessments in Risk Assessment

In recent years there has been a growth in the use of structured assessments of risk across a range of behaviours. The approaches used range broadly along a continuum from 'actuarial' to 'clinical' assessments. Empirical approaches may, for example, depend on data such as previous convictions to estimate the probability of a given outcome. To take a hypothetical example a violent offender with 99 previous convictions for violent offences may have an 85 per cent probability of being reconvicted of a violent offence within two years. In many respects this is useful information but what it does not, and indeed cannot tell, is whether the individual offender being assessed falls into the 85 per cent who will be reconvicted, or the 15 per cent who will not.

At the other end of the continuum is what might be termed unstructured 'clinical' assessments. Here practitioners will use their knowledge and experience to reach a decision about whether an offender presents a risk. Research into this type of approach has consistently shown that unstructured assessments made in this way are an inaccurate way of assessing risk (Helibrun, 1990; Heilbrun & Dvoskin, 2003). However, this overall finding masks additional complexity. For example, it is clear there is a range of performance across practitioners, with some making assessments that are better than chance. Others in contrast make predictions that are worse than chance; in other words they make predictions consistently in the wrong direction. When amalgamated, such data tends to suggest that clinical assessments are not predictive (Monahan & Steadman, 1994; Heilbrun & Dvoskin, 2003). It seems likely that 'good' practitioners are, in this context, identifying cues that are genuinely predictive; in contrast 'poor' practitioners are identifying cues that are unrelated or worse.

As noted, purely empirical approaches present difficulties because they are essentially predictive about groups of people, rather than individuals. A further weakness with such approaches is that they tell us little about what can be done to moderate or manage risks. Such predictions are often based on what have been termed 'static' factors, which refers to the fact that these are unchanging and often unchangeable. Examples of such static predictors might include age at first conviction and so on. It is generally the case that whatever changes occur with the offender historical factors such as these will not change. However, it can be argued that offenders can and do change, limiting the predictive value of such data in predicting outcomes (Heilbrun & Dvoskin, 2003).

Unstructured clinical assessments also present problems because of the range of performance by practitioners, with most performing relatively poorly. Probably as a result of these concerns there has been a recent growth in the use of what might be broadly termed structured risk assessment 'tools' within offender management community settings.

One popular risk assessment 'tool' is considered in more detail below. However, the issues relating to the use of psychological assessment methods are broadly applicable to other structured risk assessment 'tools'.

The Psychopathy Checklist – Revised (PCL – R)

The Psychopathy Checklist – Revised (PCL – R) and the various alternative versions are a psychological assessment method developed in Canada. It is an assessment that has gained ground recently as a popular method of assessing 'risk'. It is also noteworthy that a number of other risk assessment 'tools' such as the HCR–20 (Webster et al., 1997) and the Violence Risk Appraisal Guide (VRAG) (Quinsey et al., 1998) have been developed, which improve on the predictive validity of the PCL – R alone. However, both include the PCL – R within their framework, suggesting that this assessment remains a central measure in such risk assessment tools.

In a UK sample those scoring 25 and over on the PCL – R were twice as likely to be reconvicted as those scoring less than 25 (Hart, Hare & Forth, 1993; Cooke & Michie, 1997; Clark, 2000a). This increases to a ratio of 4:1 where only reconvictions for violent offending are considered (Hemphill, Hare & Wong, 1998). The PCL – R has also been shown to be predictive of institutional problems (Clark, 2000a). However, this is not a particularly surprising finding given its circularity. The PCL – R identified individuals who have presented as being more troublesome and disturbing. A number of researchers in this area have noted that it is not really surprising that these individuals have futures that are also most troublesome (Gendreau, Goggin & Smith, 1999).

Advocates of the PCL – R and related tools make a number of claims in relation to its value in two key respects. First, it is suggested that the PCL – R is a very effective predictor in relation to future violent recidivism. Secondly, it is suggested that the PCL – R is an effective predictor of responsivity to intervention (Quinsey et al., 1998). Indeed it has been described as 'unparalleled' (Salekin, Rogers & Sewell, 1996) as a risk assessment tool.

The view that those with high PCL – R scores respond negatively to existing interventions rests largely on a study that looked at treatment outcomes from the Oak Ridge Social Therapy Unit. Using a PCL – R cut-off score of 25 the researchers categorized offenders as 'psychopathic' (25 and above) or 'non-psychopathic' (less than 25). The researchers noted that the levels of reoffending for those in the 'psychopathic' group who had received treatment at Oak Ridge were higher than for untreated 'psychopathic' offenders. They also noted that the levels of reoffending amongst offenders with PCL – R scores of 25 and above were higher than for those with PCL – R scores of less than 25 (Rice, Harris & Cormier, 1992).

Clearly in the context of probation practice any method that provides an accurate estimation of future risk and also of likely response to intervention is to be broadly welcomed. It is perhaps this that has led to the recent rapid growth in use of the PCL – R and related measures.

However, the PCL – R also presents a number of difficulties that suggest a need for caution in the use of this method and call into question the appropriateness of this approach to assessing risk and assessing likely response to interventions. Some of the key concerns about the PCL – R are outlined below. However, more detailed reviews of the PCL – R are available (Gendreau, Goggin & Smith, 1999).

One striking concern about the PCL – R is the very limited base-rate data on PCL – R scores in the general community. The PCL – R manuals (Hare, 1991, 2003) provide normative data for incarcerated offenders and psychiatric patients. However, normative data for the general population is lacking, something that significantly weakens the scope to make inferences about individuals in relation to PCL – R scores.

A further concern relates to the cut-off points using the PCL – R for an individual to be categorized as 'psychopathic'. The usual cut point for North American samples is 30, although in other studies this has been 25. However, researchers in the UK have suggested 25 as a more appropriate cut point. Researchers here seem to have set largely arbitrary cut-off points and used post hoc explanations, based on social and cultural differences to 'account' for these (Gacono, 2000).

Related to this point it is worth noting that in any appropriately structured psychometric measure a normal expectation would be that confidence intervals should be specified. So, for example, an IQ test might yield a score of 100 but have a confidence interval of 10. This would suggest that the 'true' IQ was likely to be between 90 and 110. However, such confidence intervals are not presented in the PCL – R manuals (Hare, 1991, 2003).

No psychometric assessment is 100 per cent accurate'; therefore some individuals will be assigned to the wrong groups. For example, offenders may be assessed as likely to reoffend but do not (a false positive). Alternatively, they may be assessed as unlikely to reoffend but do (a false negative). The accuracy with which a method can allocate individuals to the correct group is termed 'specificity'. Freedman (2001) in looking at this in the PCL – R noted the low specificity of this method. Freedman summarizes the false positive rates for the PCL – R in predicting violent behaviour as ranging from 50 to 75 per cent.

The use of the PCL – R also raises a number of issues in relation to diversity and equality. Studies in North America have shown that black offenders score significantly higher on the PCL – R than do white offenders (Kosson, Smith & Newman, 1990). Curiously the researchers are somewhat dismissive of this finding, suggesting post hoc that this apparent bias is likely to be circum-vented by the PCL – R being completed by practitioners from a similar ethnic background to the offender being assessed. It seems likely that similar biases may be present in the assessment of African-Caribbean offenders in the UK, although this clearly awaits further research (Bhui, 1999).

Linked to this is the issue of class and culture related judgements within the PCL – R. It is axiomatic that differences in sexual behaviour have existed across countries, across time and between cultures. The PCL – R however includes a number of what appear to be moral judgements that seem likely to disadvantage particular groups. For example, in item 11, assessors are asked to make judgements about promiscuity. Linked to this, for example, item 17 of the PCL – R requires assessors to make judgements about whether indi-viduals have had 'many' short-term sexual relationships.

Iterative Classification Tree Methods

Iterative classification tree (ICT) methods have long been used in a range of areas where risks are assessed, for example in the prediction of violence (Gardner et al., 1996). The method has a number of advantages for practi-tioners and clearly integrates well with other frameworks popular in risk assessment, such as the Cambridge framework outlined below.

The advantages of an ICT approach include the fact that it is predicated on an interactive and contingent model of risk (Monahan et al., 2000). It also allows for fine distinctions to be assessed within subgroups. This contrasts markedly with approaches that group offenders into broad risk categories, such as the PCL – R outlined above.

The development of ICT within the context of forensic practice has been most effectively developed as part of the MacArthur risk assessment study. The aim of the approach is to increase the clinical utility of actuarial risk assessment methods (Monahan et al., 2000). Within this study an ICT was developed to look at the risk of violence in mentally disordered offenders. An algorithm was developed to look at the associations between 106 eligible risk factors and the dichotomous outcome measure of risk in the community.

In looking at outcomes the researchers clearly defined what they meant by high- and low-risk groups. Those in the high-risk group were defined as those showing rates of violence at twice the base rate or above. Similarly the low-risk group was defined as those showing violence at half the base rate or below. Within the sample studied the base rate for violence was 18.7 per cent.

To take two exemplars from this study, those with no history of serious arrests showed a 9.2 per cent rate of violence in the community. This relatively low-risk group however disguised additional complexity. Hence those rated as low on motor impulsivity were at lower risk (7 per cent), whereas those rated as high on this characteristic saw their risk increase to 21.2 per cent. Again within the low impulsivity group additional distinctions could be made. Those with a familial history of the father using illicit drugs showed a rate of 18.9 per cent compared to 4.9 per cent for those who had no such history.

At the other end of the range those with a history of arrest for offences of robbery, rape, assault or murder showed a rate of violence in the community of 36.1 per cent. However, where there was an absence of recent violent fantasies this fell to 26.9 per cent. Where such fantasies were present the rate increased to 52.7 per cent (Monahan et al., 2000).

Such an approach fits well with the Cambridge framework for risk assessment and management outlined below and the use of ICT approaches is particularly apposite to stage 3 of this structured approach (see figure 5.1). Having identified the risk or risks being assessed, an ICT approach provides an effective way to integrate actuarial data in a clinically useful way. It also avoids the oversimplification inherent in existing 'tools' that often place offenders into a small number of broadly defined categories. The ICT approach also feeds into the way in which clinicians intuitively tend to think about addressing risk, in that it guides the intervention process outlined in stage 4 of the Cambridge framework.

The Cambridge framework outlined below has utility in giving practitioners a logical framework within which to assess and manage risks on an ongoing basis. It also outlines the process within which the available evidence base and a range of psychometric assessments might helpfully fit into assessing and managing risk. Applied psychologists based in probation settings have the opportunity to contribute to this area in coming years by developing and enhancing the skills of multi-disciplinary teams and in helping to provide professionally defensible risk assessment and management approaches in the community.

A Framework for Risk Assessment

In looking at the area of child protection Wald and Woolverton (1990) suggested that effective risk assessment needed to do three things. First, the process must identify factors that are known to be associated with the particular future behaviour or behaviours of concern. Secondly, it is essential that the factors concerned can be accurately measured. They note as an example that it is not useful to know that current drug use is a good predictor, if it is not possible to measure accurately current drug use. Thirdly, they note that effective risk assessment is complicated by the need to balance conflicting goals in child protection. This is equally applicable to community forensic settings. If the goal was, for example, simply one of protecting the public, then this could be served by imprisoning offenders. However, the probation service is also concerned to rehabilitate offenders wherever possible. This means that an effective risk assessment process needs to balance risks. Ultimately, whatever methods and 'tools' are used to assist in the process risk assessment will involve making value judgements. All good risk assessments will involve estimating probabilities and, as noted below, psychological research can help by reducing some of the evident biases in decision-making processes. However, the fact remains that decisions about what level of risk is acceptable will require judgements.

As noted above structured risk assessment 'tools' raises a number of issues in relation to use. In reality such methods are often asked for, and indeed used, in ways that remove them from an appropriate context. For example, psychologists may be asked to conduct a PCL – R assessment on an offender without a clear rationale for its use in relation to future risk, or indeed without reference to the risks associated with the assessment method. Psychologists here have a clear ethical and professional duty not to provide tests in the absence of such a rationale and without assessing the associated risks.

Figure 5.1 below provides an outline of the Cambridge framework for risk assessment and management (Towl & Crighton, 1997). This provides, in essence, a logical structure in line with practice in other, better developed, areas of risk assessment and management that also facilitates the use of ICT approaches.

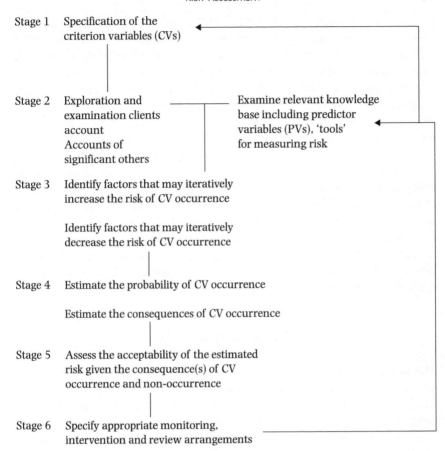

Figure 5.1 Cambridge framework for risk assessment

Within the Cambridge framework the choice of structured risk assessment methods would occur at stage 2 of the process, following the specification of the relevant criterion variable(s). This step is essential because it is evidently true that no risk assessment 'tool' is predictive for all of the risks that may need to be estimated. There is, therefore, a professional judgement to be made between defining the risk to be measured and deciding which (if any) 'tool' or 'tools' to use. Failing to do this suggests a failure to distinguish between the scientific process and the technologies that may support it (Towl, 2003a, 2003b).

A further key aspect of the Cambridge framework is that it fits with the reality of risk assessment and management as both a dynamic and ongoing process. Whilst there is evidence of consistency in behaviour it would be easy to overstate this. It would also be easy to neglect the opportunity for interventions that modify risk. It is clear within the Cambridge framework that decisions need to be made at a fixed point or points in time in relation to one or more assessed risks. For example, Multi-agency Public Protection Arrangements (MAPPA) and the panels that derive from these may need to make a decision about the risks presented by a sexual offender and decide whether or not they can be managed in a particular context. However, the process of monitoring and managing risks will be ongoing and dynamic.

A related practice issue here is that of effective communication between professionals. This is absolutely imperative to help inform accurate risk assessments and Prins (1995, 2002) helpfully highlights three aspects of adequate communication within forensic practice. First, there is a need to have good inter-professional communication. Second there is a need to have adequate communication between the practitioner and the offender with an understanding of some of the inherent tensions in such a relationship. Third, there is a need on the part of practitioners to listen.

Acceptability of Risks

The focus of this chapter has been primarily on the technical process of risk assessment and management. However risk assessment and management needs to go beyond simply stating probabilities for broad categories of behaviour. The acceptability of risks is inevitably an issue, along with a consideration of who will be subject to risk. There has to date been remarkably little direct research into this area. Such considerations are perhaps most pressing in community contexts for forensic practitioners, where the risks presented are often towards the general public. MAPPA present a positive development in this respect since they draw together a range of stakeholders to make decisions about risk in a structured manner.

Questions about the acceptability of risks are, to a large extent, trans-scientific (Towl & Crighton, 1996, 1997). However, there is a body of psychological research in the area of decision-making that is of relevance and may be of help to decision-makers. Cognitive and social psychology has gone a long way toward illuminating the processes and biases involved in making such decisions.

Nisbett and Ross (1980) drawing on research in cognitive psychology suggest that people deal with the world around them in a number of consistent ways. First, people process information. It is also evident that the interpretation of a stimulus depends both on the attributes of the stimulus and on the perceiver's prior expectations. Additionally individuals will try to organize their experiences and that such organization will generally involve selection and simplification. In turn it has been suggested that such organizing processes function to provide both a guide for action and also a basis for prediction of future events.

These basic assumptions have been well supported by research in cognitive and social psychology (Kahneman & Tversky, 1973; Nisbett & Ross, 1980; Plous, 2002). Indeed it can be argued that it would be impossible for individuals to function in a world where there is effectively an unlimited amount of information available, without being able selectively to abstract and process information.

What seems equally clear is that a number of the processes used to achieve this can lead to systematic errors and biases. For example, when dealing with complex tasks people have been shown to use a number of intellectual shortcuts or 'heuristics' (Kahneman & Tversky, 1973; Evans, 1989). In comparison to logical or mathematical analyses these heuristics can be shown to produce inaccurate results. In relation to decisions relating to risk in the mentally disordered a number of these are of particular relevance.

Representativeness

This refers to a group of heuristics used by people to make a wide range of assessments. It refers, in essence, to the tendency for people to make assessments on the basis of how 'representative' an event is, even where other information may be as, or more, important. An example, in the context of mental disorder, may be a tendency to overestimate the likelihood of violence from the mentally disordered.

Availability

This refers to the information that is actually attended to in a cognitive task. A very basic example of this is the tendency for the majority of people, when asked, to say that more words begin with the letter K than have K as the third letter. In fact this is clearly inaccurate but the outcome can be explained on the basis that it is much easier for people to retrieve from memory on the basis of the first letter than the third (Evans, 1989).

Such availability biases can also be triggered by expectancies and prior beliefs. An example being 'illusory correlations'. Chapman and Chapman (1967) found in a study of practitioners that they reported patterns of relations between clinical tests and diagnoses that confirmed their prior beliefs but were not, in fact, present in the material presented. Indeed there is now considerable evidence that information may be selectively encoded and retrieved in ways that confirm prior beliefs (Evans, 1989). Thus, for example, in mental health settings self-injurious behaviour may be dismissed as being 'manipulative' and 'attention seeking', in line with existing beliefs about the behaviour of service users. Such interpretations may not though be predictive of actual outcomes.

Vividness

Nisbett and Ross (1980) proposed this notion to explain some of the weightings given by people to social information. They argued that people have a clear tendency to overweight vivid, concrete information and in turn will undervalue dull, pallid and abstract information. They suggest that the vividness of information appears to be determined by its:

- emotional interest to the recipient
- concreteness and imaginability
- temporal and spatial proximity

In the context of risk assessment with the mentally disordered it is perhaps not difficult to see a number of implications. For example, emotional interest is likely to be high where positive relationships exist between staff and service users. It may also be suggested that concrete events such as verbal abuse will be weighted more heavily than less concrete occurrences such as delusional beliefs and hallucinations.

Confirmation Bias

This refers to an inferential error, which suggests that people have a fundamental tendency to seek information that is consistent with their current beliefs, theories or hypotheses, and to avoid potentially falsifying evidence (Evans, 1989). This is probably related to Kahneman and Tversky's (1973) notion of 'adjustment and anchoring': this bias refers to the trend for people only to adjust their views with reference to its initial starting point. In general people appear resistant to making radical shifts in their opinion, which in turn seems to be resistant to contradictory information.

Conclusions

As outlined above, the area of risk assessment and management is one of central importance to forensic practitioners in the probation service. OASys provides a key foundation to such work across correctional services, in terms of positively addressing issues of risk. It also has a number of advantages as a common platform for case management. Of itself though OASys will not be able to meet fully the need for effective risk assessment and management.

Applied psychologists, from whatever specialism, have the potential to contribute in a fundamental and valuable way to addressing this need. They can do so by working within logical structures that enable practitioners to make more accurate assessments and implement more effective interventions to reduce risk. They can also do so by developing the knowledge base in relation to factors that might act and interact to affect the levels of risk presented by offenders.

There are real and serious public concerns to control risks effectively across a range of areas. The probation service has not been exempt from these pressures and, in many respects, has been at the forefront of addressing them. This is reflected by the increasing emphasis on the public protection role of probation within correctional services and the Criminal Justice system.

There is though also a clear temptation to look for easy answers or, in modern managerial parlance, 'quick wins' and shortcuts here in the form of technical measures that have the appearance, if not the substance, of science. This has happened before, for example in the field of child protection in the United States. Wald and Woolverton (1990) noted a push to deploy inadequate and unproven methods, for a range of ill-defined reasons. Quick, easy and relatively low-cost risk assessment 'tools' have an intuitive appeal and were managerially easier than putting in place highly skilled and professionally supported practitioners. In reality though such approaches presented a mirage that failed to deliver the real goals of those child protection services.

As outlined above, probation services have, in recent years, begun to adopt 'tools' such as the PCL – R or the Structured Risk Assessment 2000 in an often uncritical manner.[2] In addition the widespread drive to adopt cognitive behavioural groupwork interventions to address offending have been implemented on a large scale and on the basis of limited evidence that they effectively reduce risk. In fact such methodologies do not provide a panacea for risk assessment and management and may present risks when used inappropriately.

In ensuring effective risk assessment and management in probation there is no real substitute for a broad-based multi-modal approach to risk assessment and management, focused on the individual and undertaken by appropriately skilled staff. Whilst specific psychometric assessments may be of value in specific cases or groups of cases no assessment will fit all needs. Such assessment 'tools' also need to be used in professionally appropriate and defensible ways.

NOTES

1 In fact both high- and low-frequency events present particular challenges. Identification of low-frequency events tends to be associated with large numbers of 'false positives' (See Reason, 1997).
2 The SRA was a structured approach to assessing risk in sexual offenders (see chapter 4 for a fuller discussion).

| Chapter | Six |

Suicide and Intentional Self-Injury

Sara Casado and Amy Beck

Introduction

In order to understand the role of community-based psychologists working for the National Probation Service (NPS) in the area of suicide and intentional self-injury (ISI) it is essential to define the terms 'self-injury and suicide'. Sutton (1999) defined self-injury 'as a compulsion or impulse to inflict physical wounds on one's own body, motivated by a need to cope with unbearable psychological distress, or regain a sense of emotional balance. This act is usually carried out without suicidal, sexual or decorative intent.'

Towl and Crighton (1996) defined suicide less colourfully as 'the act of taking one's own life'.

Some research refers to ISI and suicide as being on a continuum; other researchers see ISI and suicide as being discrete behaviours. For expository purposes the above definitions are broadly adopted, with ISI and suicide being viewed as a potential continuum, which can be helpful, specifically with regard to assessing and/or managing an individual's level of risk. In addition we refer to the term 'complete' suicide as opposed to 'commit' suicide. This is in recognition that 'commit' is a historical term used prior to the Suicide Act 1961 when suicide was deemed a criminal offence.

This chapter focuses on an overview of working with individuals at an inflated risk of suicide and ISI within the NPS, exploring the use of a multi-disciplinary approach, the general role of a psychologist, advantages and disadvantages to community care of suicide and ISI, in comparison to custody. It also explores risk assessment, risk categories, risk assessment 'tools' and external risk situations. The latter focuses on interventions addressing ISI and suicide within the NPS, such as effective interviewing practice, work with other agencies, care plans and work with 'high-risk' offenders, including the use of Cognitive Behavioural Therapy (CBT) as an effective method. We address staff training issues for the NPS, and future developments and recommendations with this type of work.

Psychologists in the NPS often manage offenders at inflated risk of suicide & ISI within a multi-disciplinary and multi-agency framework, in common with the approach used by psychologists working for HM Prison Service and the National Health Service (NHS).

The release of an offender from the prison service into the care of the NPS is a particularly stressful time and the likelihood of suicide and intentional self-injury increases. A study in West Yorkshire (Akhurst, Brown & Wessely, 1994) reported a very high incidence of ISI among offenders being supervised by the NPS. The study, which looked at 238 offenders, found that almost one third had reported one or more incidents of ISI. Of the offenders involved in the study 72 per cent had made what were classified as serious suicide attempts. The profile of offenders seen in the study was very similar to the profile seen amongst non-offenders who intentionally self-injure and included factors such as high levels of unemployment, alcohol and drug misuse, breakdown in family relationships and mental health problems.

One study (Pritchard, Cox & Dawson, 1997) looked at the suicide rate for male offenders on probation orders. Results indicated that deaths by suicide for male offenders on probation are nine times higher than for the general population. Suicide levels for male offenders on probation were even higher than for offenders in the prison system.

Studies such as these highlight the valuable role that applied psychologists can assume in order to assist in the management of offenders at risk of suicide or intentional self-injury in the community.

An Overview of Working with Individuals at Inflated Risk of Suicide and ISI in the National Probation Service

The multi-disciplinary approach

The overall management, supervision and responsibility for an offender in the community is ultimately held by a probation officer, often referred to as the case manager. In cases where an offender is considered 'low risk' the case can be held by a Case Management Officer (CMO) or a Probation Service Officer (PSO) who is deemed suitably qualified. As soon as the NPS has contact with an offender a risk assessment should be conducted, which may be before the individual has been sentenced. In most circumstances though this generally does not happen. For example, where bail application reports are prepared or where a specific sentence report is completed, risk assessments are rarely completed. At this time probation officers may be asked by the court to write a Pre Sentence Report (PSR) (see chapter 2). As part of this report the probation officer is required to make an assessment of risk, which would include an assessment of the risk of reoffending. Theoretically such reports will also include an assessment of ISI and suicide risk, although in practice this is unlikely at the PSR stage as such risks are not of great interest to the court's decision-making process. Should concerns arise at this stage the probation officer may request an assessment by a psychologist looking at the risk of ISI and suicide and how such risks can be managed effectively.

The management of the offender in the community takes on a multi-disciplinary approach towards monitoring and providing suitable intervention for offenders at risk. The psychologist will always involve the case manager (probation officer) and general practitioner, and in addition possibly psychiatrists, mental health services, including psychiatric nurses, and hostel staff. In some probation areas, there is access to clinical, counselling or forensic psychologists who are often attached to community mental health teams. In these areas forensic psychologists employed by the NPS may work collaboratively with their NHS colleagues to safely and effectively manage the offender's risk of ISI or suicide.

A referral to a psychologist may also be made if offenders are on a Community Rehabilitation Order (CRO) and if there are concerns that they may intentionally self-injure. This is particularly likely to occur should offenders be resident in probation accommodation after probation service staff have conducted an initial risk assessment that indicates suicide or ISI risk. In some probation areas, hostel staff may make a direct referral to the local community mental health team or forensic mental health service.

Once a referral and assessment request has been made to a psychologist, it may be appropriate for the psychologist to offer one-to-one work using CBT (or other therapeutic approaches) in order to manage and reduce the level of intentional self-injurious behaviour. This approach will be discussed briefly later in this chapter.

The general role of the applied psychologist

There are a number of roles in which the psychologist can be involved in working with offenders who intentionally self-injure. First, psychologists can be involved in the assessment process to assess likelihood of suicide or ISI.

Secondly, they can be involved in devising a management and intervention plan to assist in safe community management. Thirdly, the psychologist can become involved in working one to one or in delivering appropriate groupwork to assist offenders who are demonstrating ISI behaviour. Fourthly, psychologists can undertake a role in the development and delivery of staff training for the NPS. In addition they may also contribute at strategic policy levels to the organization and management of such work. This may include chairing working party groups and reviewing policy data in order to ensure best practice.

Due to the relatively recent introduction under the new national structure of psychologists to the NPS, work with offenders who are at risk of suicide or ISI is still an evolving field. One differing emphasis with psychologists working in the NPS in comparison to the prison service is that psychologists in the NPS are often deployed in a variety of roles, depending on the probation area. As a consequence of this, psychologists can spend differing amounts of time working with offenders at risk of suicide or who are vulnerable to ISI, dependent on the priorities of a particular probation area and the way in which they choose to manage the issue, something that is also true of colleagues based in prison establishments.

In addition, psychologists working in the community may be more involved in risk reduction as well as minimizing levels of ISI. Psychologists in the community have no control over offenders' access to material, which they may use to ISI. Therefore, there may be an additional educational role for the psychologist to adopt to promote and ensure harm minimization as well as working to reduce and, one hopes, eliminate the ISI. This role may differ from that of psychologists working in the prison service who may in the most serious cases of ISI seek to ensure prisoners do not have access to materials they could use to injure themselves.

Advantages and Disadvantages of Managing Suicide and ISI in the Community in Comparison to Custody

There are many advantages of supporting an offender within the community, since offenders can improve their 'coping skills' to deal with day-to-day environmental stressors. This in turn can help to improve individuals' self-esteem. In addition, being in their usual environment and possibly in close contact with their family/friends may help. Offenders should have some responsibility and should retain their usual lifestyle, providing the assessor with direct information about offenders' family dynamics and day-to-day stressors (Morgan & Owen, 1990).

Most also note the disadvantages to care in the community in that this is not appropriate for the severely suicidal. It is difficult to ensure safety and adequately close and supportive care. It is more challenging to monitor individuals and make sure that they are taking prescribed medication or following and participating in interventions considered most effective for them. It can also be problematic to provide a safe place for offenders to escape to from their environmental and/or family stressors. In addition it may cause conflict within the home, as family carers may be placed under severe strain (Morgan & Owen, 1990).

Offenders being assessed and supervised by NPS staff may be screened for ISI and suicide on contact with the service. Some structured risk assessment 'tools' in use within probation settings have included an assessment of such issues and this has been continued with the 'Offender Assessment System' (OASys) (Home Office, 2001). OASys has the potential to increase effective practice with improved working between probation and prison services. This structured assessment can also act as an initial screen for offenders at inflated risk of suicide and ISI, as it prompts the practitioner to consider a number of possible indicators. The NPS are using this assessment and the prison service is currently this system in place with full implementation planned for late 2004. This creates the potential for a better integrated approach to assessment of risk.

The assessment of suicide risk and ISI is in part the process of matching an individual with a set of 'risk factors', which have been shown to have a statistically positive correlation with these behaviours. The 'risk factors' have been derived from large cohorts of people who have completed ISI and suicide (Morgan, 1994). It is important to be mindful that 'risk factors' are correlates, and not necessarily causation factors. It has also been noted that risk factors can be more accurately predictive in the long term rather than in the immediate future (Morgan et al., 1994). A sound knowledge of the research base in this area allows psychologists to help to inform risk assessment and management in this area.

Risk assessment and the role of the psychologist

Psychologists can offer advice on risk assessment and management strategies within the NPS in particular with regard to suicide and ISI. Towl and Crighton (1996) note that many of the associated risk factors for someone that is at heightened risk of displaying intentional self-injury or completing suicide are similar to those frequent among the offender population. Thus accurate individual assessments of risk are particularly difficult with this client group, given the high prevalence of 'risk factors' across the offender population. Crighton (2000) provides a detailed review of risk assessment in this area of practice.

Whilst we can draw upon the research and data present with regard to best practice within the prison population on suicide and ISI, there are some distinct differences between offenders in custody and those in the community. Often ISI or suicide within the prison service may have direct links with the surrounding environment. This may also be true within the community, but here there are many more variables that can influence whether or not an offender may intentionally self-injure or complete suicide. The abundance of these variables within a less restricted environment means that it can be more professionally challenging to assist an offender to control ISI and attempted suicide within the community than within a closed institutional setting.

Risk categories

The traditional risk factors associated with suicide and attempted suicide are depression, alcoholism, substance misuse, mental health, and previous child abuse. (O'Connor & Sheehy, 2000)

It is important to note that diminished signs of these risk factors does not mean that an individual is 'not at risk' of self-injury, or suicide. Rather these provide a baseline 'check-list' from which the interviewer can assess risk of ISI and suicide, as the causes of ISI and suicides are usually multi-factorial. Suicide and ISI risk are not dichotomous variables in terms of risk; that is, individuals do not fall into two categories 'at risk' and 'not at risk' respectively. The term 'no risk' in the domain of ISI and suicide is not only exceptionally unhelpful; it can be dangerous (see chapter 5).

The following groups have also been identified as having an increased risk of suicide, compared with the general population: males, older age group, those with psychiatric disorders, divorced/single/widowed, socially isolated, unemployed, those with physical illness, those with a previous history of intentional self-harm, family history of affective disorder/alcoholism/suicide, bereavement in childhood, poor socio-economic status, and certain personality traits (Morgan & Owen, 1990).

Morgan and Owen also note that:

approximately 1% of people who carry out an act of non-fatal deliberate self-harm kill themselves in the following year and 10% of all deliberate self-harmers eventually complete suicide. The closer the act of deliberate self-harm resembles the characteristic profile of completed suicide, the greater the risk of eventual suicide. (Morgan & Owen, 1990)

All intentional self-injury should be taken seriously and explored within the scope of the initial risk assessment as a possible indictor of inflated risk of suicide.

Studies in the community have also examined length of unemployment and found it is an important factor when assessing for risk of suicide. Research looking at completed suicides indicated that for those individuals unemployed for more than six months the completed suicide rates were 6 times higher than for employed individuals; for individuals who were unemployed for twelve months the completed suicide rate was 19 times higher than for employed individuals (Platt & Kreitman, 1984).

Many researchers have noted hopelessness as being linked with suicidal ideation, (Nekanda-Trepka, Bishop & Blackburn, 1983), completed suicide (Beck, Brown & Steer, 1989) and those engaging in intentional self-injury irrespective of intention (Petrie, Chamberlain & Clarke, 1988). A number of themes also emerge as precursors to suicide, such as loss events, provocation and frustration, social isolation, and anniversaries of distressing events (Towl & Crighton, 1996; Crighton & Towl, 2002). When assessing an offender for risk of ISI or suicide the interviewer should be mindful of the above risk factors, and of what we know already about suicide and ISI from previous research.

Risk assessment 'tools'

Psychologists are well placed to make contributions to multi-disciplinary teams with regard to psychological methods that can be used to provide helpful information about suicidal intent, such as Dexter and Towl's (1995) four-stage typology described below:

1. Thoughts indirectly related to suicide, but no evidence of them having considered suicide as a possible or desired option.
2. Thoughts suggesting they would like to complete suicide, but have no intention of carrying it out.
3. Thoughts suggesting they would like to complete suicide, but no evidence of them having made plans to carry it out.
4. Thoughts indicating they would like to complete suicide and they have planned how to do it.

Research has shown that prisoners who had scores above the cut-off point for Beck et al.'s hopelessness scale (HS) (see Beck, Brown & Steer, 1989) fell into categories 3 and 4 of the typology (Dexter & Towl, 1995). Towl and Crighton (1996) note that in the absence of psychometric testing, this is a useful set of hypotheses to help the practitioner make some assessment of an individual's risk of suicidal intent. In addition they have provided a 'checklist for risk assessment interviews with suicidal clients', as a guide to ensure that the assessor asks some key questions. It is important to be mindful that the offender may not wish to disclose such sensitive information during the first interview. In support of the interview, psychologists can also administer, score and interpret psychometric tests specifically designed to indicate and measure one's predisposition towards behaviours such as ISI and suicide. An example is Beck's Depression Inventory (BDI), which is a useful tool as a measure of depressive state and possible suicidal intent. Other examples include the suicide intent scale, the scale for suicide ideation, the suicidal ideation questionnaire and the suicide probability scale (Eyman & Eyman, 1992). However, interviewers should remember that although psychometric tests can provide a quantitative measure, and can be helpful in the monitoring process of an individual, they are best used to inform a thorough 'clinical' assessment. In addition, the assessor should be mindful of the limitations that self-report psychometrics hold; for example, the relative ease with which individuals can misreport.

External risk situations

Statistics published by the Howard League for penal reform in 2002 indicated that more than 50 prisoners each year complete suicide shortly after their release from prison. Information from the report indicated that prison and probation officers were 'failing to adequately support these vulnerable individuals' and found that prisoners who were serving short prison sentences received little or no help in planning for release. The report suggested that although the NPS was supervising those offenders who were serving long sentences it was more orientated towards protecting the public than looking after the welfare of individual offenders. In conclusion, the Howard League recommended that the NPS must pay attention to identifying and supporting those who are at risk of suicide as much as it does to the identification of dangerous offenders and the protection of the public.

Probably the most robust finding of research into prisoner suicide is that prisoners are at an inflated risk of suicide during the initial stages of their entry into an establishment (Bogue & Power, 1995; Towl, 2003b).

Future uncertainty and the stress of change may well be particularly important when assessing risk for an offender just released from custody, especially with life sentenced prisoners, as well as others serving very long prison sentences, who may have become institutionalized and feel disorientated upon release. Another piece of research supporting this view was conducted by a group of probation staff, where a key finding was that the first three weeks after admission into a probation hostel is considered a high-risk time for those at risk of suicide (Dunkley et al., 2002). This gives rise to the need for effective communication, support and sharing of skills, between different agencies within the Criminal Justice system, when releasing either prisoners into the community or sending offenders from the community into custody. Under these circumstances, psychologists from both probation and prison settings may act as information gatherers and providers for an offender presenting with high-risk behaviours. It is important to make a judgement about the acceptability of the level of risk identified in order to look at a suitable support system and possible intervention for the offender.

Intervention: Work with Other Agencies, Care Plans and Interventions with High-Risk Cases

Effective interviewing practice

Psychologists may also assist with appropriate interviewing techniques. Towl and Crighton (1996) state that of great importance in the assessment process is obtaining the client's view of events and an account of relevant background features, and gaining an understanding of the immediate nature of their difficulties. They also note the worth of listening to offenders' use of language in their account of events, as this can provide clues as to how individuals are feeling or are portraying their own situation. The interviewer must check out that their understanding of the events is accurate and again Towl and Crighton (1996) helpfully note the usefulness and importance of using direct closed questions and a matter-of-fact approach. They note that questioning about the degree of reflection, planning, intended method of suicide, duration of suicidal thoughts and frequency may elicit useful information in informing the risk assessment process. This provides an assessment of an offender's risk psychologically, socially and physically. A history of the offender should be obtained from any relevant information/reports kept in addition to self-report.

Psychologists can either contribute to the supervision of the offender or help inform others about those at risk of ISI or suicide. Management of such an individual should link closely with the assessment of risk conducted with the offender. Examples of this may be that if an offender is assessed as at high risk of ISI and/or suicide, then that offender may be monitored at regular Multi-agency Public Protection Panels (MAPPPs), which form part of the national Multi-agency Public Protection Arrangements (MAPPA). These consist of representatives from the relevant local agencies such as probation, police, mental health services, social services and housing agencies. It is increasingly the case in the probation service that in-house psychologists participate in this process and attend meetings where appropriate. This is similar in a number of ways to the care planning process that operates in prisons, when staff from different departments within the prison devise a plan to manage the prisoner's behaviour, which is implemented by all disciplines that each has responsibility for a particular aspect of the management plan.

Multi-agency working is also in evidence, when an offender has been screened, found to be of high-risk of ISI/suicide and has been referred to the local Community Psychiatric Nurse; a psychologist may act as the lead for such links with healthcare professionals. Applied psychologists may also input on care plans and monitoring for the offender, as well as offering support and advice on how to approach the matter with the case manager. There is a need for co-ordination of community support so that the intervention is most effective for the offender; this can include support also from the offender's family or people in close contact with him or her. Voluntary agencies such as the Samaritans also play an important role for the offender, as they provide 24-hour support to despairing people, especially in times of crisis (Morgan & Owen, 1990).

Psychologists can help assist and advise the worker with effective practice in working with ISI and suicide ideation by developing care, support and management plans. Research suggests, for example, that enabling the individual to experience care and understanding by demonstrating empathy towards the underlying distress can reduce the completion of suicide (Vaughan & Badger 1995). Dunkley et al. (2002) undertook research within probation hostels. Based on their findings they suggested that 'the quality time spent with residents could be just as effective at preventing suicide, if not more so, than regular 15-minute suicide checks'.

Research in custodial settings has indicated that bullying can also lead to an increase in suicide risk, especially in young offenders (Inch et al. 1995). Therefore, it is especially important for staff working in probation hostels to be alert for signs of bullying and to have effective strategies in place to manage and support individuals involved.

Workers should maintain a non-judgemental approach that sees beyond the injury or thought and that tries to help offenders to explore what ISI means for them. It can often be helpful to discuss 'harm minimization' approaches to ISI with offenders. Such approaches may provide offenders with a number of strategies that enable them to minimize the degree of physical harm they cause to themselves. One way to approach this is to draft a flexible contract with the person, which can be reviewed regularly.

It is interesting to note the similarities between a number of the factors identified by the Social Exclusion Unit and the factors associated with suicide and ISI (Social Exclusion Unit, 2001). Research has indicated that poverty – defined by unemployment, poor housing and, curiously, car ownership is a significant risk factor for suicide. Research at the University of Bristol has indicated that geographical areas where more individuals reside alone, are unmarried, move house frequently and reside in private rented accommodation, have higher rates of suicide. A key aspect of the Government initiative to tackle social exclusion is an aim to reduce suicide rates by 2010 (BBC Online Network, 1999).

Many of the factors identified and linked with inflated risk of suicide, such as failure at school and unemployment, are reflected in a number of the social factors identified in longitudinal developmental studies (e.g. Farrington, 1993) as factors associated with crime (Towl & Crighton, 1996). Offenders in the community may well be at similar levels of inflated risk for suicide as offenders in prison.

Cognitive Behaviour Therapy

This approach may be potentially effective with ISI. Cognitive Behaviour Therapy (CBT) works on the principle that self-injury is a learned behaviour driven by self-destructive thoughts and beliefs that are maintained by positive reinforcement (e.g. attention and nurturing) and negative reinforcement (e.g. relief from distress). The CBT model indicates that it is possible for individuals to 'unlearn' their self-injuring behaviour.

Psychologists working with this model will often focus on the offender's current life in order to try to understand and identify what thoughts, emotions and behaviour trigger intentional self-injury.

It therefore seems that the role of a psychologist with regard to assessment and intervention of ISI and suicide is as a specialist practitioner. However, another key potential skill of the psychologist is in sharing information, theory or practice that may be used in the area of staff training.

Staff training and support

It has previously been identified that working with offenders who intentionally self-injure or who are at an inflated risk of suicide can present significant challenges (Towl, McHugh & Jones, 1999). Psychologists in the NPS have an important role to play in helping other colleagues understand the precipitating factors behind self-injury and how it can best be managed:

- Evaluation of training requirements with needs analysis
- Review of current training material
- Devising specific training plans
- Delivering specific training interventions to provide knowledge and understanding of the areas of suicide and ISI
- Evaluation and review of training delivered

In particular a needs analysis is essential, as indications from some NPS areas suggest that in meeting the needs of staff training in this area, a 'one size fits all' approach has been adopted. Due to the variety of roles within the NPS, training has often been delivered at a basic level to increase awareness, with the intention to develop knowledge and understanding in this area. The result of such an approach may be that some staff have not been provided with the advanced training in this area they may need. In future, it is possible that psychologists could be used to assist in the development of further training on a more advanced level for Case Managers who are specifically working with clients who are at risk of ISI/suicide.

In some NPS areas, psychologists are already involved in the development of staff training. The aims and objectives of any training delivered should be specific and measurable. Typically, training in the area of suicide and ISI has been delivered in formal training sessions and has sought to address the following issues:

- Definition of ISI/suicide and examination of the motivation behind both
- Review of the ways individuals can ISI and their likely needs
- Feelings that may precipitate ISI/suicide
- Factors that may make an individual more likely to ISI or be at greater risk of suicide
- Outward signs may indicate ISI or inflated risk of suicide
- The links and differences between suicide and ISI
- Knowledge and understanding of the Probation Area's local policy on managing offenders at risk of suicide or who ISI
- Positive, constructive and effective ways to manage an offender at inflated risk of suicide or ISI, including increasing staff confidence in their ability to work in this area
- The impact of working with individuals who ISI and support services available to staff

By addressing the areas outlined, individuals on training courses are provided not only with knowledge but also an opportunity to deploy practical skills. Psychologists should give consideration and utilize a range of training styles. Consideration should also be given to the basics of training such as the number of training places and tutor ratios. Training in small groups will generally facilitate the delivery of better quality training.

For psychologists working in this area it is essential that they keep abreast of recent research developments and attend training in groupwork skills if delivering training. In addition, the impact of this work cannot be underestimated and appropriate professional supervision must be in place.

There may also be a role for psychologists in working to support colleagues who have been supervising an offender who completes suicide. This may be particularly useful when there were no identified overt signs that the individual was contemplating suicide. In cases such as this, it is not uncommon for the professionals to blame themselves and feel there was something else they could or should have done. Sometimes the shock of a sudden death can leave the professional feeling traumatized, confused and with unanswered questions. There is a role for the psychologist in debriefing the professionals involved and assisting them to recognize, address and manage their feelings.

Research has indicated that the bereavement process can be hindered when an individual feels responsible for the death of another person (Hauser, 1987). It is possible that survivors of suicide (those still living when someone close has completed suicide) begin an exhaustive and often frustrating search for the reasons behind the death, which may never materialize. Guilt and feelings of responsibility are not unusual emotions for survivors to experience (Wertheimer, 1991). Therefore it is essential that practitioners previously involved with an individual who completes suicide be given appropriate support.

Psychologists in the National Probation Service may also work with other agencies in the community to increase awareness of suicide and ISI. External agencies that have been assisted by psychologists include accommodation providers such as probation staff in residential accommodation and the police service. In particular, the delivery of training to accommodation providers is crucial. Homelessness has been found to increase the likelihood of suicide greatly (Craig et al., 1996).

The main purpose of external training has been to increase awareness of the issues 'behind' suicide and ISI and to implement ways of appropriate and safe management. This can result in the effective minimization of intentional self-injurious behaviour. The involvement of applied psychologists in delivering external training to other agencies can lead to valuable links with other agencies, significantly improving effective multi-agency working.

Future possibilities

- Better links between psychologists working across correctional services, when issues of suicide or ISI have been identified. There would be numerous benefits to such better communication and co-working
- Where appropriate, present findings of investigations if an offender has completed suicide whilst on a Community Rehabilitation Order to NPS Management with recommendations to address areas where service could be improved. Looking for and identifying patterns and trends to inform future policy
- Devising training courses for probation staff / external agencies on the subject of suicide and ISI and being involved in their implementation and management
- Conducting research in the area of suicide and ISI, especially its management in the community, and whilst offenders are undertaking community groupwork interventions devised to address offending behaviour
- Contribution to the devising of appropriate strategies and policies, which involve the safe management of offenders in the community who are at risk of suicide or ISI. Evaluating these strategies/policies and recommending improvements on current practice should be an ongoing process
- Offering support and advice to Case Managers and Case Management Officers who are working on a daily basis with offenders who exhibit ISI
- Providing one-to-one interventions for offenders who ISI and assisting in the development of groupwork where appropriate
- In everyday practice, treating offenders with respect, encouraging and supporting self-efficacy beliefs

SUMMARY

There is much applied psychologists can contribute within the NPS regarding suicide and ISI. This includes specialist assessment, devising management strategies, intervention methods and delivery and development of staff training. The role of a psychologist can be specialist and he or she may act as an overall consultant on ISI and suicidal behaviours.

The framework is similar to that of applied psychologists (from whatever specialism) in HM Prison Service. Specifically this involves using a multi-disciplinary, multi-agency approach. Managing ISI and suicide in the community is fraught with difficulties with regard to close monitoring, although there are advantages, in that assessment and intervention work can take place when offenders are in their home environment, and therefore assessment can directly address how offenders adapt to day-to-day environmental stressors. As we have seen, potential stressors such as homelessness and unemployment may play a very significant role in psychological and social pathways to suicide.

Much of the research emphasizes the importance of care and the monitoring of ISI and suicide within the initial stages of change within one's environment (Bogue & Power, 1995; Dunkley et al., 2002; Towl, 2003a, 2003b). Therefore there is a need for better joint working and information sharing across agencies working with offenders.

The relatively new introduction of 'in-house' applied psychologists within the NPS means that there is much scope for developing the role and contribution of applied psychology within probation settings, in particular with improving practice with assessment and management of ISI and suicide.

Chapter Seven

Groupwork-based Interventions

Anne Williams

Introduction

The range and growth of groupwork interventions running in the National Probation Service (NPS) is largely attributable to the results and literature of what has become termed 'what works' (McGuire, 1995a, 1995b), and has become one of the core aspects of potentially effective practice in working with offenders (HM Inspectorate of Probation, 1998). The NPS established a number of what were termed 'pathfinder' programmes. The aim of these was to draw on the available evidence base and to build on existing examples of good practice across probation services, including the groupwork interventions. 'Pathfinders' met a range of criteria in terms of quality and delivery and were used as the basis for implementation.

Groupwork-based interventions are assessed by an independent panel. This panel advises on whether an intervention is suitable for delivery on a national basis. A programme is defined for these purposes as:

> a planned series of interventions over a specified and bounded time period which can be demonstrated to positively change attitudes, behaviour and social circumstances. Usually it will be characterised by a sequence of activities, designed to achieve clearly defined objectives based on an identifiable theoretical model or empirical evidence. (HM Inspectorate of Probation, 1998)

Thus, these groupwork interventions are based on research and use methods that are potentially likely to be effective in reducing reoffending (Home Office, 2002c, 2002e). Proponents of the 'what works' literature have argued that, based on meta-analytic reviews, structured treatment interventions can potentially reduce reoffending. The National Probation Service (NPS) adopted and developed various 'pathfinder' interventions (e.g. the 'sex offender programme' by Thames Valley), which were rolled out in different NPS areas. A number of these involve joint working between prison and probation services (Law, 1999).

The probation (and prison) service is set targets for the delivery of 'accredited' interventions. These targets relate to the number of offenders who have completed the intervention and are weighted by indicants of the quality of delivery. The major issue that has plagued the delivery of these groupwork interventions is the problem of attrition in respect of attendance. It is evident that the largest proportion of dropouts occurs prior to the start of the intervention or in the early stages (Hollin et al., 2002). This problem is believed to be linked to inappropriate targeting of prospective participants and to some of the materials being unsuitable for different groups of offenders. Some research has indicated that a wide range of completion rates have been found, with some groupwork interventions achieving a high percentage of completion rates and others being significantly lower (McGuire, 2002).

The joining of HM Prison and National Probation applied psychological services and the appointment of the first joint head of this service has meant a steady influx of psychologists into probation service areas. Initially, a working party designed to set up psychological services in the probation service identified that one of the priorities for psychologists working in the probation service was to support the delivery of accredited offending behaviour interventions to meet targets and standards (Wilmott, 2002a). The role of psychologists working in probation service areas in relation to groupwork was initially to attempt to help ensure the quality of delivery of such interventions, and to have a central role in their management and evaluation (Towl & McDougall, 1999).

In practical terms this has involved applied psychologists contributing in a variety of ways. This includes psychologists being facilitators, assessing offenders for suitability for groupwork (e.g. assessing intellectual functioning, 'psychopathy', deviancy levels and psychometric profiles), contributing to the development, roll out, research and evaluation of interventions, being a 'treatment manager' and delivering consultancy services (including training and assisting in audits). The role of psychologists in relation to groupwork has often been dependent on levels of skills, knowledge and experience. In addition, these roles are likely to broaden now that work has a clearer emphasis on resettlement (HM Prison Service and National Probation Service, 2003a).

Current Policy and Practice

General offending groupwork interventions

These interventions address thinking and behaviour associated with offending, and teach offenders a range of social and 'cognitive skills'. They are based on the premise that anti-social behaviour (including offending) stems from offenders' inabilities to reach their goals in pro-social ways, because of a lack of 'cognitive skills' (Clark, 2000b). These 'deficits' are related to styles of thinking and attitudes that lead to anti-social behaviour, rather than intellectual functioning or level of education (Clark, 2000b) and include self-control, concrete and rigid thinking, interpersonal problem solving, egocentricity and critical reasoning. General offending behaviour groupwork interventions aim to influence these 'cognitive deficits' by using a variety of therapeutic methods, including structured learning therapy, critical thinking, lateral thinking, values education, assertiveness training, negotiation skills training, interpersonal problem solving, social perspective training and role playing and pro-social modelling (Ross, Fabiano & Ewles, 1988).

The general offending interventions that ran in the community have included Enhanced Thinking Skills (ETS), Reasoning and Rehabilitation (R&R) and Think First (TF). All of these interventions target male and female offenders who are assessed as medium- to medium-high risk as assessed by the Offender Group Reconviction Scale (OGRS) and more recently the Offender Assessment System (OASys) (Home Office, 2001). For 'high-risk' offenders, a general offending behaviour intervention can be sequenced with other interventions; for example an offence-specific intervention.

Enhanced Thinking Skills (ETS). This groupwork intervention consists of 20 sessions of 2 to 2.5 hours, with a maximum of 10 offenders. It employs a sequenced series of structured group exercises to teach interpersonal problem solving (National Probation Directorate, 2003).

Reasoning and Rehabilitation (R&R). This consists of 38 sessions, lasting between 2 and 2.5 hours. It is designed to teach interpersonal problem solving via structured sessions. This intervention is designed to run with 8–10 group members.

Think First (TF). This has a total of 22 sessions of 2 to 2.5 hours each. It first teaches offenders problem-solving skills and then aims to motivate offenders to apply these skills to their offending behaviour. Finally, offenders rehearse self-management and social skills. The optimum number of group members for this programme is 10 (National Probation Directorate, 2003).

Violent offending groupwork interventions

There are now two interventions running in the community, with plans to 'roll out' another shortly (the HM Prison Service 'Controlling Anger and Learning to Manage it' – CALM). These are 'Aggression Replacement Training' (ART) and 'Domestic Violence Duluth Model'.

Aggression Replacement Training. This is designed for men and women offenders who are convicted of assault, public order or criminal damage, and who have a 'medium risk' of recidivism. The intervention consists of 18 sessions, each lasting two hours, with an additional 4 catch-up sessions if required. It aims to reduce aggressive behaviour through teaching social skills, anger management techniques and by improving moral reasoning. It uses techniques from skills training and Cognitive Behaviour Therapy. The intervention can be run with a minimum of 3 group members and a maximum of 10.

Domestic Violence Duluth Model. This intervention is targeted at men who are in heterosexual relationships and whose offence involves domestic violence. It involves 24 sessions of 2 hours each. This offender-focused intervention does require partner involvement and is designed to challenge attitudes and beliefs associated with domestic violence. It also teaches social skills and enhances victim empathy. The approaches behind this intervention are feminist, cognitive behavioural re-education with an emphasis on victim safety (Lindsay & Brady, 2002). It can be run with a maximum of 12 group members.

Sexual offending groupwork interventions

There are three accredited interventions being run in the probation service that target sexual offending. They are the Community Sex Offender Groupwork Programme – West Midlands (C-SOGP), Thames Valley Project (TVP) sexual offender intervention and Northumbria Sex Offender Rolling Programme. All of these interventions target male offenders who have committed a sexual offence, and they all aim to reduce offending (National Probation Directorate, 2003).

Community Sexual Offender Groupwork Programme (C-SOGP). This intervention consists of different modules. The first module is the induction (50 hours), which is designed to decrease levels of denial and minimization of their offending and to enhance motivation to change. Men who have been assessed as low risk / low deviancy (using psychometric testing and clinical judgement) would complete this and then go directly onto the relapse prevention (50 hours). In addition, if men have successfully completed the Sexual Offender Treatment Programme (SOTP) in HM Prison Service, they can go directly on to the relapse prevention module. Those men who are assessed as high-risk / high deviancy would undertake the full programme (250 hours), which in addition to the induction module, consists of six modules. These modules address cognitive distortions and offending cycles, relationships and attachment styles, self-management and interpersonal skills, the role of fantasy in offending, victim awareness and empathy and relapse prevention (National Probation Directorate, 2003). This intervention is designed for 8 group members, with a maximum of 10.

Thames Valley Project (TVP) intervention. This consists of a foundation block (10 consecutive days), a victim empathy block (60 hours), a life skills block (40 hours), a relapse prevention block (44 hours) and a partner's block (36 hours). Men who are assessed as high-risk / high deviancy would complete the whole programme, whereas those assessed as low risk / low deviancy could omit the life skills block. Men who have successfully completed the HM Prison Service's SOTP can go directly on to the relapse prevention block. The optimum number of group members for this programme is 8, with a maximum of 10 group members.

Northumbria Sex Offender Rolling Programme. Presently, this programme involves a total of 160 hours. This includes a core programme (four modules) and an additional relapse prevention programme. Men can join at the beginning of any module. A shorter pathway for low risk / low deviancy men and a long-term maintenance programme is still under development (National Probation Directorate, 2003). Like the other two sexual offending interventions, the optimum number of group members is 8, with a maximum of 10.

Other Groupwork Interventions

These include interventions that target substance abuse and drink-related driving offences. Two groupwork interventions are being run in the community that are either fully or provisionally accredited (National Probation Directorate, 2003). These are Addressing Substance Related Offending (ASRO) and Drink Impaired Drivers (DIDs) interventions.

Addressing Substance Related Offending (ASRO). This is a module-based groupwork intervention that involves 20 sessions of 2.5 hours each and aims to teach offenders skills to reduce or stop substance misuse. It targets men and women offenders of a medium to high risk of offending as currently assessed by the Offender Assessment System (OASys) (Home Office, 2001). However, individuals of a 'lower risk' may be included if there is evidence of repeat offending and 'higher risk' individuals can be included if this intervention is sequenced appropriately with another intervention. The group size of this structured intervention is 8–10 group members.

Drink Impaired Drivers (DIDs). Comprises 14 sessions of 2 hours each. It combines cognitive behavioural work and education to reduce the risk of future drink-related driving offences. It targets men and women offenders who have committed a drink-drive related offence, and priority is given to those whose offence has an aggravating factor such as a repeat offence or a high alcohol reading. This structured intervention is designed to run with 8 to 10 group members.

Theoretical Basis

The majority of the accredited groupwork interventions are cognitive-behavioural in approach (Towl, 2002) although not exclusively. Some structured interventions draw on a multi-modal approach. This would include skills training and the modelling of pro-social behaviour. The meta-analytic reviews suggest that cognitive behavioural techniques are particularly effective. However, generally the following principles are thought to be associated with effective interventions: effective risk management, targeting offending behaviour, addressing specific factors linked with offenders' offending, relevance to offenders' learning style, promoting community reintegration and maintaining quality and 'integrity' of delivery (Home Office, 2002c, 2002e).

Each groupwork intervention, in order to become accredited, must present a clear model of change that is backed up by research evidence. This usually involves the development of a theory manual that uses evidence from existing research to support and explain why the targets and methods used are likely to work for the offenders selected. Such interventions are required to use methods that are effective with offenders and those which are considered, based on evidence, most likely to work. They must also be skills orientated whereby they teach skills for offence-free living (Home Office, 2002c, 2002e).

Selection Criteria

Each groupwork intervention has to select offenders who need to change and whose risk is appropriately targeted and likely to be reduced by the intervention. Proposals for interventions must identify the characteristics of the offenders who are suitable and also develop criteria for those who need to be excluded. Generally, offenders are excluded from attending groupwork-based interventions if they lack the offence-related needs, have serious mental health problems (e.g. not stabilized by medication) and an inability to learn in a group setting (National Probation Directorate, 2003). The latter can include having a severe drug dependency, low intellectual levels, poor literacy skills and those deemed to have 'severe personality disorders'.

Offenders are selected if they meet the level and range of deficits that the intervention targets. For offence-specific interventions they must have an offence or established pattern of offending behaviour that the programme targets (e.g. have committed a sexual offence or have displayed aggressive behaviour/offence). Each programme has a detailed selection and exclusion criteria. The treatment manager is responsible for ensuring that these criteria are adhered to.

The Process

It has been argued that for an intervention to be effective it must be structured and delivered as specified in the treatment manual, as with a range of manualized approaches to working with clients. This includes interventions being carried out by trained and skilled practitioners (with a warm, therapeutic style), it being well managed and having a tight design (HM Prison Service, 2003a).

In addition, responsivity, learning and enforcement also contribute to the effectiveness of delivery (HM Inspectorate of Probation, 1998). The 'responsivity principle' highlights that approaches to treatment should be matched to the intermediate targets and to the learning style of the offender (Muller-Isberner & Hodgins, 2000). The intermediate targets include reducing anti-social attitudes and behaviour, increasing support and self-management skills, replacing anti-social behaviour with pro-social alternatives and modifying the rewards and costs of criminal and non-criminal activities (Andrews et al., 1990, in Muller-Isberner & Hodgins, 2000). Facilitators must be able to adapt their approach to a range of learning styles as individuals learn through different avenues (e.g. by concrete experience, reflective observation, abstract conceptualization and active experimentation [Kolb, 1984]).

It is also important that groupwork facilitators have an understanding of the process of change (HM Inspectorate of Probation, 1998). The process of change refers to different stages individuals must work through in order to change and maintain their behaviour (Prochaska & DiClemente, 1984). Thus, facilitators must be aware of why some offenders may be resistant to change and what approaches may be most effective to help offenders move forward.

The principles of motivational interviewing underpin such groupwork interventions, and this approach involves a set of motivational techniques that encourage offenders to argue for the benefits of change to empower them to make a decision to alter their behaviour (Miller & Rollnick, 1991). This approach highlights that individuals who engage in problem-based activities are often ambivalent about them (McMurran, 2002).

Groupwork-based interventions must use methods that are known to promote effective participation by group members. During group sessions, facilitators display empathy and warmth and use positive reinforcement and pro-social modelling to maximize group cohesion. The type of questioning style most often adopted in accredited groupwork interventions is Socratic questioning. These are open, thought-provoking questions designed to help group members think through something or change their beliefs and attitudes in a non-threatening way.

Staffing

To become a groupwork facilitator for an accredited groupwork intervention, staff are required to pass an assessment and an intensive training course to assess their suitability and hone their skills. The content of this training varies according to what type of groupwork is being taught. Generally, all training courses involve gaining an understanding of the underpinning theory and research, learning and developing skills and techniques linked to the programme (usually motivational interviewing and cognitive-behavioural approaches) and how both of these relate to the achievement of delivery targets (as specified in treatment manuals). Once groupwork facilitators have delivered a certain number of sessions (usually each session twice) they can attend another training course to assess if they are fully accredited as facilitators. This usually means that facilitators have demonstrated skills, knowledge and a sufficiently full understanding of the intervention.

In probation areas, accredited groupwork interventions are increasingly being delivered and managed by multi-disciplinary teams. These usually involve probation officers, probation service officers, senior practitioners, divisional managers, senior probation officers and, less frequently, psychologists. They are managed by a 'treatment manager' who is responsible for the quality of delivery and supervision of facilitators and by a 'programme manager' who deals with organizational and delivery issues like staffing and physical resources.

All groupwork facilitators undertaking the work outlined above should receive regular supervision and feedback from video-monitoring by the 'treatment manager', who usually attends a course on supervision skills, and are expected to have a good understanding of the knowledge base and experience of direct delivery of the groupwork intervention. Those facilitators who deliver sexual offender treatment interventions are also expected to have regular counselling to help them cope with the effect of working with sexual offenders and to minimize the impact on their personal lives.

Conclusions

It is likely that the role of applied psychologists in relation to groupwork will change to adapt and expand to the changing needs of staff undertaking work with offenders (HM Prison Service and National Probation Service, 2003a). Psychologists sometimes facilitate, manage treatment, provide consultancy services and contribute to the development and research of accredited programmes.

There are a number of groupwork interventions being run in the probation service, and more are being piloted or researched. Those being run in probation target general, violent, sexual and substance abuse related offending. Interventions that are currently being developed, researched and/or piloted include women's acquisitive crime, violence booster, 'cognitive skills' booster, substance abuse, domestic violence, black and Asian offender research and racially motivated offenders (National Probation Directorate, 2003). The majority of these are cognitive-behavioural in approach. All have a clear model of change, selection and exclusion criteria for targeting and are monitored and evaluated to ensure adherence to the manuals. In addition, they utilize motivational interviewing techniques and different learning experiences to encourage offenders to change their offending behaviour.

Chapter Eight

Cognitive Skills Groupwork

Derval Ambrose

Introduction

The prevailing view in the early 1970s was that no interventions with offenders were having substantial impact in reducing reoffending. This is particularly notable in the phrase 'nothing works', taken from a much-cited article by Martinson (1974) where he expressed his general conclusion on the intervention approaches of the time. He believed that his work revealed a 'radical flaw in our present strategies – that education at its best, or that psychotherapy at its best, cannot overcome, or even appreciably reduce, the powerful tendency for offenders to continue in criminal behaviour' (Martinson, 1974).

Lipton, Martinson and Wilks (1975) supported this view in their review of a number of 'treatment' interventions aimed at the reduction of recidivism. They concluded that irrespective of different methodological approaches the consistent finding was that no intervention could be relied upon to reduce recidivism effectively. Brody (1976) echoed this view in relation to the United Kingdom.

However, from the outset a number of researchers in the field of intervention work with offenders expressed reservations concerning the conclusions of Martinson and others, and challenged the conclusion that 'nothing works'. For example, Gendreau and Ross (1980) produced a review of a series of research studies demonstrating a number of positive outcomes from intervention work with offenders. More specifically they concluded that 'amongst other attributes, interventions that acknowledged the role of cognitive processes, and particularly styles and patterns of thinking and problem-solving, appeared to be effective in reducing criminal re-convictions' (Thomas & Jackson, 2003).

In addition Blackburn (1980) re-examined a number of studies conducted in the late 1970s, applying the criteria for analysis set out by previous studies, such as follow-up time and matched control groups, and concluded that reductions in recidivism were obtained amongst 'treated' as opposed to 'untreated' groups. It is noteworthy that Martinson himself had gone on to re-evaluate his opinion that 'nothing works' in the late seventies and acknowledged errors in his earlier studies.

The development of meta-analytic research (a statistical method initially derived to facilitate the review process and enable reviewers to combine the findings from a large number of randomised control trial studies) has had a substantial influence on what has come, amongst some, to be accepted as effective interventions with offenders (Blud, 1999, 2003). The meta-analytical reviews published to date have assessed a wide range of outcomes, including reoffending.

Two larger scale meta-analyses have obtained consistent, parallel patterns of results and have drawn together a set of conclusions (Andrews et al., 1990; Lipsey, 1992). These studies addressed young offenders and adult offenders respectively. The overall conclusions of these meta-analytic studies indicated the net effect of interventions was, on average, a reduction of recidivism of between 10 and 12 per cent (Andrews et al., 1990; Lipsey, 1992, 1995). However, for some intervention approaches they claimed that this increased to approximately 30 per cent.[1]

However, a note of caution is expressed regarding the reliability of meta-analytic studies. First, the outcome of meta-analytic studies is only as reliable as the studies that are included in the analysis. Secondly, the statistical approaches used in doing this are still somewhat contentious (Hunter & Schmidt, 2003). In addition the research base of studies for meta-analysis in the behavioural sciences has not, to date, been overly encouraging. It is predominantly made up of small sample studies with limited methodologies (e.g. a lack of randomised control trials). Furthermore there is a bias inherent in meta-analytic studies in that they are based on published research. It has been argued that researchers tend to submit positive results for publication and are less likely to submit, or have accepted for publication, findings that are less favourable (Pettiti, 1999; Hunter & Schmidt, 2003).

Early research by the prison service into the effects of groupwork interventions within HM Prison Service suggested encouragingly positive results in terms of reducing criminal reconvictions over extended follow-up periods (Home Office, 1996a). However, this has been followed up by large-scale and long-term evaluation work by the Home Office, looking at group-based interventions to reduce criminal reoffending. The results of these evaluations have recently been published and show no difference between the two-year reconviction rates for a sample of adult male prisoners who had participated in a 'cognitive skills' based group, during the evaluation period of 1996 to 1998 compared with a matched control sample of offenders who had not participated in such groups (Falshaw, Friendship & Bates, 2003a; Falshaw et al., 2004).

Beyond the average effect size the findings of meta-analytic reviews indicated that particular approaches were more effective than others. For example, Izzo and Ross (1990) compared interventions that contained a 'cognitive' component with those that did not, and found a marked superiority in terms of reduced recidivism following the former. Skills-based cognitive behavioural approaches were reported as the most successful interventions (McGuire, 1995a). These interventions are broadly based using a variety of methods and typically involving behavioural and social learning principles including interpersonal influence, developing skills and use of methods to produce 'cognitive change' (Blud, 1999).

In light of this emerging evidence a number of intervention approaches have been developed, for both prison and community-based settings. Some have argued that offenders present differently with regard to the number and range of 'cognitive deficits' that they exhibit. Ross and Fabiano (1985) and Clark (1993) suggest that these 'deficits' can be effectively addressed by structured group interventions and additionally note that a number of features may increase the effectiveness of groupwork interventions. It is suggested that these include

- having a clear theoretical framework supported by empirical research
- clear assessment of risk of reoffending and allocation to services accordingly
- targeting offending behaviour or closely related behaviours, which can be altered by intervention
- the application of interventions that consider the concept of responsivity, employing clear approaches and targeting the learning styles of most offenders
- adopting a multi-modal, skills oriented, cognitive-behavioural approach
- using community-based interventions, since these are more effective than those based in institutions
- demonstrating that the intervention is carefully planned (see McGuire, 2000)

Palmer (1996) has added to the above list, proposing the term 'breadth principle'. This is based on the recognition that a large number of offenders are faced with multiple challenges in their lives. Palmer classified offenders into three groups. Group A comprised offenders with 'skills deficits' – developmental or social challenges in educational, employment or interpersonal domains. Group B referred to external pressures and disadvantages, including family stressors and limited social support. Group C referred to internal challenges such as self-esteem, attitudes or personal commitments. The most effective intervention to reduce reoffending would, Palmer suggested, ideally address multiple components.

Policy and Practice Development

The probation service has a long history of providing groupwork for offenders in the community. A survey conducted in 1989 covering 43 out of 56 probation services then in operation supplied information on 1,500 groupwork interventions (Brown & Caddick, 1993). An earlier study by Barr (1966) yielded similar results. Derived from the above debate and research on the effectiveness of interventions with offenders, the concept of 'accrediting' interventions has developed. Such 'accreditation' of groupwork interventions involves the evaluation of the structure and nature of interventions against pre-set criteria. This is similar to the process used in education where a new course will need to meet set criteria in terms of the coverage of materials, the way the materials are delivered, the way individuals are supported, and the way the course is maintained and evaluated.

Future development of the 'national curriculum' for offending behaviour groups was to be guided by a number of principles. It is intended that offending behaviour groupwork will involve the targeting of 'medium' and 'high' risk offenders only, as the available research does not support their use with low-risk offenders. It is also noted that longer duration of interventions may be necessary with 'high' risk offenders and that this should be achieved through the sequencing of interventions, building on 'cognitive skills' groupwork, which would provide the foundation level for further work. Systematic provision should be made for the following major categories of offenders: acquisitive offenders, motoring offenders, substance-misusing offenders, violent offenders, racially motivated offenders, and sex offenders. All interventions, whether for those on community orders or licence, should contain elements reinforcing and applying learning linked to ongoing case management work. Furthermore, the 'responsivity needs' of women and offenders from minority ethnic groups should be addressed in all groupwork interventions. This is to recognize the potential differing needs of female offenders and offenders from minority ethnic groups (National Probation Directorate, 2002, 2003).

The National Probation Service takes a broad view on the key elements of the 'what works' approach. Specifically five particular elements are identified:

1. *Offending Behaviour Groupwork.* Through the 'Pathfinder' pilots (piloted community-based intervention with offenders), the National Probation Service has developed a number of groupwork interventions. These include 'cognitive skills' groupwork and specialist interventions addressing specific offending, such as the sexual offending. Once a groupwork intervention is accredited in this way it becomes part of the Core Curriculum.[2]

2. *Offender Assessment.* The National Probation Service recognizes the importance of matching offenders to appropriate interventions. The recent development of a new system for the assessment of offenders (OASys) (Home Office, 2001), a detailed computerised risk assessment 'tool', increases the likelihood that pre-sentence reports will include a substantial assessment of risk of offending behaviour and make clear recommendations for the most appropriate form of intervention.

3. *Community Reintegration.* Community reintegration is an integral part to any long-term alteration in offending behaviour. New interventions are being developed to support offenders' reintegration into the community. New 'Pathfinders' will include an employment project, a joint prison and probation basic skills project and an 'approved premises' project.

4. *Community Punishment.* 'Pathfinder' projects have been in operation to explore the effectiveness of various techniques and approaches to an offender's supervision in the community. The Enhanced Community Punishment Scheme (ECPS) was introduced in 2003, and is a further development of Community Punishment Orders (CPOs). The scheme is designed to increase the effectiveness of community punishment orders by ensuring that they are completed in line with 'what works' standards.

5. *Evaluation.* An independent research programme has been commissioned to evaluate the effectiveness of accredited groupwork interventions, examining the impact on the offender and reconviction rates.

Specific Cognitive Skills Groupwork Interventions

The National Probation Service underwent significant changes between 2001 and 2004. There are a number of specific 'cognitive skills' groupwork interventions now in operation nationally. Below is outlined a selection of these interventions.

Reasoning and Rehabilitation (R&R). A group-based intervention designed to run over 38 two-hour sessions, and directed at more 'high-risk' offenders. The following areas are covered:

1. *Self-control.* Skills development is focused on the reduction of impulsivity by the use of thought analysis and behavioural change.
2. *Social perspective taking.* Group exercises encourage participants to develop the ability to see situations from a variety of perspectives.
3. *Interpersonal problem solving.* Participants are encouraged to examine how problems are defined and resolved.
4. *Critical reasoning.* Group and individual exercises encourage participants to reflect on past thinking patterns and behaviour.
5. *Cognitive style.* Rigidity and inflexibility of thought is challenged. Group members are also encouraged to examine irrational thinking and stereotyping, particularly generating the consequences of such thinking patterns.
6. *Moral reasoning.* Participants are encouraged to explore their own value base through group 'moral debate' exercises.

Think First. A group-based intervention targeted at 'general' offending behaviour and similar in structure and process to 'Reasoning and Rehabilitation'. It is aimed at encouraging offenders to develop social problem solving skills and associated skills, with a view to enabling life management and reducing reoffending. It aims to develop a number of skills such as problem solving, self-management instruction, social interaction training and values education. 'Think First' is intended to cater for men and women who have committed a wide variety of offences.

In addition 'Think First' has four 'pre-group' sessions and six 'post group' sessions. 'Pre-group' sessions focus on case managers introducing offenders to the approach and completing a more detailed assessment. The 'post group' sessions are conducted by the case manager and focus on reviewing progress, refreshing problem solving skills, relapse prevention and drawing up personal plans, and reviewing plans and larger lifestyle plans being made.

Priestly one-to-one. A groupwork approach to 'general' offending behaviour similar to 'Reasoning and Rehabilitation' and 'Think First', but intended for one-to-one use with offenders. It aims to develop social skills, problem solving, empathy, self-management, goal setting, to explore attitudes and values about crime, and consists of 20 one-hour sessions.

Addressing Substance Related Offending (ASRO). A 20-session group for men and women aged 17 years or over, who have a substantial history of substance abuse assessed as being linked to their pattern of offending behaviour. ASRO is described as a 'bio-psychosocial developmental model' and integrates findings from a wide range of research. Four particular stages are addressed: (1) motivation of offenders to change, (2) the 'personal scientist', (3) relapse prevention, and (4) lifestyle modification. 'Cognitive skills' work is one of the techniques applied in the programme.

Drink Impaired Driving. An offending behaviour group developed by South Yorkshire Probation area, and employing a combined cognitive-behavioural and educational approach. The programme is aimed at men and women over the age of 17. Priority is given where

- it is a second drink driving offence
- includes a breath or blood alcohol reading of at least twice the legal limit
- includes aggravating factors such as failing to provide a specimen, or involvement in an accident

The objectives are to address a wide range of areas, such as lack of knowledge about alcohol and driving, increase planning skills and skills to generate alternatives. Therefore, the group addresses change with regard to problem solving skills, anti-social attitudes and knowledge deficits.

Selection Criteria

Offenders are identified as potentially benefiting from 'cognitive skills' groupwork in a number of ways. The Criminal Justice and Court Services Act 2000 introduced a number of new provisions including the replacement of the probation order with the Community Rehabilitation Order (CRO). Sentencers can impose a CRO and set conditions, which may include completion of a specific 'cognitive skills' groupwork intervention. It is however worth noting that the courts' power to set conditions as part of the CRO derives from the Criminal Justice Act 1991.

Offenders are primarily assessed at the Pre Sentence Report (PSR) stage of sentence (see chapter 2) whereby the reporting probation officer can recommend particular interventions, which the offender should complete as part of a Community Rehabilitation Order. In many areas probation staff may have delivered 'cognitive skills' awareness presentations to the judiciary and magistrates in order to give sentencers some understanding of what participation in such groupwork interventions entails.

Offenders who receive an order, of which the completion of an intervention is an integral part, are bound by the court to complete that intervention. Offenders who do not complete, or who drop out, are in breach of their orders and must be returned to court. This produces a number of challenges within the process. Attrition rates in the community are unsurprisingly higher than in a prison environment. Brown and Caddick (1993) refer to some of the difficulties that arise from the marriage of enforcement and 'treatment':

> A major practice issue in groupwork with offenders is the difficult question of compulsion versus voluntarism. This is by no means a new issue, but there are increasing statutory pressures to coerce people into groups thereby running the risk of reducing the offender's commitment to change and development through personal decision. (Brown & Caddick, 1993)

In addition the recommendations made by the reporting probation officer are dependent upon a number of variables. With regard to 'cognitive skills' groupwork interventions the offender is referred to the relevant interventions unit, where a more detailed assessment is conducted on the basis of the requirements of the intervention recommended. Offenders may be excluded where they have a learning disability that would disadvantage them in the process. Similarly they may be excluded if there is evidence of a psychotic disorder, which is not adequately controlled.

Evaluation

Offenders who undertake and complete 'cognitive skills' work in the community complete a series of psychometric tests before and after the group. These tests are broadly based on the psychometric tests in operation for prison-service-based 'cognitive skills' interventions. In addition an extensive independent research project has been commissioned by the National Probation Service to evaluate ongoing work in this area. This project will focus primarily on the impact on offenders and reconviction rates (National Probation Directorate, 2003).

With regard to previous evaluative research on 'cognitive skills' groupwork, evaluation data for 'Reasoning and Rehabilitation' has been produced in Canada over the past decade. Robinson (1995) explored the impact of 'cognitive skills' training on post-release recidivism among Canadian federal offenders. His report focused on 4,072 offenders released into the community. Recidivism data concerned approximately 2,000 offenders who had been released on licence for at least 12 months. The study included three separate categories, 1,444 offenders who had completed a 'cognitive skills' group, 302 offenders who had started a 'cognitive skills' intervention but not completed it, and a control group of 379 offenders.

The broad findings of this study were that there was no significant impact for those who had breached their licence conditions but who were not returned to custody. There was an 11 per cent reduction in offenders recalled to prison due to breach of licence conditions, and a 20 per cent reduction in reconviction rates was reported for those who had completed a group (Thomas & Jackson, 2003).

In addition 'cognitive skills' groups were reported to have differing impact levels dependant upon offence and risk of recidivism assessment. Specifically, those offenders categorized as 'high-risk' did not appear to benefit from the intervention. Conversely, a 20 per cent reduction in recidivism was reported for those offenders classified as being at a lower risk of recidivism. Robinson (1995) also reported that offenders convicted of sexual offences demonstrated a greater reduction in reconviction rates. Offenders convicted of violent and drug offences displayed a 35 per cent reduction in reconviction rates, yet non-violent property and robbery offenders showed minimal effect. This group was also classified as being at the highest risk of reoffending. This may in part be due to such offending having minimal connection to 'cognitive deficits' (Thomas & Jackson, 2003).

Robinson (1995) went on to suggest that the minimal impact on high-risk offenders may suggest that this group need more intervention work, or alternatively that they may respond to different types of intervention. With regard to the differences between offence types it was suggested that this might be due to sexual and violent offenders having greater motivation to change than other types of offender. It would seem clear that further exploration of this reported effect is needed.

There are though a number of methodological concerns expressed about Robinson's study. Primarily, participation in a 'cognitive skills' group may not have been the only factor that differentiated the 'treated' group and the control group. In light of the complex number of factors that can influence offending behaviour, it would seem that a more in-depth exploration of group differences might be called for. One example of this might be a need to consider the employment status of offenders released into the community on licence.

The recent evaluation research by the Home Office, referred to earlier, reports no difference between the two-year reconviction rates for a large sample of adult male prisoners who had participated in a 'cognitive skills' groupwork intervention between 1996 and 1998 (Falshaw et al., 2003). This study represents one of the best-controlled and most methodologically adequate studies in this area to date.

A number of possible explanations for the findings were explored, including quality of delivery being negatively affected by large expansion of groups and motivation of offenders who completed the groups being lower then previous studies that suggested positive results. In addition the authors recognized that there may be significant gaps in our understanding of 'what works' in practice and with whom.

The National Probation Service aims to reduce reoffending by 5 per cent by 2004. Evidence published in October 2002 indicates that reconvictions for those on community penalties have reduced by 3.1 per cent against the predicted level. In addition, Community Rehabilitation Orders and Community Punishment Orders indicated a 4.9 per cent reduction against the predicted reconviction rates. Although these are encouraging figures, it is noted that Community Rehabilitation Orders may have groupwork completion as a condition of the order, but not necessarily 'cognitive skills' work. In addition Community Punishment Orders have not traditionally involved the completion of accredited groupwork. Such orders will also generally include ongoing individual casework with probation officers and others.

The evaluation of the impact of 'cognitive skills' groupwork in the community is in its early stages. Psychologists can play an important role in this evaluation. However, the effects of similar approaches in operation in the prison settings have not yet been adequately demonstrated to have a significant impact on reoffending (Falshaw et al., 2003, 2004). Groupwork within the community also presents a number of challenges that custodial interventions do not. For example, offenders have access to a wider number of choices as to how they fill their time. Also, offenders have the opportunity to work, and may therefore need to attend groupwork intervention outside normal working hours. These extra factors and stresses should be considered as part of any evaluation.

The Role of Applied Psychologists

Applied psychologists chiefly from the forensic specialism, have been involved in the development of a number of group interventions run in the community. Probation Officers and Probation Service Officers (PSOs) have traditionally been at the forefront of delivering such work in the community. As the employment of 'in-house' forensic psychologists in the probation service is a relatively new initiative, the involvement of psychologists in 'cognitive skills' groupwork has been minimal. Psychologists have taken the role of 'treatment managers' in some probation service areas.[3] Some have also contributed to the delivery and evaluation of groupwork interventions.

Clinical, counselling, educational, health and forensic psychologists are well placed to do individual work in areas such as social skills and what might broadly be termed 'cognitive skills'. Such work could be targeted at 'high-risk' offenders who do not appear to respond to existing groups.

Developing Evidence-based Practice

The National Probation Service has taken a broad approach to the concept of 'what works' and positive reintegration of offenders into the community. As referred to earlier, the framework of 'what works' is being applied to different services provided by probation and focusing on some of the wider social and economic factors that can contribute to reoffending.

An example in this area would be the introduction of Enhanced Community Punishment (ECP) that came into use early in 2003. This is a community-based approach to working with offenders and takes advantage of the high levels of contact and supervision of those on Community Punishment Orders (CPOs). The approach aims to reduce levels of reoffending and involves four key elements: case management, pro-social modelling, guided skills learning in employment related areas and good quality placements (HM Prison Service, 2003a).

In addition April 2003 saw the launch of the Intensive Change and Control Programme (ICCP). This is a strict and closely monitored community sentence, targeting offenders in the 18–20 age group. This age group has the highest rate of reoffending, accounting for 20 per cent of all reconvictions, and often presents with a range of problems, such as inflexible thinking styles and drug misuse. The ICCP offers a range of interventions. For the first three weeks offenders must attend for 25 hours a week. For the following three months they attend for 12 hours a week. ICCP includes attendance at an offending behaviour group, education, employment and training services, and mentoring. ICCP also requires offenders to complete 100 hours of community service, adhere to a curfew order and pay a financial penalty or compensation order (London Probation Area, 2003).

There is some convincing evidence to support the connection between gaining employment and the reduction of reoffending (Lipsey, 1992). This meta-analytic study reported employment to be the single most effective factor in reducing offending. Furthermore, it was reported that employment can reduce reoffending by up to 33 per cent. The National Probation Service Employment Pathfinder project is designed to enable offenders to gain employment. This is approached by assessing 'thinking skills' and attitudes in relation to employment, providing practical assistance, such as advice about disclosing convictions and CV preparation. Other elements of the programme include offering advice on all aspects of seeking employment, such as benefit entitlements and engaging in direct work with employers, including post placement support for 13 weeks. The process includes a ten-session 'employment skills' group and placement follow-up support.

The probation service has also initiated 'pathfinder' interventions to assess ways of improving literacy and numeracy issues amongst offenders in the community.

Conclusion

In conclusion, in-house psychological services have had a short history in the National Probation Service (HM Prison and National Probation Service, 2003a). The National Probation Directorate in London has employed psychological staff to contribute directly to the development and management of offending behaviour groupwork. Clinical, counselling, health and forensic psychologists have a number of competencies and skills that could usefully be applied to the area of 'cognitive skills' groupwork and add to effective multi-disciplinary working. For example, providing a consultancy role with regard to risk assessment and management as well as broader research and evaluation issues. In addition psychologists can contribute to interventions with offenders who do not meet the criteria for groupwork, or for whom groupwork is inappropriate.

The National Probation Service has very ambitious and demanding targets for 'cognitive skills' groupwork with a national commitment for 2003 to 2004 of 25,000 completions. It can be suggested that there has been a tendency within the probation service to look to creating new groups for offenders whose needs are not necessarily addressed under current provisions. Some caution is needed with regard to this development. Interventions with offenders can be addressed in a variety of ways, not all of which require the completion of groupwork interventions. The National Probation Service, as outlined above, has sensibly approached 'what works' in an eclectic manner. As a result there are a wealth of opportunities for psychologists to contribute to effective multi-disciplinary and multi-agency work with offenders in the community (see chapter 12). This might particularly be in the areas not addressed by 'cognitive skills' groupwork, and in additional support and relapse prevention for offenders who have completed 'cognitive skills' interventions.

NOTES

1   It is perhaps worth noting that the percentage changes reported were calculated in differing ways by different researchers and therefore the comparability of these findings is unclear.

2 The Core Curriculum is being introduced in every probation area and refers to interventions deemed to be high quality.

3 Treatment Managers are responsible for what might broadly be termed the 'clinical' aspects of groupwork interventions. They tend to be senior practitioners with relevant experience of groupwork.

Chapter Nine

Multi-agency Public Protection Arrangements

Tania Tancred

Introduction

In recent years an increasing focus has been placed on the importance of the risk assessment and management of serious violent and sexual offenders. Failure to do so can result in a high cost for victims, services involved with offenders and offenders themselves. Traditionally the National Probation Service has worked in a multi-disciplinary way with other agencies in the community such as the police service to manage such offenders. This relationship was made statutory in the Criminal Justice and Court Services Act 2000 (sections 67 and 68) when the police and probation were given statutory responsibility for joint risk assessment and management of sexual and serious violent offenders through the creation of Multi-agency Public Protection Panels (MAPPPs). This lead to the introduction of the Multi-agency Public Protection Arrangements (MAPPA) in April 2001. The police service and National Probation Service are referred to in the Act as 'responsible authorities' and are responsible for MAPPA in each of the 42 areas of England and Wales.[1] This chapter will cover the development of MAPPPs and relevant policy, an overview of the process, a brief description of some of the risk assessment 'tools' in use and the role of the applied psychologist within MAPPA.

Policy and Development of MAPPA

MAPPA has been developed in three phases. Phase 1 was to set up formal arrangements building on the multi-agency work that had begun as a result of the Sex Offender Act (1997). Phase 2 was to achieve consistency in the development of arrangements based on the first year's annual reports. Phase 3 will involve preparation to implement the provisions of the Criminal Justice Bill. One of the key provisions of this bill is to make HM Prison Service part of the 'responsible authority' with the police service and National Probation Service (NPS). This will have implications for applied psychologists based in HM Prison Service in addition to those based in the NPS. In addition the Criminal Justice Act 2003 makes reference to the 'duty to co-operate.' This places responsibility on a number of other agencies such as health authorities and NHS trusts, housing authorities and registered social landlords, social services departments, social security and employment services departments, youth offending teams (YOTs), local education authorities and electronic monitoring providers to assist MAPPA by co-operation with the 'responsible authority.'

It has been argued (Kemshall, 2003) that best practice in public protection could be considered under the following headings:

- Ensuring defensibility of decisions made
- Risk assessment procedures
- Risk management plans and delivery
- Audit and evaluation of service delivery

The headings describe the process of MAPPPs and will be referred to in more detail below.

Each area (geographical police and probation areas that have common boundaries) is required to have a strategic management board (SMB) responsible for the statutory duty to review, monitor and make necessary changes to the risk assessment and management processes. The SMB prepares an annual report that evidences monitoring and evaluation.

The recent Home Office guidance on MAPPA advises a commonality of approach and practice. This is beneficial for staff in a number of ways. First for staff moving to different areas and also for staff within areas to manage the transfer of an offender from one area to another. However, it is difficult to ensure that all areas will adopt a uniform approach due to differences in working practice and the geography of areas. For example, some NPS areas may be predominantly urban areas, whereas others may be more rural, leading to differences in factors such as the number and risk level of offenders. The way in which the process is staffed may also lead to varying practice. Due to these factors the way in which MAPPPs are organized within areas inevitably varies. As such there are some variations in the terminology used to describe the MAPPP process. For example the term 'RAMP' (Risk Assessment Management Panel) may sometimes in the past been used interchangeably with the term Multi-agency Public Protection Panel. Despite the variations the under-lying principles of policy and practice are the same – a multi-agency approach to the management of high-risk offenders in order to protect the public.

Another important factor for MAPPA work, in addition to public protec-tion, is a clearer focus on child protection. The importance of considering child protection was highlighted by Laming's report on the Climbié Inquiry (Department of Health, 2003a, 2003b). The MAPPA will have a role in taking forward these developments through MAPPPs staff regularly attend-ing or linking with Area Child Protection Committees (ACPCs). This ensures that agencies such as social services are kept up to date on information to do with an offender where there are child protection concerns. In practical terms this could result in a child being removed from circumstances where he or she is considered to be 'at risk' or a refusal to allow an offender to return home until a child protection conference has taken place. This may be the case where an offender has a conviction for sexual offending or domestic violence. Multi-agency working is important in reducing domestic violence (Hague, 2000) (see chapter 10).

Similarly an increased focus on the victims of an offence is suggested by the Home Office (Home Office, 2003a). The guidance highlights the importance of assessing and managing the risks to the victim whilst recognizing the important role that a victim may play in providing information about an offender whom they are best placed to know. The guidance adds an extra dimension to the excellent victim support work that has been taking place in probation areas that was imposed by the Criminal Justice and Court Services Act 2000 section 69. The act placed a statutory role on the NPS to consult with and notify victims of sexual or other violent offences about the release arrangements for offenders where they are sentenced to one year or more in prison.

The annual reports for the second year of MAPPA were prepared in 2004. Each NPS area in conjunction with the police area is required to produce an annual report on MAPPA. These reports provide a valuable insight into arrangements in any particular area, and are generally available on the Internet or via the particular local police or probation area.

An Overview of the Multi-agency Public Protection Arrangements (MAPPA)

In order to give a practical rather than theoretical overview of the MAPPA process one NPS area (Kent) is described in detail. Kent probation and police area run Multi-agency Public Protection Panels (MAPPPs) in a way that closely follows the guidelines provided by the Home Office and as such provide a helpful illustrative example of the reality of practice.

It is important to note that due to the dynamic nature of risk an offender may be subject to a MAPPP at any time during a sentence. This may mean that it is held prior to release, to plan for an offender's return to the community. It may have been deemed necessary to put a number of environmental controls into place to contribute to improving public safety. Alternatively an offender's risk may escalate during a community sentence necessitating MAPPP procedures.

The co-ordination of the MAPPPs is carried out by a 'public protection manager' (a senior probation officer) and a detective chief inspector (DCI) in conjunction with the MAPPP co-ordinators who are administrative staff jointly employed by Kent Police and Kent probation area. This team acts as a central point of contact for staff to refer offenders. The team also co-ordinate and organize MAPPP meetings and disseminate and collate all of the information pertaining to MAPPP offenders. They also maintain records of the meetings and provide data and analysis for the SMB and prepare the annual report. The senior management board (SMB) in Kent is chaired by an Assistant Chief Officer (ACO) from the probation service and attended by representatives from Kent Police and Kent Social Services. In future members will also be joining from HM Prison Service and Victim Support.

The Home Office MAPPA (Home Office, 2003d) recommends that certain types of offender should be considered under the MAPPA arrangements:

Category 1 – Registered sex offenders (those offenders who have been convicted or cautioned of certain sexual offences since September 1997 under Part 1 of the Sex Offender act 1997).

Category 2 – Violent and other sex offenders (those offenders who have received a sentence of 12 months or more).

Category 3 – Other offenders (those not in categories 1 or 2 but whose offending behaviour is considered by the responsible authority to pose a risk of serious harm to the public).

In order to explain the two-tier process used in the Kent area it may be helpful to outline the geographical set up of the probation service across the county. Probation offices in Kent are located in the main towns to serve the petty sessional court areas. For example the Mid Kent offices are based in the towns of Maidstone and Tonbridge and serve four petty sessional areas. Offenders living within those boundaries would report to their probation officer in their regional office. In addition to the regional offices there is an office to provide the headquarters function of senior management. In Kent

MAPPPs take place at two levels. First the Local MAPPP (LMAPPP). LMAPPPs are initiated and organized by the probation officer and the Senior Probation Officer within the local offices. They would have identified an offender as 'medium' or 'high-risk' and hold a local MAPPP to collate information and decide whether the offender was very high-risk which would necessitate a County MAPPP or KMAPPP. LMAPPPs may be held as the need arises and on a more regular basis in conjunction with the police when the police hold sex offender panel meetings or violent offender panel meetings. These panel meetings are held to review the risk of sexual or violent offending and, in the case of sex offenders, to review those on the sex offender register.

In order for offenders to warrant a KMAPPP they would have been assessed as 'very high-risk' of harm and/or at 'very high-risk' of reoffending. This assessment would be made using the Risk Matrix 2000 and Offender Assessment System (OASys) (see chapter 5). Offenders are assessed as medium- or high-risk if the following criteria apply:

- May require unusual or highly specialized resource allocation
- Serious community concerns
- Media implications
- Need to involve other agencies not usually involved

The imminence and seriousness of the risk would also be considered when deciding whether to discuss the case at a local or county level.

The county MAPPPs are held on the same day every week, which enables a schedule to be planned both for initial meetings and review meetings. The public protection manager chairs the KMAPPPs and 'standing' members include representatives from Kent Police and Kent Probation area. Other types of staff that may be asked to attend might be from amongst police, social services, housing, probation/case worker, victim liaison officer, employment officer, HM Prison Service staff, youth offending teams, health service staff and psychologist. When a panel operates on such a multi-agency basis, it constitutes a good example of effective partnership working within the criminal justice sector.

The Kent Probation Area (KPA) public protection policy 2002 outlines the role of an initial MAPPP conference as follows:

- Share risk assessments and form an opinion on the risk factors, the level of risk and the associated risk indicators
- Agree (or otherwise) on endorsing the initial KPA risk level and registration

- Agree on the aims and objectives for the risk reduction plan and agree to authorize appropriate resources to achieve those objectives
- Agree on a multi-agency 'Risk Assessment Plan'
- Consider the need for community disclosure and other community issues
- Agree a media strategy where appropriate
- Appoint the local SPO as case co-ordinator

Following the initial meeting a series of further review meetings is planned to review action points and changes in the level of risk to decide if the case is kept at a county or local level.

During the initial meeting agencies would inform the meeting of the relevant information they had about an offender. This might include demographic information, police intelligence including previous convictions, relationships, living arrangements, employment, engagement with staff and so on. This information together with information from actuarial risk assessment 'tools' would enable the panel to agree a level of risk and to develop the risk management plan based on the identified factors and available resources.

As referred to earlier the defensibility of decisions is an important aspect of the process. As such reference is made to the Human Rights Act 1999 at the end of each meeting to ensure that the decisions made are proportional and do not contravene anyone's human rights.

The risk management plans incorporate the notion of SMART (Specific, Measurable, Achievable, Realistic and Time bound) objectives. As such the risk management plans and the minutes of the meeting are circulated promptly after the meeting has finished.

It is important that cases are managed at the appropriate level so that resources can be deployed effectively.

Risk Assessment 'Tools' Used to Inform MAPPPs

Broadly there are two main approaches to risk assessment. First, actuarial methods based on statistical information and techniques, and secondly, clinical methods such as interviews. Whist actuarial methods are generally viewed as more reliable than clinical methods a combination of the two provides the best range of information (Kemshall, 2001, 2002).

The two main actuarial risk assessment 'tools' used for MAPPPs are Risk Matrix 2000 for the risk assessment of sex offenders and OASys (Home Office, 2001) for the assessment of all offenders.

Risk Matrix 2000 (Thornton et al., 2002) is an actuarial risk assessment 'tool' used to give a risk level for sex offenders and is used by specialist sex offender liaison police officers in addition to probation officers. It uses the same classifications of risk as OASys – low, medium, high and very high.

The Offender Assessment System (OASys) is being introduced across the National Probation Service and HM Prison Service when the electronic version (EOASys) is available. OASys is the new national system for assessing the risk and needs of an offender. The following information is taken from the OASys manual (Home Office, 2001).

OASys is designed to:

- Assess how likely an offender is to be reconvicted
- Identify and classify offending-related needs, including basic personality characteristics and cognitive behavioural problems
- Assess risk of serious harm, risks to the individual and other risks
- Assist with the management of risk of harm
- Link the assessment to the supervision or sentence plan
- Indicate the need for further specialist assessments
- Measure change during the period of supervision/sentence

There are five main components to OASys:

1. Risk of reconviction and offending related factors (OASys 1 and 2).
2. Risk of serious harm, risks to individual and other risks.
3. OASys summary sheet.
4. Supervision and sentence planning.
5. Self assessment.

In Kent staff are asked to complete the full OASys risk of reconviction and offending related factors (OASys 1 and 2), risk of serious harm, risks to individual and other risks and OASys summary sheet to inform the meeting. In turn the MAPPP may inform the supervision plan element of the OASys document.

In addition to actuarial risk assessment 'tools' it is important to consider 'dynamic risk factors'. 'Dynamic risk factors' have been described as those factors that change over time or that can be made to change through treatment and intervention. Researchers also point out that the assessment of 'dynamic risk factors' is often more complex as the factors may relate to an offender's environment or social networks. They suggest that some factors may change over time due to maturity, whereas others will need intervention such as housing or employment (Quinsey et al., 1998).

As referred to earlier a key part of any risk assessment of an offender is to consider the victim. Consideration should be paid to the victim's demographics – age, gender, race, religion, sexuality and vulnerability in order to assist the risk assessment of any potential future victims or the repeat victimization in cases such as domestic violence. The assessment of the victim could also inform any potential risks for staff such as homophobic or racist offences. The Victim Liaison Officer provides a very useful role in gathering information from the victim who may be best placed to give a view on the motivation for offending and risk presented.

A new database system is under development for use in the National Probation Service and Police Service in England and Wales. The Violent and Sex Offender Register (ViSOR) is now being piloted. It is hoped that the system could be used to provide a single database for all offenders under MAPPA. This would offer a valuable information source to inform risk assessments especially for those offenders moving from area to area.

The Psychologist's Contribution to MAPPPs

MAPPPs provide a wide client base with which psychologists may be required to assess or provide intervention work. Men, women and children may all be assessed as high-risk and be referred to a psychologist for assessment or intervention work. In addition the psychologist may have a role to play in effective liaison or referral to mental health services.

The best practice headings proposed by Kemshall (2003) have been used to provide a framework to describe the ways in which psychologists may contribute to MAPPPs.

Ensuring defensibility of decisions made

An important issue for working in MAPPPs is the notion of defensibility. The public sector is subject to close scrutiny by the media and the public. This is especially evident when things go wrong. Due to this it is particularly important that psychologists ensure that their decisions about a client and/or victim are defensible. Kemshall (2003) proposes the following minimum standards of practice:

- All reasonable steps have been taken
- Reliable assessment methods have been used
- Information has been collected and *thoroughly evaluated*

- Decisions are recorded (and subsequently carried out)
- Policies and procedures have been followed
- Workers and their managers adopt an investigative approach and are proactive

As such psychologists need to ensure that they are well informed about the benefits and limitations of any methods they may employ. Similarly the importance of informing a client about the limits of confidentiality is important. The psychologist should also be mindful of confidential information that cannot be shared with an offender due to risk to the victim and or public. Further guidance on ethical issues is available from the British Psychological Society in the Code of Conduct for Psychologists (British Psychological Society, 2000a), the British Psychological Society Division of Forensic Psychology Ethical Guidelines on Forensic Psychology (2002) and the Professional Practice Guidelines in Applied Psychology (HM Prison Service and National Probation Service, 2003b).

Risk assessment procedures

Psychologists have a clear role to play in contributing to risk assessments. Clear guidance on structuring risk assessments for violent offenders and sex offenders is available in the literature (Towl & Crighton, 1996, 1997). Similarly they provide an outline for the risk assessment of suicide. This is particularly important, as the risk to self may be as high as the risk to others when an offender is subject to MAPPA. A useful overview of the risk factors associated with domestic violence is also available in the literature (Walby & Myhill, 2000).

The psychologist could be asked to interview an offender or complete a risk assessment on file information. This may be the case for an offender assessed as too high-risk to be interviewed. In addition to risk to the public, practitioners should also be aware of any risks to themselves prior to seeing an offender and ensure the interview environment is safe and appropriate.

In addition to contributing to risk assessments the psychologist has an important role in informing other disciplines attending a MAPPP about the risk assessment 'tools' used and potential outcomes for clients. Other staff may not be aware of the limitations or ethical issues involved for clients of using particular tools. For example, the implications and ethical considerations for the offender of using a tool such as the Psychopathy Checklist – Revised (PCL – R) (Hare, 2003) in terms of an offender being potentially and somewhat contentiously labelled a 'psychopath' and all that may mean for him or her in the Criminal Justice system (see chapter 5).

Risk management plans and delivery

Psychologists may contribute to the risk management plan in a number of ways. First they may have something to offer in the initial information exchange if they know the offender. They may have been allocated work in terms of recommendations from the risk management plan. This could be to undertake a risk assessment as outlined above. Or it could be to deliver some intervention work.

A typical case study of someone who would be managed by a MAPPP might be as follows.

John Smith aged 29, a white male. Previous convictions for unlawful sexual intercourse (victim aged 12) numerous indecent assaults on women and girls aged between 10 and 58. He is on community supervision having served six years of an eight-year custodial sentence for rape. Mr Smith has been unemployed since leaving school. He has a history of drug and alcohol use, most recently using amphetamines. He also has a history of domestic violence when in relationships. Mr Smith is due for release from prison where he has undertaken the Sex Offender Treatment Programme (SOTP). Whilst in prison Mr Smith has been subject to suicide and self-injury monitoring procedures (F2052SH) due to self-injurious behaviour. A MAPPP is being held to share information and develop a risk management plan for Mr Smith's release.

Some examples of potential risk management objectives that may be assigned to a psychologist in a case such as this may be:

- To liase with the local NHS medium secure unit to obtain a current psychiatric assessment
- To complete an assessment of the risk of completing suicide or intentional self-injury
- Psychological assessment to be undertaken regarding issues of abuse/ power towards women and report of SOTP
- To undertake work with JS in relation to his attitude to women
- To write a report to support the application for a Sex Offender Order on JS
- In addition to the community-based psychologist undertaking assessment or intervention work the prison-based psychologist would be invited to the MAPPP to give information about Mr Smith's participation in intervention work whilst in custody and their assessment of future risk. Other prison-based staff may also be invited to give a view on Mr Smith's behaviour whilst in custody

Audit and evaluation of service delivery

A key skill of the psychologist is research and evaluation. Processes such as MAPPPs benefit from regular audit and evaluation. Psychological staff could be usefully employed in carrying out an evaluation of service delivery. This could take the form of a qualitative reviews of MAPPA or statistical review of numbers of offenders and risk management objectives that could inform a review of resources required to run MAPPA effectively. This work could be used to inform the annual report of areas and, in turn might, at a national level inform best practice.

Conclusions

The management of high-risk offenders in the community using the MAPPA is a developing area of work to which applied psychologists are well placed to provide an effective contribution. The multi-disciplinary and multi-agency nature of the work provides a variety of tasks and experience both for the trainee psychologist and qualified practitioner. In this chapter an outline of the process of MAPPPs, the types of risk assessment used and the ways in which psychologists may contribute has been provided.

NOTE

1 Multi-agency Public Protection Arrangements (MAPPA) applies across England and Wales and sets the framework for public protection from high-risk offenders under the supervision of the NPS. Part of MAPPA is a system of Multi-agency Public Protection Panels (MAPPPs). Area-based panel systems often built on previously existing local approaches with a variety of terms being used to describe these.

Chapter Ten

Domestic Violence Work with Male Offenders

Jane Lindsay, Dermot Brady and Debbie McQueirns

Introduction

This chapter explores intervention options for male perpetrators of domestic violence supervised by the National Probation Service (NPS) for England and Wales, including those on community orders or on release from custody. The policy context within which developments are taking place is discussed. The theoretical approach and practice models being evolved by the National Probation Service as it works to develop effective interventions for domestic violence are examined. One of the key features of this approach is the aspiration of contributing to an integrated and co-ordinated community response to domestic violence. The steps being taken to promote a multi-agency and inter-professional response are outlined.

The key features of the community-based Integrated Domestic Abuse Programme (IDAP) are outlined and used as a framework to consider what role applied psychologists working with the probation service might play in supporting work with domestic violence perpetrators. The IDAP intervention in September 2003 has research Pathfinder status.

A critical element within the NPS approach is the recognition of the responsibility of the service to promote the safety of the victims of men attending community domestic violence interventions. The NPS also acknowledges the contribution these women may wish to make to the assessment of offenders and the centrality of their role in evaluating the effectiveness of interventions. A new role, Women's Safety Worker, has been developed to carry out this work. The challenges these workers encounter in their work and the potential role of psychologists in supporting them in their work is discussed.

What Is Domestic Violence?

The NPS defines domestic violence as being:

> Any form of physical, sexual or emotional abuse, which takes place within the context of a close relationship. In most cases the relationship will be between partners (married, co-habiting or otherwise) or ex-partners. Domestic violence also takes place in gay and lesbian relationships and occasionally in heterosexual relationships when the man is the victim, and in inter-generational relationships. It may happen in any section of the community regardless of class race or religion, but women from minority ethnic groups may face particular difficulties that result from a combination of sexism and racism. (National Probation Directorate, 2003)

This is a broad definition, but is important in that it signals that domestic abuse includes not only the isolated incidents of physical abuse most likely to lead to conviction for offences but that is part of a pattern of abusive behaviour which can include ongoing emotional and psychological abuse and intimidation. The term 'domestic violence' masks many different forms of abusive behaviour, which are anything but homogenous. The definition also indicates that both racism and sexism may exacerbate the effects on victims of abuse. This chapter focuses on male perpetrators' abuse of their female partners or ex-partners as, to date, the main developments of interventions within probation are with this group of offenders.

The national context and prevalence

There has been a significant increase of awareness about domestic violence in British society in recent years, which is in no small part due to the persistent efforts of organizations working with women. Women's Aid, Refuge and many voluntary organizations representing women have striven to get this issue on the agenda of successive governments, often pointing out shortcomings in service delivery that do nothing to end domestic violence and the damage it causes in society. Government policy sets out a three-strand approach to the problem, placing emphasis on *prevention* (which includes working with offenders to prevent reoffending), increased legal *protection* for victims and their families and on providing the *support* victims need to rebuild their lives (Home Office, 2003). Victim services and support have also recently been highlighted in the criminal justice agenda, which aims to ensure that victims' 'interests are at the heart of the Criminal Justice System' (Home Office, 2002a). The aim of government policy is to develop a new national framework for victims of crime and to promote integrated working by all agencies within the criminal justice system to promote victims' rights and safety. The probation service's development of approaches to work with perpetrators of domestic violence is framed within these broad aims.

Estimating the prevalence and incidence of domestic violence is difficult. Domestic abuse is under-reported and prosecution rates for domestic violence are low. The most recent estimate (1996 survey) of the British Crime Survey (BCS) is that one in four women and one in six men will be a victim of domestic violence in their lifetime. Domestic violence occurs across society regardless of age, gender, race, sexuality, wealth and geography (Mirrlees-Black, 1999). A more in-depth study by BCS on sexual and interpersonal violence was conducted in 2001. The results of this study were due to be published in the autumn of 2003 and it is anticipated that this confidential study will reveal higher levels of domestic violence than previously estimated.

Nearly half of all female murder victims are killed by partners or ex-partners (an average of two women per week). Of all murders of men, 8 per cent are homicides by female partners or ex-partners and some of these may include those committed in self-defence following a history of abuse by a partner (Flood-Page & Taylor, 2003). Domestic violence has the highest rate of revictimization of any crime (Kershaw et al., 2000). The effects of domestic violence on victims include both physical and mental health problems. It is estimated that 50 per cent of women in touch with mental health services have had violent or abusive experiences (Home Office, 2003e).

It is less commonly understood that children are also regularly victimized. Children living in contexts of domestic violence may experience both indirect and direct abuse both by witnessing abuse and by intervening to attempt to stop the violence (Mirlees-Black, 1999). Domestic abuse within the family can also have a negative impact on children's school attainment and the likelihood of school exclusion (Home Office, 2003e). The links between domestic violence and the needs of children are being increasing recognized and supported by research (see e.g. Hester & Radford, 1996; Mullender, 1996; Mezey, 1997; Hester & Pearson, 1998; Humphreys, 2000).

The extent of domestic violence within probation caseloads has not been routinely measured to date. A recent National Probation Directorate (NPD) pilot of the Offender Assessment System 'tool' (OASys) (Home Office, 2001) that includes specific questions on family violence and relationship problems found that nearly one fifth of all offenders assessed reported domestic violence. It is anticipated that, as use of OASys increases within the probation service, a more accurate profile of the extent of domestic violence within the probation caseload will be available. It is likely that the demand for the provision of interventions for perpetrators will increase with the concurrent need to provide relevant services for women and children associated in different ways with those offenders. Other potential growth areas include the development of approaches to working with women subject to supervision who are experiencing domestic violence or who have done so in the past, and to working with offenders of both genders who have childhood experiences of domestic violence.

Developing a probation response to domestic violence

The provision of specific interventions for perpetrators of domestic violence in the UK has a relatively short history and limited evaluation and effectiveness research. Mullender and Burton's (2001) literature review, commissioned as part of the Home Office Crime Reduction programme's Violence Against Women Initiative in 2000, highlights the national paucity of interventions in comparison with developments in the USA, Canada and Australia. In the UK, non-governmental organizations took an early lead in initiating intervention programmes with male perpetrators. By 1999 though, over half the recorded national provision was located in the statutory criminal justice sector (14 of 27 groups – Network Directory, cited in Mullender & Burton, 2001). Most of these providers are associated with the National Practitioners Network and its umbrella organization, Respect, an umbrella organization working across statutory and voluntary sectors. Most also subscribe or aspire to the principles and minimum standards of practice developed by Respect (2000).

Given the limited growth of interventions, it is perhaps unsurprising that the two main external evaluations of perpetrator interventions in the UK (the CHANGE programme / Lothian Domestic Violence Probation Project [Dobash et al., 2000] and the Violence Prevention Programme / Domestic Violence Intervention Project [Burton, Regan & Kelly, 1998]) are based on relatively small samples with significant attrition rates and draw modest conclusions in terms of the effectiveness of the intervention approaches utilized. These studies are helpful in pointing to methodological and ethical requirements for evaluation research on domestic violence interventions (Bowen, Brown & Gilchrist, 2002). As domestic violence is increasingly treated as a 'crime',

Mullender and Burton (2001) predict that the main growth area for intervention provision may be within the statutory probation sector. Whilst acknowledging that this may lead to more comprehensive provision of interventions and the standardization required for effective evaluation, they question whether such developments may stifle the creative and innovative contributions made by the non-governmental sector.

The National Probation Directorate (NPD) launched a research Pathfinder for intervening with male perpetrators of domestic violence in early 2001. Research 'Pathfinders' are one of the strategies utilized by the 'What Works?' unit of the NPD to identify evidence-based best practice in working effectively with offenders. Structured interventions designated as research 'Pathfinders' are evaluated independently both for effectiveness and for 'value for money'. In developing the community-based domestic violence interventions, the NPD works collaboratively with HM Prison Service for England and Wales, who are concurrently developing intervention programmes for male prisoners assessed as being domestic violence perpetrators (The Healthy Relationships Programmes [Moderate and High Intensity] based on the Correctional Service of Canada's Family Violence Prevention Programmes [Stewart et al., 1999]). The NPD also consults a reference group whose members include representatives from key voluntary sector organizations providing interventions with perpetrators and women's organizations. Elements of the research 'pathfinder' on domestic violence include research on the offending related needs of offenders with domestic violence histories (Gilchrist, yet to be published), a cross-national study on the Spousal Assault Risk Assessment (SARA) developed by Kropp et al. (1995), and the development of community-based interventions.

The first community-based intervention, the Integrated Domestic Abuse Programme (IDAP) (piloted in West Yorkshire and London probation areas) was due to be reviewed by Correctional Services in the autumn of 2003. Although this intervention had only 'pathfinder' status in September 2003, it provides a useful example of the development of an intervention and offers a framework for considering what role applied psychologists working with the probation service might play in supporting the work with domestic violence perpetrators.

The Integrated Domestic Abuse Programme (IDAP)

The Integrated Domestic Abuse Programme (IDAP) is based on the intervention model (often known as 'The Duluth programme') developed by the Domestic Abuse Intervention Project (DAIP) in Duluth, Minnesota, USA. The decision to select this intervention for the research 'pathfinder' was informed by the findings of existing research carried out in North America that appear to hold out some promise for the efficacy of this approach (Gondolf, 2002). It was also known that there was a certain level of practitioner familiarity with this approach. Existing work in the UK with male perpetrators of domestic violence had utilized concepts inspired by the Duluth model (Mullender & Burton, 2001). Finally, the philosophy underpinning the Duluth approach, which promotes a co-ordinated community response to domestic violence (see box 10.1) was seen to be congruent with the UK governmental promotion of a multi-agency strategic approach to domestic violence (Home Office, 2000). The 'Pathfinder' intervention could be situated and developed within a wider local and national environment in which agencies work together to develop 'joined-up' services (e.g. community safety agendas such as Crime and Disorder Partnerships and Crime Reduction interventions and child protection initiatives [Department of Health, 1999a, 2000b, 2003b]). It was considered that the intervention could form part of a wider holistic community approach that prioritizes and centralizes women and children's safety and contributes to the overall government initiatives on domestic violence.

Box 10.1 The eight key components of the community intervention projects (Duluth)

1. Creating a coherent philosophical approach centralizing victim safety
2. Developing 'best practice' policies and protocols for intervention agencies that are part of an integrated response to domestic violence
3. Enhancing networking among service providers
4. Building monitoring and tracking into the system
5. Ensuring a supportive community infrastructure for battered women
6. Providing sanctions and rehabilitation opportunities for abusers
7. Undoing the harm that violence does to children
8. Evaluating the co-ordinated community response from the standpoint of victim safety

(Shepard & Pence, 1999)

The philosophy underpinning the IDAP

The IDAP adopts the Duluth principle of locating the men's intervention within a wider framework. It is predicated on the position that no single intervention can in itself be sufficient in treating domestic violence and preventing recidivism (Stubley, 2003). The IDAP promotes and requires co-operation and inter-agency working with both statutory agencies (including the police, Crown Prosecution Service, the courts and social services) and non-governmental organizations to promote women and children's safety, manage risk and to ensure that men are held to account for their actions.

The IDAP's philosophy holds that perpetrators of domestic violence use violence as a way of imposing control on their partners, and that this behaviour is intentional. The power that men exercise in this way is seen as a direct result of the patriarchal structures that exist in our societies, which benefit men and give them power. The IDAP uses the Duluth wheels (Power and Control / Equality) to symbolize both the range of abusive behaviours that men use, and the alternatives or non-controlling behaviours that the intervention seeks to teach participants. It is predicated on the idea that domestic violence is gender based and that anger management as a primary focus for intervention would not be appropriate. It is held that men who assault their partners often equate anger with abusive behaviour and misattribute the reason for their actions to their highly charged emotional state. This is viewed as a form of denial and minimization and a tactic in avoiding taking responsibility for their actions.

Theoretical basis of the IDAP

The study of domestic violence is an evolving field and emerging explanations are much debated with competing emphases being placed on either sociological or psychological factors. The IDAP (in common with the Healthy Relationships domestic violence intervention being provided by HM Prison Service) utilizes the 'nested ecological model' (see Stubley, 2003) as a broad theoretical framework to describe the aetiology of domestic abuse. The strength of this model is that it incorporates key psychological and sociological explanations, viewing domestic violence in terms of the outcome of the interaction of biological, psychological, interactional, family, community and social factors operating within an ecological system. It directs practitioners to consider both risk and protective factors in developing both their understanding of why domestic violence occurs, recognizing that this is likely to be multi-determined. It is also seen to be helpful in framing appropriate targets for intervention both at an individual and systems level. The nested ecological model describes four contextual levels of explanation, and suggests that each level is influenced by the other (see box 10.2).

Box 10.2 The Nested Ecological Model

1. *Macro system*. This encompasses the broad attitudes and beliefs regarding partner assault that are held by one's culture, for example, the influence of patriarchy and the social and cultural prescriptions that endorse male aggression and their power and control over women. Dutton suggests that macro-system socialized norms (e.g. patriarchy) may influence men's interpretation of arousal states when they perceive a loss of control in their intimate relationships and this mechanism may increase the likelihood of an aggressive response being selected.

2. *Exosystem*. This level consists of social structures that influence the immediate context in which the assault occurs; for example, workgroups, friendships or other groups that connect the family to the larger culture. Dutton hypothesizes that work stress, unemployment or the lack of social support could increase the risk for family violence. Association with other men who endorse violence towards women may also increase the risk that men will be violent in their intimate relationships.

3. *Micro system*. The third level consists of the patterns of interactions within the family unit or immediate environment within which the abuse takes place. It examines the level of conflict within the family unit and between the couple, the factors that led up to the abuse and the consequences of the abuse. Dutton suggests that whilst micro-system processes may contribute towards abusive behaviour, individuals' particular response to the experience of this may be learned.

4. *Ontogenic level*. The last level focuses on the features of the individual's developmental experience that shape responses to factors at other levels and which can help to shape an abusive personality. Cognitive appraisals and emotional and behavioural reactions are viewed as learned predispositions, shaped by the individual's experiences; for example, the individual's develop-mental history, his possible experience of abuse at the hands of his parents and/or watching his father abuse his mother, his degree of empathy, his ability to manage his emotions, his response to handling conflict and the level of anxiety over relationship changes. Dutton postulates that power and intimacy needs learned in the family of origin could interact with stress and conflict at micro-system and exosystem levels.

(Adapted from Stewart et al., 1999, and Stubley, 2003)

The IDAP draws on social learning theory as an explanatory framework to account for how abusive behaviour develops, incorporating the role of cognition and mediating thought processes, and stressing choice and responsibility for individual action. This forms the basis of the programme's model of change. The intervention orientation of the programme is cognitive behavioural, teaching participants to analyse thinking patterns and then to change the premises, assumptions and attitudes that underlie those thinking patterns. Once individuals are able to develop a critical awareness of beliefs underlying sexist and violent behaviour, they are then introduced to alternative beliefs, actions and behaviours. The specific goals of intervention are shown in box 10.3.

Box 10.3 IDAP: intervention goals

Goal	Means by which this is achieved
To increase participants' understanding of the causes of their violence and for participants to understand their underlying purpose in using acts of violence as a means of controlling the victim's actions, thoughts and feelings	By examining the social, cultural, experiential and psychological factors that have been instrumental in shaping their behaviour and by examining the intent of their acts of abuse and the belief systems from which they operate
To increase participants' motivation to engage in the process of positive change	By examining the negative effects of their behaviour on their relationships, partners, children, friends and themselves
To provide participants with practical skills to change abusive behaviour	By exploring and practicing non-controlling and non-violent ways of relating to women
To encourage participants to become accountable to those they have hurt through their use of violence	By encouraging them to acknowledge their abuse and accept responsibility for its impact on partners and others

(derived from Pence & Paymar, 2003)

Approach to evaluation on the IDAP

The evaluation of the IDAP Pathfinder seeks to assess the extent to which the intervention has changed perpetrators' attitudes and behaviour; whether the intervention is more effective with those with specific psychological and behavioural characteristics; and the degree to which it contributes to a co-ordinated community response to domestic violence. Its impact on pro-offending attitudes and behaviour is assessed by pre and post intervention measures[1] completed by the offender (pre programme, post programme and at a follow-up stage six months after the end of the programme), and also by information sought from the victim and any subsequent partner. The evaluation replicates the approach taken by Dobash et al. (2000) in seeking to compare perpetrator and victim reports. Victims are asked to contribute voluntarily to this process and a set of victim report measures is used at similar intervals to those administered to the offender.[2] The attrition rate in securing the conviction of male perpetrators of domestic violence is well reported (Morris & Gelsthorpe, 2000) and reconviction records are unlikely to provide a reliable measure of further offending. It is intended that evaluation will also utilize police 'call out' records and information from victim agencies to supplement the data provided by the victim and the offender. Reports of further domestic violence incidents are recorded.

The evaluation also seeks to tap into the question of whether different offenders respond differently to this intervention. Typologies of domestic violence perpetrators are beginning to be identified (Holtzworth-Munroe & Stuart, 1994; Holtzworth-Munroe et al., 2000; Waltz et al., 2000). It is hypothesized that pro-feminist cognitive-behavioural re-education interventions such as a Duluth programme may be more effective with some groups of offenders than others. Alternative interventions may be needed for those assessed as having high dependency and 'borderline personality disorder' characteristics. The Pathfinder programme utilizes the Spousal Assault Risk Assessment (SARA) (Kropp et al., 1995) as a risk assessment 'tool' supporting programme referral and to collect data as part of the evaluation. It is thought that this risk assessment may contribute to identifying subgroups for whom the intervention is most suitable (National Probation Directorate, 2001a)

The extent to which the intervention is contributing to a co-ordinated community response to domestic violence is less easy to assess. An independent process evaluation is being conducted as part of the overall evaluation and a stakeholder evaluation has been proposed (National Probation Directorate, 2001b) with specific attention being paid to protection and safety issues in relation to victims and related vulnerable children and adults. The achievement of treatment compliance (Hollin, 1995; HM Inspectorate of Probation, 1998) is also a critical feature in evaluating effectiveness. The extent to which treatment compliance has been achieved forms part of the process evaluation of the pathfinder programme. The evaluation of this Pathfinder should also prompt a review of the evaluation approach taken. It is possible that the measures now used will be revised.

IDAP design

The intervention is as an integrated case management and groupwork intervention with effective communication and collaboration required between facilitators, case managers and women's safety workers.

The intervention as a whole can be seen as having five stages: pre-sentence assessment, post sentence assessment and orientation, groupwork with integrated case management, end of groupwork and post groupwork with the case manager. In parallel to these processes with the offender, women's safety work is undertaken (see box 10.4). Tracking and monitoring of the offender in liaison with the police community safety units, social services and Multi-agency Public Protection Panels also forms part of the wider integrated approach and is linked into each of these stages. There may well be opportunities for applied psychologists to contribute at each of these stages.

Selection and Assessment on the IDAP

The Integrated Domestic Abuse Programme is designed to target 'moderate' to 'high-risk' adult male heterosexual domestic violence perpetrators. Assessment for perpetrators will be through OASys, which is due to be fully operational by the end of 2004. OASys is designed to identify and classify offending related needs (including basic characteristics and cognitive behavioural problems). The SARA (Kropp et al., 1995) is included as part of this process.

The SARA consists of a checklist of 20 offender-critical risk factors for domestic violence including an examination of the offender's criminal history, psychosocial adjustment, mental health, and the current or index offence. In cases where the offender is thought to have a mental health problem, a specialist assessment may be required. A further section of the SARA allows for other factors particular to the individual offender to be considered, and critical items, those adjudged to be particularly pertinent to the risk of reoffending are also identified.

This structured clinical assessment draws on interviews with the perpetrator and collateral information including any reports, case records and criminal histories that are available. It is intended that this should, as far as possible, include information from the victim and other known partners. A structured interview schedule is used (Victim's Contribution to the SARA) with the victim's consent, to obtain information to gather further information about the offender. Further information is sought from relevant community agencies.

Box 10.4 Integrated Domestic Abuse Programme Stages

Stage 1. Pre-sentence/pre-release assessment

Is the person suitable for the IDAP? Should a condition of his sentence or licence be a condition to attend?

- A man has appeared in court and has pleaded or been found guilty of an offence. Domestic violence features. The court has asked for a pre-sentence report to be prepared. Should it be proposed to the court that he is required to attend the IDAP as a condition of a Community Rehabilitation or Community Punishment and Rehabilitation order?
- A man is in prison and may be released on licence. Domestic violence features. Should it be recommended that he attend the IDAP on release from prison?
- A probation officer makes an assessment and prepares a report using the SARA (the Spousal Assault Risk Assessment).
- If possible during the remand period, the Women's Safety Worker makes contact with the victim and provides her with information about safety planning, about the programme and about where she may access help. The Women's Safety Worker asks the victim to help with the risk assessment of the man and completes the Victim's SARA.

Stage 2. Post sentence: assessment and orientation to the groupwork programme

Men who are required to undertake the programme as part of their supervision by the Probation Service first undertake an orientation to the programme. This consists of at least three pre-programme sessions with the case manager designed to prepare them and motivate them

- A supervision plan is drawn up by the case manager, based on a risk assessment and the outline plan drawn up in the Pre Sentence Report and OASys.
- The man is prepared to undertake the programme and completes pre-programme measures designed to help to find out if it has been effective.
- A three-way meeting is held between the case manager, a groupwork facilitator and the offender to help him become familiar with the format and exercises used on the groupwork.
- The Women's Safety Worker provides the woman with information about the programme, discusses safety planning and provides information about where she may access help. The Women's Safety Worker asks the woman to help with the assessment of the man and to contribute to the overall evaluation of the men's programme. She asks the woman to complete pre-programme evaluation measures.

Stage 3. Groupwork programme delivery with integrated case management

The man attends the groupwork programme. Contact is maintained with the woman.

- Men undertake a groupwork programme, which normally lasts between seven and nine months. There are 27 weekly sessions. These are divided into nine modules of 3 sessions per module. Participants can join at the beginning of each module (except Sexual Respect), having completed the one-to-one pre-group sessions, which include preparation for joining (e.g. becoming familiar with the format and exercises used in the sessions).
- Offenders work to an agreed action plan for changing their behaviour. If they fail to attend the programme, they are taken back to court.
- Each offender meets with his case manager at least once a month.
- There is a review halfway through to assess his progress with a groupwork facilitator and the case manager.
- The Women's Safety Worker responds to any contact from the woman and makes contact with her halfway through the groupwork. She provides information about the man's attendance and enquires about his behaviour outside the group. She reviews safety planning arrangements and ascertains if there are any emerging risk issues.

Stage 4. End of groupwork programme

The man has completed the groupwork.

- An end of groupwork review is conducted with the man, his case manager and a programme tutor.
- The man is asked to complete end-of-programme measures.
- The Women's Safety Worker contacts the woman. She provides information about the offender's attendance on the programme and enquires about his behaviour outside the group. She asks the woman to complete the end-of-programme evaluation measures. She reviews safety planning arrangements and ascertains if there are any emerging risk issues.

Stage 5. Post groupwork stage work with case manager

Follow-up work with the man to help him put what he has learned on the programme into action and prevent relapse.

- The case manager sees the man regularly, completing relapse prevention material with him and monitoring risk. These sessions are designed to build on and reinforce his learning on the programme and to help him to work on his action plan to stop behaving abusively in relationships.
- Six months after he has finished the groupwork programme the offender is asked to undertake more tests for evaluation purposes.
- The Women's Safety Worker contacts the woman six months after the man has completed the groupwork programme to ask her for feedback. She provides information about the offender's attendance on the programme and enquires about his behaviour. She asks the woman to complete the final set of evaluation measures designed to find out if the programme has been effective in stopping the man's violence.

In the 'Pathfinder' pilot areas protocols for the exchange of information were signed between the relevant social services department and police services. As relatively few domestic violence offences result in prosecution, reliance on criminal records may not give a full picture of the extent of police involvement with the offender. There may be information about police call-outs that can enable a better assessment of the risk of revictimization to be made. This also assists in challenging the idea, often proposed by perpetrators, that their offence was a 'one-off' incident and out of character. It may also help to contribute to community risk management processes; for example through the work of Multi-agency Public Protection Panels (MAPPPs: see chapter 9).

In completing Pre Sentence Reports writers should include an outline supervision plan for all cases. The offender assessment may indicate a range of offending related needs in addition to specific interventions relating to domestic violence (e.g. alcohol or substance misuse, basic skills). In these cases, careful attention should be given to sequencing interventions.

As a final prerequisite for attendance, the offender is asked to sign release of information and statement of understanding forms. These aim to ensure that the offender understands what he will be required to do if he is sentenced to the IDAP. Offenders are also informed that a women's safety worker will contact the victim of the offence and any current partner. There are a number of reasons why an offender might not be suitable for the IDAP, as is commonly the case with any intervention approach. Declining to sign these forms would mean the man was unsuitable. Assuming that the offender is then sentenced to a community order with a condition of attendance on the IDAP, the assessment process will continue, and the case management aspect of the intervention will start.

Case management

The case management role can be seen as the lynchpin of the IDAP in terms of risk assessment and management and co-ordinating an integrated and co-ordinated community approach in relation to individual offenders. This role includes liaising with all relevant community agencies (e.g. social services and the police; with women's safety workers and the groupwork staff). Working with perpetrators will always need to take the needs of their children into account at every level. Child protection concerns must always be considered thoroughly. The case manager ensures that social services departments are informed when men are undergoing intervention work in all cases where men are either living in the home or have contact arrangements in place. On the IDAP, the case manager has the main responsibility for operational decisions about child protection and risk issues, although responsibility for identifying and sharing information about these issues is shared by all.

Case managers also deliver the range of evaluation of measures at each required stage and this is seen as an opportunity also to engage the offender in the process of change. Case managers, who are usually specially trained and qualified probation officers, undertake individual work with offenders to reinforce motivation and attitudinal change and to promote skills development. They are also expected to address any other crime-related needs that are evident from the OASys assessment.

The case manager co-ordinates regular three-way meetings with the offender and groupwork staff. The first of these meetings is held before the offender commences the groupwork element of the intervention, and this is used to examine the index offence in great detail, using one of the main learning tools of the intervention, the control log. The second meeting is held at the midway point in the intervention and is used to review the man's progress and learning and his application of the non-controlling behaviour strategies taught on the groupwork element. The final three-way meeting is held following completion of the groupwork element and is used to assess the man's achievement on the groupwork and to set the agenda for follow-up individual sessions with the case manager to reinforce learning. Once the groupwork is completed the case manager provides a number of relapse prevention sessions. These sessions serve to reinforce learning, and also to identify what the offender has learned from the work he has done, and high-risk situations in the future.

Groupwork content of the IDAP

Nine themes, each representing an aspect of non-violent and respectful relationships, are addressed on the groupwork element of the programme:

- Non-violence
- Non-threatening Behaviour
- Respect
- Support and Trust
- Accountability and Honesty
- Sexual Respect
- Partnership
- Responsible Parenting
- Negotiation and Fairness

Each theme is explored over three sessions that follow the same sequence for each subject covered. Three exercises are used. First, the group produces a definition of theme. Following this, the group watches a short video vignette that depicts a man using a series of controlling and abusive behaviours related to the theme. Participants analyse the scenario using a 'control log'. They are asked to consider if they have used similar abusive behaviour. The last exercise within the session requires the participant to identify one goal for change and commit to use one or more specific steps to achieve that goal. Men are asked to complete a personal control log on an incident of their own abusive behaviour related to that theme in preparation for the next session.

Control logs are a primary learning tool on the programme and provide a framework to facilitate analysis of an abusive act. They are divided into seven sections, which include:

1. naming behaviours that constitute abusive *actions*
2. identifying the *intent* of the abuser in using that action and the underlying *belief* system that justified it
3. identifying *feelings* that motivated him to act
4. identifying the ways he *minimized* his action or *blamed* the victim or others for his behaviour or *denied* his actions
5. examining the *impact and effects* of his actions on himself, his partner and others
6. acknowledging the relationship of his *past use of violence* to his action and the victim's reaction to him
7. identifying *non-violent, non-controlling behaviour strategies* – alternative ways of dealing with conflict in a relationship

The second session of the theme is used to analyse men's own use of controlling and abusive behaviours using the control log. Particular attention is given to section 7 of the control log and the use of non-controlling behaviour strategies is reviewed and learning reinforced.

The third session focuses on exploring and practising non-abusive and non-controlling behaviour (teaching skills and reinforcing attitude change). On the IDAP men learn and practise 11 non-controlling behaviour strategies. The groupwork offers a 'skills repertoire' approach. Some men will find some of the techniques to be unsuitable for a number of reasons. Group members are told that they can and should choose from the repertoire of skills they will learn. Facilitators should encourage all participants to become competent in using all the methods so that they can choose knowledgeably which ones will work best for them. All 11 strategies are taught in sessions 2 or 3 over the course of the 27 weeks and are reviewed in session 2 in response to participants' control logs (particularly in relation to section 7 of the control log (non-controlling behaviour strategies).

The strategies covered are:

1. Taking time outs
2. Recognizing anger cues
3. Using positive self-talk
4. Coping with jealousy
5. Acknowledging women's fear
6. Using assertive behaviour
7. Accepting women's anger
8. Being aware of non-verbal cues
9. Communicating feelings and thoughts
10. Letting go
11. Non-violent conflict resolution

Offenders work to an agreed *action plan* for changing their behaviour, which is reviewed in each group session and with the case manager.

The role of women's safety workers: working with women and children

It is a requirement of both probation and prison-based domestic violence interventions that systems be in place to initiate and maintain contact with the victims of offenders and any new partners of men. This provides an opportunity to engage with victims in a unique way and to work in a manner in which the offender is not necessarily the primary consideration. Specialist women's safety workers are appointed to undertake this work.

Women offered services by the women's safety workers include women still living with the perpetrator; women who are separated from perpetrators but who are still in regular contact with them, often with children involved; women who are separated, with no contact with their ex-partner, and women who have formed relationships with perpetrators since commencement on the IDAP. All contact with women should be undertaken on the basis of promoting and centralizing women's and children's safety. Whilst every effort is made to contact women, this is clearly a voluntary contact. Women may not wish to have any contact with the probation service, and it is only right that this is respected.

Box 10.5 The key tasks of women's safety workers

Women's safety workers:

a) Contribute to promoting women's (both women and children) safety by supporting women to construct a realistic safety plan. Whilst the needs of women and children are often similar this is not always the case and the safety of children must always be paramount
b) Provide realistic information to women about the men's domestic violence programme and the possible outcomes of intervention with offenders
c) Provide women with information about men's attendance on the programme
d) Facilitate referral of women to local women's services for support, advice and assistance
e) Contribute to risk management by

- Ensuring that women are informed about any current or emerging risks posed by men attending the domestic violence programme
- On each contact with the woman, ascertaining if any changes have taken place that have implications for her or her children's safety
- Ensuring that any relevant information provided by women is shared promptly with the case manager responsible for risk management of the offender and the programme team

f) Contribute to the evaluation of the men's domestic violence programme by

- Requesting and seeking information from women to inform the initial and ongoing assessment of the offender
- Requesting and obtaining feedback from women at regular intervals throughout the programme, at the end of the programme and at a specified follow-up interval about reoffending for evaluation purposes
- Ensuring that evaluation information is properly recorded and forwarded to those managing the programme evaluation.

g) Contribute to the development of a co-ordinated community response to domestic violence by working with probation and prison services colleagues, other local agencies and local women's services in a positive and inclusive way.

(Lindsay et al., 2003)

Women's safety work includes initial assessment tasks, work undertaken during the groupwork phase and post intervention work. In the initial assessment phase the purpose of contact with women is to provide information about the IDAP, to promote safety planning, and to facilitate the referral of women to relevant community services. Women's safety workers also seek information from victims to inform the initial and ongoing assessment of the offender and risk management. The objective of women's safety work during the period that men are undertaking the groupwork is to provide women with information about men's progress, to facilitate referral to relevant services and to provide a contact point for women about any new issues or concerns. The women's safety worker reviews the impact of the intervention with women, identifies any emerging risks, and provides feedback about women's concerns within a context of explicit awareness of safety issues. In the final phase women are asked to contribute to the post intervention evaluation both at the end of the groupwork and at a specified follow-up interval. Women's safety workers provide regular feedback to groupwork staff and case managers throughout the process of intervention.

There are of course ethical issues that must be considered is gathering information from women and then using it. The first concern must always be victim safety and it is a challenge to ensure that the women who are contacted and who agree to participate are approached with this is mind. It is important to ensure that information provided by women is used for appropriate ends and is not communicated directly or indirectly to the offender.

The women's safety worker's role includes facilitating women's referral to statutory agencies and local women's services for support, advice and assistance. The probation service does not have the resources to provide a full advocacy and support service, and in this may attract criticism. It is argued given the complexity and multi-faceted nature of problems experienced by victims and their children, 'organizational individualism' (Hudson et al., 1999) in which one organization attempts to meet all needs without reference to services provided by other agencies, could be seen as counterproductive and possibly dangerous. Women's safety workers and case managers are expected to be aware of the range of services available locally and to develop effective communication channels with relevant agencies both for the purposes of enabling women to access specialist support and for the purposes of risk management.

The ethos of domestic violence interventions, demanding that victim safety should be central to all activities, gives rise to a complex set of relationships and ethical tensions that need to be handled sensitively. In the UK there are not yet sufficient appropriate services available to women who experience domestic violence in the community and it can be the case that women's safety workers identify this unmet need on a regular basis in their work. It is perhaps incumbent on the probation service to work with partner agencies and other stakeholders to ensure that this changes. Probation interventions must not only work towards goals of ending violence by individual perpetrators, but also of ending tacit societal acceptance of domestic violence. Nowhere is this more evident than in work with such victims.

Opportunities for Developing Contributions from Applied Psychological Services

To date applied psychological services have been involved with domestic violence interventions within the probation service in two key ways. First, applied psychologists have contributed to the identification of the theoretical models that underpin the programmes of interventions being utilized by the probation service. These theoretical models specify and state the psychosocial principles and processes whereby change can occur and thereby introduce criteria for measurement of change. Secondly, and linked with establishing theoretical models, psychologists have been involved in developing evaluation criteria including the use of evaluation measures, in consultation with the programme development team. Measurement of change using reliable and valid measures will perform a key basis of both effectiveness and the participants' change from pre to post intervention.

To date, applied psychologists have acted largely as 'consultants' with other disciplines in order to drive forward effective intervention and introduce measures of change and effectiveness. However, as research and practice develops in the field of domestic violence, it is becoming evident that applied psychologists are well placed to support the probation service in their work in this area in a number of ways. These areas while initially perhaps appearing subsidiary to the main thrust of work with survivors and perpetrators of violence are crucial to ensuring the quality of intervention at several different levels: development of staff skills, support and consultation with staff, development of a robust research base, ensuring effective and relevant collection and collation of data, individual assessment work with offenders and development of communication and links between agencies, in particular between the prison and probation service.

Development of staff skills: training

The introduction of programmes such as the Duluth model of intervention necessitates a broad skill base for those working with the perpetrators and survivors of abuse. This intervention requires those working with victims to be able to administer risk assessment and evaluation measures. Due to the nature of the offences and the position of the victim, these interviews require considerable skill. Practitioners working with perpetrators of violence require skills in assessment and intervention as well as having a sound knowledge of the theoretical basis of intervention. Applied psychologists may be well placed to contribute to training both at an induction (basic) level and at a more advanced level to meet the requirements of these practitioners.

Consultancy services

Applied psychologists are usefully employed in a consultancy capacity in many areas and fields. An example of this is the role of a forensic psychologist as a negotiator advisor in hostage situations within the prison service. Such roles could, of course, be undertaken by a range of applied psychology specialisms; for example counselling psychologists. The primary advantage of consultancy is that the 'consultant' is outside the process and can potentially provide clarity of approach and information based on his or her skills and knowledge. With the development of domestic violence interventions there tends to be a 'triangulation' of practitioners working within the intervention (the women's safety worker, the case manager, the groupworker). The potential for conflict is apparent, particularly due to the highly emotive nature of the work. Psychologists are well placed to offer a support role to other practitioners as they may stand independent of the process and can therefore usefully provide support based on their observations and knowledge. This role is distinct from the provision of individual counselling support with practitioners in that it is the overall intervention process that is being reflected upon, rather than the impact of such intervention work upon individual practitioners.

Research

Whilst the body of research into domestic violence is growing steadily there still remains a paucity of research in comparison, for example, to Canada and other countries. The focus on developing accredited interventions and standardized assessments nationally presents an interesting challenge for the development of research with a national context. This is a requirement for continual assessment to evaluate effectiveness, but for this to be relevant, effectiveness needs to be measured not only broadly in terms of risk of reoffending but also in relation to, for example, age, ethnicity, individual psychometric criteria, perceptions of survivors and so forth. Applied psychologists, from a range of specialisms, often have the skills and knowledge to contribute to the development of this research.

Collection and collation of data

The development of psychometric assessment 'tools' to accompany interventions should be based on examination of the theoretical model and finding or developing 'tools' that can measure the processes described in the model. The theoretical model can suggest appropriate and relevant measures, but this is not implicit; and what is usually the case (as in the IDAP model), is that the development team devise and develop a battery of measures that provide the 'best fit' for the theoretical model. Simplistically, the better the 'fit', the better the quality of the evaluation. However, it is only with experience and evaluation that the quality of the measures employed can be evaluated fully, and consequently there is a process of development and evolution where the quality of collection and collation of data is improved. Applied psychologists have a potentially key role to play in this.

Offender assessment

Perpetrators of domestic violence often have a range of psychological issues that may be related to their offence history or that may impact on the range of treatment options they are suitable to undertake. These may include chronic substance misuse, mental health issues and a diagnosis of 'personality disorder'. For example, there is a developing body of research which suggests that domestic violence perpetrators tend to have high scores in terms of some 'personality disorder' traits, whilst not always reaching clinical thresholds. In addition, on occasion an offender's educational level may preclude him from benefiting from a particular type of intervention where literacy is essential. There is therefore considerable scope for applied psychologists to undertake individual assessment work with those offenders where the case manager or treatment manager have concerns, with the aim of providing a comprehensive assessment and recommendations as to appropriate interventions.

Development of links and communication between agencies

The broader vision of the development of work within the field of domestic violence is to reduce the risk posed to victims or potential victims. The essential component in reducing risk is effective and timely communication between the agencies involved. These agencies may range from prison establishments to police, social services departments, education and health. Communication is the concern of all practitioners involved. Where it is considered there is a high risk, the case may be brought to a Multi-agency Public Protection Panel (MAPPP) (see chapter 9) and psychologists are a valuable source of information and can be called upon to provide specialist assessments when required. When an offender has received a custodial sentence it is essential that there is communication between staff in the prison establishment and community agencies, including the probation service, and in particular, practitioners who will be involved in their supervision upon release and those who have contact with the victim (women's safety workers). Applied psychologists working in the probation service are ideally placed to forge essential links with their professional colleagues in the prison service in order to foster liaison and cultivate communication between the prison and probation service. This may, for example, include routine attendance at case reviews of those offenders who have undertaken domestic violence programmes in prison, or assessment interviews with offenders prior to release with the view of contributing to the setting of any conditions on licences and/or the recommending of further work required whilst the offender is subject to licence.

Staff supervision and counselling

Finally, working with domestic violence perpetrators and victims is personally demanding work, which has the potential to damage staff if they are unable to make sense of the stresses they experience. Staff may, for example, experience vicarious trauma, and this is something that services need to be aware of. Applied psychologists, in particular clinical or counselling psychologists, might play a role in the early identification of these processes, assist in the supervision and support of practitioners and develop strategies to manage the work in order to minimize the stresses experienced.

NOTES

1 Violence Assessment Index, Controlling Behaviour Index, Injury Assessment Index, Revised Attitudes to Offence Scale, Locus of Control Scale, Inventory of Beliefs that Support Wife Beating Revised Short Scale, Quality of Life Interview (see National Probation Directorate, 2001b)
2 Violence Assessment Index (Victim version), Controlling Behaviour Index (Victim version), Injury Assessment Index (Victim version), Quality of Life Interview (Victim version) (see National Probation Directorate, 2001b)

Chapter Eleven

Work with Life Sentence Offenders

Debbie McQueirns

Introduction

Life sentence offenders (LSOs),[1] both those serving sentences and those on licence to the probation service in the community are a growing population in the United Kingdom. Britain imprisons more people for an indeterminate period than the rest of Western Europe combined (Shaw, 1999). This population comprises those who have committed the most serious of offences including murder and who by the nature of their offences present challenges to the Criminal Justice system with respect to the assessment and management of their risk, and implicitly, the protection of the public. The serious and emotive issues that arise due to the nature of such offences have concerned successive governments and since the 1980s there have been substantive legislative reforms with respect to procedures for dealing with LSOs. There have been the introduction of the automatic life sentence, new guidelines for working with the victims of LSOs and new categories of offence included within those for which a discretionary life sentence can be passed.

LSOs on average are now serving half as long again in custody as they did in the 1970s (Shaw, 1999). The number of lifers beginning their sentence exceeds those being released at a ratio of approximately 3 : 1. However, there has been a fall in reconviction rates for male lifers for serious offences, in marked contrast to the higher reconviction rates for other offenders (HM Inspectorate of Prisons and Probation, 1999). Since 2001 the probation service has recalled to custody approximately 25 life sentence offenders annually, which constitutes less than 2.1 per cent of those under supervision. A joint thematic review by HM Inspectorate of Probation and HM Inspectorate of Prisons undertaken in 1999 suggested that the work in prison with LSOs, along with the close supervision by the probation service whilst on licence, may have contributed to this decline. With the growth in the use of the life sentence, the importance of fair, accurate and thorough assessments of risk in reducing the risk of reoffending is vital in order that the stakeholders, including the offender, the victim or victims and the public can remain confident in correctional services and the broader Criminal Justice system.

This chapter provides an overview of the lifer system. This is followed by a review of the roles of practitioners in the probation service in working with this group of offenders. The current and potential roles of applied psychologists are then considered.

Overview of the Lifer System: Types of Life Sentence

Adult offenders

For England and Wales, the Homicide Act 1957 brought an end to capital punishment for murder, and the death penalty for other offences was suspended in 1965 and was subsequently abolished for all offences in 1970. Following the suspension of the death penalty, life imprisonment became the mandatory penalty for persons over the age of 21 convicted of murder. Thus offenders convicted of murder are known as 'mandatory lifers' because life imprisonment is the only sentence that a court can pass by law for that offence.

Life imprisonment is the discretionary maximum sentence for over 50 offences committed by offenders over 21 years of age. Whereas in theory a large number of offences can officially attract a maximum term of life imprisonment, many seldom do so and some of the offences in this category are largely of historical interest (e.g. committing arson in a naval dockyard). Discretionary life sentences are typically imposed for a small number of offences including manslaughter, attempted murder, rape, buggery, arson, armed robbery and some drugs offences. The life sentence will only be imposed where the court considers the offender to be sufficiently 'dangerous' to warrant a life sentence. Implicit in the definition of 'dangerousness' is some evidence of instability and/or 'personality disorder'. A discretionary lifer's tariff is set and given in open court by the trial judge following conviction.

Automatic life sentences (or 'two strikes and you're in') were introduced in 1996 following the publication of the White Paper *Protecting the Public* (Home Office, 1996a). Under Section 2 of the Crime (Sentences) Act 1997, a life sentence became the automatic sentence for any second serious violent or sexual offence. This was revised under the Powers of the Criminal Courts

(Sentencing) Act 2000 (PCC(S) Act) giving trial judges the discretion to award a life sentence for a second serious violent or sexual offence, rather than making it an automatic life sentence.

This change allows for cases where offenders were automatically receiving life sentences when they committed, for example, an offence of 'wounding with intent to do grievous bodily harm' because they had a previous minor conviction for a minor assault. The amendment to the 1997 Act allows the trial judge to use discretion when an indeterminate sentence is felt to be a disproportionate punishment to the series of offences in question. Automatic life sentences have been the subject of extensive criticisms but remain an aspect of the legislative framework.

Young offenders

No child under the age of 10 years may be convicted of a criminal offence. Children and young persons under the age of 18 who are convicted of murder are sentenced to be detained at Her Majesty's Pleasure (mandatory). The 'specified part' of the sentence (tariff) is set in open court by the trial judge. Children and young persons under the age of 18 years who are convicted of other offences of exceptional gravity are sentenced to detention for life (discretionary). For young people between the ages of 18 and under 21 years, if convicted of murder or other serious offences, the sentence passed will be custody for life. Whilst the same terminology 'custody for life' is used for both murder and other serious offences, in practice when imposed for murder it will be administered as a mandatory life sentence and for other serious offences as a discretionary life sentence.

Length of Sentence and Tariff

Bailey (1995) notes that the life sentence is composed of two parts: (1) time spent in custody and (2) time spent on life licence in the community. All LSOs are indeterminate in that all offenders will stay in prison until the degree of risk implicit in release is assessed as acceptable and all are subject to ongoing supervision in the community and can be recalled to custody at any time. Figures published by HM Prison Service in May 2003 showed that the average periods served in custody by lifers (of those released) were 13 years for mandatory lifers and 10 years for other lifers. This compares with 14 years for mandatory lifers and 13 years for other lifers in 1997 (HM Prison Service, 2003b). The figures for 'others' may be influenced by the influx of automatic lifers during the late 1990s, whose 'tariffs' are often shorter than that of mandatory or discretionary lifers.

The 'tariff' is the minimum period which LSOs have to serve in custody to satisfy the requirements of retribution and deterrence. The tariff for a mandatory lifer was, prior to the Anderson Judgement in 2002, recommended by the trial judge, and the Lord Chief Justice to the Home Secretary who made the ultimate decision. In the 2002 judgment in the case of Regina v. Secretary of State for the Home Department (Respondent) Ex Parte Anderson (FC) (Appellant) the House of Lords declared that the Home Secretary's power to set tariffs for mandatory lifers was incompatible with the European Convention on Human Rights. The Secretary of State therefore decided, with effect from 25 November 2002, no longer to set tariffs. Amendments introduced into the Criminal Justice Bill provide for tariffs to be set by trial judges and announced in open court. Until now, consideration of release of mandatory lifers has taken place by means of a paper hearing before the Parole Board. Mandatory lifers are referred to the Parole Board three and a half years before their tariff expires.

The progress of the lifer is considered at this stage, with the chief concern being the risk that the lifer presents to the public. Depending upon that informed judgement, recommendations will be made by the Parole Board on suitability for transfer to open conditions and a future date, generally between one and two years, when suitability for release can be considered. The release decision was then taken to the Home Secretary in consultation with the judiciary.

In the Stafford Judgment (Case of Stafford v. The United Kingdom, 2002) the European Court ruled that a 'courtlike' body should determine the release of mandatory lifers, not the Home Secretary. The court accepted that this requirement is met by having an oral hearing before the Parole Board. New legislation did not come into immediate effect to meet the requirements to comply with this legislation. In the meantime, the Prison Service introduced transitional arrangements, which were agreed by Ministers, to comply with this judgment. The main effects of this judgment are that mandatory LSOs whose tariffs have expired are entitled to an oral hearing before the Parole Board. All other types of LSOs and juvenile murderers already have that entitlement. Decisions on the release of tariff-expired mandatory lifers is therefore now the responsibility of the Parole Board. The test for the release of mandatory lifers has changed to that used in discretionary cases. The Parole Board now has to consider whether mandatory lifers represent a risk to life and limb (i.e. serious harm) in deciding whether or not to release them. This is a significant change to the previous test applied to mandatory lifers, which was the risk of their committing a further imprisonable offence after release.

Discretionary LSOs are informed of the 'relevant part' (or tariff) of their sentence in open court and can appeal against the decision. Cases are managed and reviewed by the Parole Board before tariff expiry in the same way as those for mandatory lifers. Once the tariff has expired, for those remaining in custody, the Parole Board sits as a Discretionary Lifer Panel (DLP) to assess suitability for release. The LSO may attend the DLP and be legally represented at the oral hearing.

Young people sentenced to life imprisonment at Her Majesty's Pleasure are now dealt with in a similar way to discretionary lifers, following a judgment in the European Court of Human Rights (Case of Hussain v. The United Kingdom, 1996). Release is decided at oral hearings by the Parole Board (HMP panels). The tariff however continues to be set by the Home Secretary. Progress of the all lifers subject to detention under Her Majesty's Pleasure whose tariff have not expired is considered annually through reports by prison service staff including probation officers and applied psychologists. If exceptional progress has been made, consideration by ministers will be given to the reduction of the tariff. In addition, at the halfway mark in the tariff, progress reports are examined by ministers to consider whether the original tariff continues to remain appropriate. Prisoners may request a review of their unexpired tariff at any point during the sentence.

The Lifer Population

In the United Kingdom life sentence offenders, both those serving sentences and on licences, are a growing population. The number of persons serving life sentences in Prison Service establishments in England and Wales at the end of February 2003 was 5,352. This represents an increase of approximately 1,000 LSOs since 2001. It is forecast that this rate of increase will continue and reach between 6,000 and 7,000 by 2005 (Shaw, 1999). In addition to those serving sentences, there were 1,207 life licences under supervision by the probation service at the end of February 2003. Again, this number is likely to increase substantially over the next few years as demonstrated by the number of LSOs released for the first time on life licence, which has increased from 135 in the period April 2001 to March 2002 to 178 in the period April 2002 to February 2003. According to statistics published by HM Prison Service at the end of February 2003, 5,188 (97%) of the total population of lifers were men and 164 were women. Of the total population 162 were young offenders, 71 per cent of male lifers and 78 per cent of female lifers were serving a mandatory prison sentence for murder, and 16 per cent of lifers were from ethnic minority groups. The number of LSOs released for the first time on life licence from April 2001 to March 2002 was 135. Subsequently there were a further 178 first-time releases up till the end of February 2003, making the total number of LSOs under active supervision from the probation service 1,207 (HM Prison Service, 2003b). In addition, according to *Probation Statistics for 1994*, the probation service was responsible for pre-release contact with 3,359 lifers, as of 31 December 1994. This number is likely to have risen to the total population of LSOs serving sentences in accordance with the statutory requirements of the probation service.

Management of Life Sentence Offenders

The increase in the numbers of LSOs both serving and on licence has implications for both the probation service and the prison service in relation to effective practice with respect to risk assessment and management and in ensuring that resources are co-ordinated appropriately in order to achieve this. One result of the increasing size and complexity of the lifer population was the introduction by HM Prison Service in 1989 of a 'revised strategy'. This incorporated seven main principles, which can be briefly outlined as follows:

- Lifers should be treated as a separate group whose special needs should be recognized not by separation or privileges but due to the indeterminate nature of their sentence, there may be a particular need for support and guidance.
- The first allocation of a lifer should be to a 'main centre', which specializes in the induction and assessment of new lifers.
- A wider variety of prisons should accommodate lifers.
- Lifers should proceed, where appropriate, to conditions of lower security. For example, lifers should move to establishments of sufficient level of security that their risk could be managed effectively. Lifers should be tested in conditions of low security prior to release in order to ensure a progressive movement through the system in line with the lifer's career and life sentence plan. There are two stipulations relating to this. First, lifers should not move beyond category B conditions unless they have addressed their offending behaviour and, secondly, lifers will not be transferred to open conditions before the first formal review of their case.
- Lifers should have a planned and structured career through the system. The use of the Life Sentence Plan assists in identifying risk factors and the specification of individual needs from the commencement of the life sentence in order to plan appropriate intervention to address these needs through the sentence.

- There should be more routes out of prison and into the community. This element of the strategy focuses preparing those lifers who have spent very long periods in custody for return to the community.
- Allocation and administration should be centralized.

Stages of the Life Sentence and the Revised Life Sentence Plan

There are five phases to the life sentence: Remand/Trial Stage, 'Main Centre' or First Stage, Second Stage, Release Stage and Life Licence Stage. These stages are reflected in the revised Life Sentence Plan (HM Prison Service, 2001a, 2001b) that was redesigned by the Lifer Unit HM Prison Service in response to recommendations laid down in the Lifers Joint Thematic Review (JTR), carried out in 1999 by Her Majesty's Chief Inspectors of the prison and probation services. The revised LSP was introduced in January 2002. It requires sections to be completed by probation and prison staff working with LSOs at all stages in custody, from local prisons and remand centres through first, second and third stages. It covers potential lifers on remand and trial, newly convicted lifers awaiting transfer to first stage prisons, lifers serving in Second stage prisons, security category B and C prisons, working towards release in open prison conditions and lifers recalled to custody from life licence.

The five phases of a life sentence are represented by the following stages:

- Remand/Trial Stage – spent at a local prison
- First Stage (or Main Centre Stage) – the first stage after conviction and sentence. The Multi-agency Lifer Risk Assessment Panel (MALRAP) and Life Sentence Plan initial recommendations will be completed in this stage
- Second Stage – for offenders with long tariffs this will be the longest part of the custodial period and will be spent in a number of prisons progressing to ones of lower security
- Release Stage – the custodial period between the decision to release and the release date. Risk assessment continues throughout this and the next stage
- Life Licence Stage – in the community and under the supervision of the probation service

Should the continuous risk assessment on licence identify a developing risk that cannot be effectively managed in the community, the offender may be recalled to custody. In these instances he or she will be returned to the nearest 'Main Centre' where the decision to recall will be upheld or release will be ordered. If upheld, the 'Main Centre' with input from the Lifer Policy Unit for HM Prison Service will identify the appropriate second stage prison for transfer.

Role of the National Probation Service with Lifers

A probation officer *must* be appointed in the home area of every defendant who would face a possible life sentence on conviction. The probation service works with lifers from the point that they are defendants awaiting trial for offences for which they could or will be sentenced to a life sentence if pleading guilty or found guilty, through to supervision of them as life licensees in the community. The life licence can include a range of additional conditions such as specifying areas where the offender cannot go, where the offender can live and contact with the victim's family. These recommendations are often made by the probation service, which has a specific statutory responsibility with respect to victim contact work and therefore knowledge of the views and wishes of victims' families. The life licence may be revoked and the lifer returned to prison at any time. The lifer in all instances is entitled to make representations against recall.

The supervision element of the life licence may be cancelled by the Lifer Review Unit (LRU) following a recommendation from the probation service after a minimum of four years. However, it can be reimposed at any time should the offender's behaviour or circumstances give rise to concern. The licence remains in force for the whole of the offender's life. This continuity of contact assists in reducing the fragmentization of the life sentence and thus provides consistency with respect to risk assessment. There are usually at least three different probation officers involved: the 'home probation officer', the 'seconded probation officer' and the 'supervising probation officer'. The responsibilities and duties of each of the probation officers are clearly laid down in the 'Lifer Manual' (HM Prison Service, 2001a). However, it is useful at this point to provide a summary of these duties in order that the role of psychologists within the probation service can be considered within this context.

Home probation officer

The probation officer allocated to the lifer or potential lifer at the point of arrest in the area where the offender resides is termed the 'home probation officer'. Duties include the creation of a 'home file' containing press clippings illustrating the local reaction to the offence and documenting all contact with the remanded prisoner and his family, friends and so forth. In addition, the 'home probation officer' will provide information to the court including pre-trial and post trial reports as required. He or she will visit the prisoner in order to develop a rapport, although this should not include any discussion of the offence where a not-guilty plea has been entered. Contact with the victim's family with respect to honouring the requirements laid down in the 'Victim's Charter' should also take place, and it is important that the probation officer working with the victims is not the same one working with the offender (Home Office, 1990b). Such work should also be in line with the guidelines published by the National Probation Service in relation to contact work with victims of crime (National Probation Service, 2003b). This latter duty is both complicated and sensitive, requiring specialist skills and knowledge. Probation areas now also have specialist Victim Liaison Workers (VLWs) to deal specifically with this duty and liase with the home probation officer. Upon sentence the 'home probation officer' will attend the Multi-agency Lifer Risk Assessment Panel (MALRAP) which is held at the prison or young offender institution holding the offender. They will contribute to the multi-disciplinary identification of initial risk factors, which will form the basis of work to be addressed during the life sentence.

Seconded probation officer

The probation officer seconded to the prison where the lifer is serving his sentence is termed the 'seconded probation officer'. As the lifer moves through the stages of his life sentence this probation officer will change. The duties of the 'seconded probation officer' include establishing contact with the lifer as soon as possible and opening a file, close liaison with the 'home probation officer', contributing to most aspects of the LSP, including the preparation of life sentence reports for the Parole Board, risk assessment and intervention work. In addition the 'seconded prison officer' will deal with the lifers' ongoing needs, in particular informal contact with family and friends, and liaise with the supervising probation officer when the lifer reaches the preparation for release stage. He or she will prepare a pre-release report, which states any area of risk that continues to need to be addressed for the future and ensures that appropriate resettlement plans have been made.

Supervising probation officer

The probation officer responsible for the supervision of the lifer on licence is called the 'supervising probation officer'. His or her responsibilities are to supervise the licence in accordance with national standards (Home Office, 2002d), provide reports to the Parole and Lifer Review Group (PLRG) if there is concern about the licensee (e.g. if licensees fail to report or their conduct gives rise for concern) and take responsibility for recommending recall to the relevant member of probation senior management who will forward with further recommendation to the Parole Board.

Mentally disordered offenders

Lifers can be transferred to psychiatric hospital for treatment of mental disorder under the transfer directions of s.47 of the Mental Health Act 1983, usually coupled with restriction conditions under s.49 of the same Act. A mental disorder under this Act means that the person is suffering from mental illness, psychopathic disorder, mental impairment or severe mental impairment. A prisoner's life sentence continues to run during any period of transfer and time spent in hospital counts towards the fulfilment of the lifer's tariff period. The role of the probation service with transferred lifers is similar to that for other lifers, whether they are conditionally discharged from hospital or released on life licence. The guidelines contained in *Probation Circular 90/1995* (Home Office, 1995), state that the relevant probation office should be informed when a lifer is transferred to hospital. The supervising probation officer should be involved in his or her management whilst in the hospital system and be involved in resettlement plans in preparation for release. The supervising probation officer will be responsible for the management of the licence in the same way as for any licensee.

The Role of Applied Psychologists

The Joint Thematic Review of Lifers (HM Inspectorate of Prisons and Probation, 1999) pointed to the paucity of referral to the role of psychology with lifers found in the Lifer Manual. The manual does however state that:

> Wherever possible a report should be provided by the psychologist. (paras 6.6.7 and 7.1)

> the report should include any other information, such as specialist advice, that might assist in the review. (para 7.3.8)

The Thematic Review noted that psychologists within the prison service carried out a range of tasks and that in two-thirds of the cases reviewed there was no contribution by psychologists. Indeed within the prison service over the preceding years, the roles of psychologists in working with LSOs has progressively reduced. The Review recommended that:

> The Prison Service and Probation Unit should review the respective roles of all staff, including home probation officers, involved in work with life sentence offenders by:
>
> (a) setting clear expectations regarding their retrospective responsibilities within a multidisciplinary framework;
> (b) developing a means to ensure that both seconded probation officer and psychological input with lifers is uniform across the lifer estate (para 7.34).

Furthermore, the thematic review supported the view that applied psychologists should have a key role in assessing and reviewing need in relation to risk, whilst probation staff deliver offence-focused work in individual cases. It went on to specify the value of psychologists in giving advice and in the provision of specialist work in problematic cases. It is also worth noting that the limited involvement of psychologists in work with LSOs in prison has been changing more recently. This has included the introduction of a 'named psychologist' system for LSOs in custody, which clarifies which psychologist is responsible for undertaking assessment and intervention work with a particular LSO.

The revised Life Sentence Plan is largely based on the recommendations of this joint thematic review and specifies the role of the psychologist at different stages of the life sentence. This role reflects the specific requirements of the lifer with respect to psychological assessment. First, of the offence and offending history, and secondly, the psychological factors involved in serving long periods in prison and the uncertain nature of an indeterminate sentence.

The National Probation Service has historically sought the services of applied psychologists to conduct assessments and/or treatment of certain life sentence and other offenders. Each probation area has in the past tended to have links with applied psychologists, for example clinical or counselling psychologists working within the National Health Service, and/or with psychologists in private practice. However, the creation of the joint Prison and Probation Psychology Service in 2001 offered the opportunity for probation areas to strategically plan what applied psychological services they required 'in-house' in order to meet their identified requirements.

'In-house' psychologists commenced work with the probation service in early 2001, after the publication of the revised LSP. Their role with LSOs is therefore in its infancy and not to date guided by strategy, protocol or published guidelines. Moreover, different probation areas vary in how they wish to incorporate the skills of 'in-house' psychologists within their framework of operation and the 'specialism', numbers and grades of psychologists that they have employed or intend to employ to meet these objectives. Therefore as yet the role of predominantly forensic psychologists and trainee forensic psychologists employed in the probation service in working with lifers is largely undefined. In order to look forward and strategically plan for the future it is important first to identify the role of applied psychologists with lifers. Secondly, to attempt to identify the needs of the probation service with respect to the assessment and management of LSOs and identify how applied psychologists might help meet these identified needs in a cost effective manner.

The Needs of the Probation Service with Respect to the Management of Lifers

The thematic review (HM Inspectorate of Prisons and Probation, 1999) viewed the work of the probation service in the supervision of lifers positively and reflected that the fall in numbers of licensees who committed serious offences reflected the comprehensive and effective supervision that probation officers offered. This was in contrast to previous research, which suggested the contrary (Coker & Martin, 1985; Bailey, 1995; Cullen & Newell, 1999), indicating a positive change to the effectiveness of probation services interventions with LSOs. However, there were a number of issues raised by the review that probation areas have moved to address. These include the level of reporting by licensees being unnecessarily high in some cases, indicating a tendency for some supervising officers to err on the side of caution with respect to management of risk, and post-sentence reports not being completed on all prisoners' sentenced to life (Bailey, 1995).

The revised LSP goes some way to formulate a more formalized approach to addressing some of these issues. However, with the growth in numbers of lifers both serving and in the community, plus the recent restructuring of the probation service, which has resulted in significant resources being ploughed into the delivery of interventions based on the 'what works' principles, the management of licensees stands the risk of becoming less well resourced.

In addition, probation officers have often referred the more problematic lifers to external psychologists, generally clinical, counselling or forensic psychologists based in the National Health Service, for assessment and intervention. Whilst this is useful and prudent in management of risk, it seems likely that 'in-house' psychologists may complete such work more cost effectively, freeing NHS psychologists to work more intensively with mentally disordered offenders. This approach is recommended in the recent strategy document on applied psychology for Probation and Prison Services (HM Prison Service and National Probation Service, 2003a). Lifers upon release provide substantial challenges for the probation service. The psychological impact of release is often significant and lifers often go through a period of adjustment where considerable support is required. If resident in probation approved premises accommodation, managing the licensees on a day-to-day basis can prove arduous to staff. In addition the risk of suicide and self-injury and prevalence of mental health issues in the lifer population may continue post release and may be linked to factors associated with risk.

It is therefore timely and prudent that strategic consideration is given to the role that applied psychologists can take in supporting the work of the probation service with LSOs.

The Role of Applied Psychologists

Applied psychologists based in prisons have a long history of working with LSOs. During the 1970s and 1980s work with this group of high-risk offenders was seen as a focus for much of the work of psychologists working within correctional settings. During the 1990s this area of work was perhaps relatively neglected. However, recent changes have produced a renewed focus on such offenders.

The role of applied psychologists based in prisons in working with LSOs is reviewed in detail elsewhere (Wilmott, 2002b). In summary this work falls under four broad headings: mental health, risk assessment, offending behaviour focus and preparation for release and resettlement. However, it is worth noting that whilst these areas may need to be replicated to an extent with LSOs in the community, it is unlikely that the requirements of the probation service with respect to psychological services with LSOs in the community should mirror that of the prison service.

A number of criticisms of the way psychologists have had inputs into this area of work are evident. First, the focus of psychologist's assessment and intervention work has broadly been in the early stages of imprisonment. Input at the later, and arguably more critical stage leading up to release, has been more limited. Similarly, psychologists' engagement in what has been termed 'resettlement' has often been poor. A final and major criticism of psychologists' involvement though has been the tendency for such input to end at the prison gate, with a lack of follow through to the community. The levels of involvement with psychologists after release has been very variable. There appear to have been pockets of good practice where effective psychology input into the management of such offenders has been delivered, generally through the involvement of NHS psychologists on an ad hoc basis. Examples of this might include co-working between probation and NHS community forensic services. In general though, the contributions of psychologists to multi-disciplinary teams managing LSOs in the community has been minimal (Bailey, 1995).

This is something of a paradox given what is known about risk assessment. Within prison settings LSOs present clear challenges and, particularly in open prison settings, are carefully monitored and assessed. However, in contrast to community settings, open prison settings provide a very structured and controlled environment. Given what is known about effective risk management (Monahan & Steadman, 1994; Prins, 1995, 1999; Monahan, 1997; Towl & Crighton, 1997; Crighton, 2004a, 2004b) there is a clear case for ongoing work in community settings with those offenders assessed as high-risk. Applied psychologists based within probation areas have a significant potential contribution to the public protection role of probation with this high-risk group of offenders.

The development of MALRAPs are in a large part recognition of the value of a multi-agency approach to the identification, assessment and management of risk for LSOs. MALRAPs provide a multi-disciplinary and multi-agency framework for ongoing assessment and management of LSOs. Similarly, the development of the National MAPPA (Multi-agency Public Protection Arrangements) guidelines provides a structure for the ongoing risk assessment and management of high-risk offenders in the community, including those who are imminently being released from prison settings, and including LSOs.

MALRAPs and MAPPA provide an ideal framework for applied psychologists based in the probation service to work into. Below are outlined some of the ways in which psychologists might best contribute to effective multi-disciplinary working in risk assessment and management as well as provision of support to staff, and research and development in this area.

Helping to Meet the Needs of the Probation Service

Assessment and intervention work

Approaches to assessing risk in offenders has moved on rapidly in recent years. These developments have drawn on practices in a range of other settings where risk needs to be assessed and subsequently managed, and applied psychologists have contributed significantly to this (see chapter 5). In parallel to this a number of psychometric risk assessment evaluation tools have been developed and marketed. These have been aimed at a range of risks including risk of offending, risk of violence and risk of sexual offending. Examples of these would include the HCR-20 (Webster et al., 1997) and the Sex Offender Risk Appraisal Guide (SORAG) (Quinsey et al., 1998).

Input from psychologists might have utility at several stages in the life sentence. First, there is the pre-trial stage. The majority of LSOs will be in custody at this stage but a number will not. Both groups present significant risks both to themselves and to others. Assessment of LSOs at this stage in relation to the charges being faced will, of necessity, be limited by the legal process. Based on current knowledge though it seems evident that such offenders will be at elevated risk of suicide and possibly self-injury (Bogue & Power, 1995; Towl & Crighton, 1997). The probation service is of course committed to treating offenders with humanity and a key part of this must include preventing serious harm or death.

Following sentence HM Prison Service has a well-developed system of assessing LSOs through their life sentence in prison custody. This includes the need for psychological assessments at key stages during the period of custody. The development of a joint psychology service for corrections has allowed the rapid development of an infrastructure of professional applied psychologists within probation service areas, in place of, or in addition to, previous ad hoc arrangements (see chapter 1). This in turn presents an excellent opportunity to strengthen risk assessment and management work with LSOs.

As during the pre-trial phase, it seems likely that LSOs following sentence will present risks to others and also to themselves. Many of the risks presented to others will have begun to be addressed whilst in custody. So increasingly it is unlikely that LSOs with serious anger management problems, or substance misuse problems, will be released without having undertaken considerable assessment and intervention work. However, intervention work in custodial settings is generally limited in comparison to that in community-based settings. For example, it is possible to develop with LSOs in prison strategies for avoiding alcohol abuse. However, alcohol is difficult to obtain in custody when compared to the community and consequently addressing the risk and management interventions take on a different meaning in the community.

There is little good quality research looking at levels of morbidity and mortality amongst LSOs following release. However, there is some indicative evidence to suggest that LSOs show high levels of both (Bailey, 1995). To some extent this will be familiar to practitioners across the probation service. Offenders tend disproportionately to come from socially excluded groups and, as such, tend to suffer from poorer health outcomes. It remains unclear whether LSOs show poorer outcomes than those from similarly disadvantaged groups in the community. However, it does seem likely that they present higher risks of suicide and self-injury. An association between life sentences and suicide risk has been observed for those in custody (Towl & Crighton, 1997). It is at least a possibility that this will follow through into the community.

The legal responsibility for managing the risks with LSOs in the community rests with the supervising officer – a qualified officer in the area the offender settles in. Research though has suggested that this has often been an isolated and unsupported role (Bailey, 1995) with supervising officers struggling to manage a wide range of risks whilst putting ad hoc support in place. Supervising officers have also been directly in the 'firing line' when LSOs reoffend, whilst getting little recognition for successful case management, which, by definition, remains largely invisible. Structural changes in probation, with the development of MALRAPs and MAPPAs, as well as an infrastructure of 'in-house' psychologists provide an opportunity to share responsibility amongst disciplines. It also provides scope for risk assessment and management to become more effective in protecting the public.

Finally, it is worth noting the challenges of effective communication in risk assessment. Prins (1995, 1999, 2002) notes that failings in communication have often acted to impede effective risk assessment and management. Different agencies often communicate poorly with each other to the detriment of all. The development of partnership working in psychology shows considerable promise in avoiding such pitfalls. For example, all qualified psychologists seconded to the probation service have experience of HM Prison Service approaches to LSOs. With LSOs as with other offenders this increases the scope for effective communication regarding risk and adds to the promotion of seamlessness in risk assessment across correctional services.

There is of course considerable scope for this to be developed further and more effectively and strategically. A full discussion of this is outside the scope of this chapter. However, as an illustrative example there would appear to be advantages in community-based psychologists undertaking work with LSOs in open prison conditions. Likewise there is a case for psychologists based in prison settings to become more involved in working with LSOs being recalled, or at risk of recall, in the community.

Support Role to Staff

Probation staff assessing and managing LSOs in the community are often faced with difficult issues and concerns related to their risk. This may include, for example, approved premises staff where there is a high population of LSOs, supervising probation staff and so forth. In addition the guidelines for the probation service on working with victims specifies a range of work required with the victims of life sentence prisoners. This is often an emotive area of work that requires staff being supported.

Applied psychologists are well placed to offer relevant training and consultancy to the probation service to support their work with this group of offenders and their victims. Ultimately this could serve to contribute to the reduction of staff anxieties and potential for work-related stress.

Research and Development Role

In the broad area of risk assessment with LSOs there is a poverty of information related to what is effective in reducing risk. In addition, there is generally a lack of information regarding probation areas' population of LSOs and the issues that are relevant for this population in order that resources can be directed productively. Applied psychologists are well placed to be commissioned to undertake research and development and assist in providing the probation service with a sound body of knowledge and information in order that effective strategic management can ensue and appropriate training plans be devised and implemented, leading to better awareness.

Finally, it is notable that there is considerable overlap between specialisms in psychology that would be well placed to provide input in the areas outlined. For example, with respect to mentally disordered LSOs or LSOs with learning disabilities, work in relation to risk assessment might effectively be undertaken by clinical, counselling or forensic psychologists. The way forward in making this decision may not be to choose between specialisms but by electing to have a range of specialisms and utilize their skills and expertise according to specific criteria on a case-by-case or task-by-task basis. This would ultimately provide the best 'fit' in order effectively to reduce the risk posed by LSOs in the community.

Conclusions

The future of applied psychological services in working with lifers

The value of psychological assessment on lifers in the prison service has been clearly recognized (HM Inspectorate of Prisons and Probation, 1999). Forensic psychologists working in the probation services have similar competencies and skills in relation to assessment. The view that psychological assessment is no longer necessary upon release is short sighted. In addition applied psychologists working in prisons together with colleagues in probation settings can effectively serve the role of addressing risk management for resettlement plans.

Within the concept of the 'seamless sentence' it is implicit that there is excellent communication between prison and probation. The structures that have been set up to attempt to ensure this quality of communication include the MALRAPs and the MAPPA. In addition, the liaison between the seconded, home and supervising probation officers ensures the effective transfer of information and communication of all matters in relation to the probation service's management of the lifer. The development of an 'in house' applied psychology service for the National Probation Service offers an opportunity to extend communication and foster further seamlessness with respect to lifers. This may be more effective, however, if psychologists are seconded from the prison service, in much the same way as seconded probation officers are generally experienced in the community. Secondment across correctional services allows a depth and breadth of experience not otherwise possible if practitioners have a more limited range of experience. It may also facilitate work that has commenced in prisons to be smoothly continued into the community with the ultimate result that risk assessment and management may be more consistent and thereby be more effective. Thus a protocol for joint working with lifers across correctional services can be foreseen as being an effective move forwards.

In addition, with the development of community-based psychology services, this role needs to be included within the LSO during custody, in order that the potential contribution and value of ongoing work in the community may be fully realized.

NOTE

1   The term 'life sentence prisoner' is generally used to refer to offenders subject to life sentences. The term 'life sentence offender' (LSO) is used throughout this chapter in preference, since the term is technically more accurate. Life sentence offenders are, in reality, never free from their sentence, since on release from prison they are subject to 'life licence', which provides for ongoing supervision and the potential for recall to custody at any time.

Chapter Twelve

Partnership Working: Organizational Roles, Structures and Interfaces

Trudy Leeson and David Crighton

Introduction

In this chapter we look at the nature of partnership working and the structure of some of the major organizations that work in partnership with the National Probation Service (NPS). In understanding these structures it is possible to explore the potential role and contributions of multi-agency and multi-disciplinary teams in the development and management of supervision and rehabilitation of offenders in the community. The relatively recent arrival of psychologists in the probation service as directly employed staff will also be outlined as well as what applied psychologists may have to offer in the development of multi-agency and multi-disciplinary working.

Partnership working is increasingly seen across Government as being fundamental to the effective delivery of public sector services. Without such working it has become increasingly evident that clients often fall between agencies or receive less than effective services (see chapter 1). The need for working across agencies is in many ways particularly apposite across the National Offender Management Service (NOMS) and the criminal justice system. It is therefore important to have an understanding of how and why organizations work together and how the benefits of such an approach might be optimized. Collaborative approaches are also an international phenomenon seen to enable organizations to achieve aims that would be impossible alone

(Huxham, 1996). However, partnership working also presents direct and indirect challenges that come with collaboration.

Rumgay (2003) identifies four distinguishable areas of policy that affect how the probation service operates, and the extent of the impact of each. This provides a helpful framework for examining how the National Probation Service works in partnership with other agencies at present and how such working might be enhanced and developed in future. These four areas are contracting for supervision services, community crime prevention, targeting of special groups and co-ordinated social planning and provision (Rumgay, 2003).

Outline of Current Structure of the National Probation Service, HM Prison Service, Health and Social Services

The National Probation Service (NPS) was created on 1 April 2001. The system of local probation committees, which had oversight of the work of NPS area services, came to an end in April 2002. The creation of this drew heavily on the traditions of existing services but also led to a number of new features in terms of organizational structure. Along with this reorganization, a number of new national priorities and also new titles for community penalties were introduced. The structure and roles of new NPS is described in 'A New Choreography' (National Probation Service, 2001c).

In brief the NPS is a key statutory criminal justice agency that works closely with prison and police staff, as well as working with courts, local authorities, health, housing, education and other various statutory and non-statutory organizations.

A locally based probation structure was largely retained in the form of NPS areas, each of which has a Chief Probation Officer (CPO). This means that most probation staff continue to be employed by locally based and locally accountable probation boards. Policy for the probation service nationally now rests with the Director General for the NPS. In turn the Director General of the Probation Service, along with the Director General for Prisons, report to the head of the National Offender Management Service (NOMS) within the Home Office.[1]

Responsibility for local-area-based services rests with Chief Probation Officers. Probation Boards exist in each operational area and are broadly responsible for performance and financial management of area services (Home Office, 2003b). They consist of a range of representatives of the local community. In addition the NPS has a structure of regional managers, each responsible for linking between the NPS and across a number of area services.

There has been a reduction from 54 local probation services, which were previously chiefly funded by central Government, to 42 probation areas entirely funded by central Government. These 42 areas fall in line with the geographical areas of the police service. The implementation of 42 probation areas from 54 is a significant move from the previous independent locally governed probation boards. The 42 probation boards still retain scope to develop good probation practice in response to local and national needs (Wargent, 2002). However, it has been suggested that careful monitoring is needed of how probation boards manage the balance of national direction and local implementation of its objectives (Whitfield, 2001). It appears likely that in order for boards to maintain their independence locally they may increasingly have to provide evidence of a national focus in approach to their governance.

Another change in probation structure has been the removal of the family court welfare work of the probation service. This work has passed to a new organization called the Children and Family Court Advisory and Support Service (CAFCASS), which serves the family courts and is accountable to the Department for Constitutional Affairs.

Alongside the changes in the structure and management of the NPS came five statutory aims. These were intended to highlight the importance of this restructuring into national service and were

- protection of the public
- reduction of reoffending
- the proper punishment of offenders
- ensuring offenders' awareness of the effects of crime on the victims of crime and the public
- the rehabilitation of offenders
                    (see Home Office, 2002b, 2002d, 2002g, 2002h, 2002i)

The articulation of these five aims has as its prime focus the protection of the public and the enforcement of community orders of the court. These aims are a significant indication in the change of probation working practice, which has historically had a greater focus on care and support work with offenders under supervision.

A further duty placed on the NPS has been the requirement to undertake victim contact work, part of supporting the national aim of public protection (National Probation Service, 2003b). For many probation staff, work with victims is a relatively new and developing role, which has traditionally been carried out by voluntary sector organizations such as Victim Support. The move to work with victims has been a result of wide-ranging criticism of criminal justice systems, for not addressing the needs of the victims of crime

(National Probation Service, 2003b; Home Office, 2002a, 2002h). This has led to the introduction of legislation to ensure implementation of improvements in the Victim's Charters of both 1990 and 1996.

The key priority in relation to the introduction of work with victims of crime set by the Home Secretary for the NPS, involves three main aims. These are to have more accurate and effective assessment and management of 'risk and dangerousness', more involvement and contact with victims of serious sexual and violent crime and the development and delivery of interventions that can be shown to reduce reoffending (Home Office, 2002i).

It is important to recognize the significant contribution that the NPS makes in the supervision of offenders in England and Wales. On a daily basis the NPS supervises over 200,000 offenders. Out of this number there will on average be 70 per cent on a community sentence and 30 per cent will be on licence, having been released from prison as part of a custodial sentence (Home Office, 2002g). Some 235,000 reports are also prepared by NPS for judges and magistrates in order to assist with sentencing decisions. The assessment and management of risk is central to the process of supervising offenders.

There are a number of other major statutory and voluntary organizations that work in partnership with the NPS and these would include the police services, HM Prison Service, social services, NHS and local authority housing services. The role of such organizations in relation to probation work, and how these organizations form together, in order to ensure effective public protection, will be discussed later. The acknowledgement of the contributions that other organizations can make in order to improve practice and shared learning, will also be examined. The idea that partnership working was a positive step forward between statutory and non-statutory organizations was inherent in the Crime and Disorder Act 1998. This looked at reducing crime and disorder through multi-agency working, bringing together relevant organizations such as the police, local authorities and a range of other local voluntary community agencies. Local crime problems such as domestic burglary, vehicle crime, drug abuse, persistent young offenders and anti-social behaviour could be tackled by this multi-agency approach by the development, implementation and monitoring of action plans identified locally.

In order to understand how the work of other major organizations relates to that of the NPS it is helpful to have an understanding of the structure of some of the key partner organizations. HM Prison Service has a structure based upon 12 geographical areas that are largely coterminous with local Government and NPS regions. Within each of these areas are a range of different types of prisons. There is also one 'functional' area for high security prisons. Each geographic area has an area manager who reports ultimately to the Director of Operations for the prison service, who in turn is accountable to the Director General for public sector prisons (Towl, 2003a, 2004). Prisons managed under contract by the private sector report through a senior operational manager based in NOMS.

The structure of social services is somewhat different. Departments are divided into county and city council areas, and there are two main aspects to their involvement with the NPS. First, they are involved in the Youth Offending Service (YOS), and secondly, they are involved on a much more general level offering services of child protection, mental health and working with vulnerable individuals and contributing to the Multi-agency Public Protection Arrangements (MAPPA). There is close partnership working between social services and the NPS, including the existence of agreed protocols between the two organizations in delivery of services to offenders and information sharing.

In April 2002 there was a significant change in the organization and structure of the NHS. These changes involved a pivotal role for the 302 primary care trusts (PCTs), referred to as local health groups in Wales. The NHS Executive and regional structure of the NHS was removed. In brief the changes to the NHS have been designed to give a focus to services based upon primary care practitioner services, community-based services and secondary care or hospital services. Primary care now includes family practitioner and community-based services such as primary care medical and dental practitioners, along with primary care opticians, nurses and professions allied to medicine. Secondary care includes the services of NHS hospital and mental healthcare trusts. The aim of these NHS changes was to shift the power balance from secondary to primary care, meaning that frontline staff have more autonomy in how services are developed and designed to best meet patients needs.

The Role of the National Probation Service in Working with Offenders in the Community

The key role for the NPS is to assess and manage the risk presented by offenders and to reduce the risk of reoffending. The NPS does this through providing a range of community orders and supervision orders that will generally involve multi-agency partnership working.

The Drug Treatment and Testing Order (DTTO) is a particularly good example of how a community order with the probation service is generally managed through partnership working with specialist substance abuse services provided by the voluntary sector or health services. Here such specialist services will provide a range of drug treatment work and also drug testing and the probation service will provide supervision.

The delivery of a variety of interventions to reduce offending, such as ETS (Enhanced Thinking Skills) are available within the NPS and offenders can be required to attend these. In addition a wide range of interventions exist for substance abuse, violent and sexual offending. One of the key aims of these interventions is to get offenders to take greater responsibility for their own behaviour. In some probation areas, for example in Derbyshire, local non-statutory agencies such as the National Society for the Prevention of Cruelty to Children (NSPCC) are working in partnership to deliver the community-based sex offender groupwork with the NPS (see Department of Health, Home Office and Department of Education and Employment, 1999; Department of Health, 2003a, 2003b). The NSPCC works alongside the NPS in the supervision of offenders participating in this intervention work. The skills of applied psychologists based in the probation service may be used to play a key part of the multi-disciplinary assessment of offenders' suitability to participate, and also in the delivery and management of such interventions.

Employment, Training and Education (ETE) is an intervention that the NPS also uses with a large number of offenders who may require help with basic educational and employment skills. There is a basic skills screening assessment designed to identify offenders who have particular educational or employment skills deficits. 'Work and learning' assistants are employed to ensure that effective links are made with local employment agencies and educational providers that offenders may use.

Community Punishment Orders (CPOs) (which were formerly termed Community Service Orders) are generally delivered by the probation service in partnership with a wide range of agencies. A wide range of community-based work is undertaken by offenders on behalf of the local community and, as well as providing a form of reparation, such work may often be based around community safety needs, for example typical work might include repair of criminal damage, or making alleyways safer by cutting down over-grown vegetation. Offenders may also be required to undertake work, making things that are of value to the community, such as providing furniture and other items for the community. Because offenders on CPOs are generally assessed as being less at risk of reoffending, the scope for psychologists' involvement with offenders on such orders is generally lower than for those on community rehabilitation orders (CROs).

As discussed above, the NPS is also involved in partnership working with the Youth Offending Service (YOS), alongside other agencies and disciplines working with young people. Restorative justice and reparation arrangements as well as supervision are provided by the YOS. In some youth offending services, the involvement of clinical, counselling or forensic psychologists is made available to young people who may need psychological assessment and intervention. The exact structure of YOSs is locally determined and there is therefore a degree of variance nationally in the extent of partnership working with non-statutory organizations, but the vast majority of services include probation, social services, police, NHS and education staff.

Probation staff teams can also be found located within HM Prison Service establishments. These practitioners are involved in direct assessment and intervention work with offenders, the delivery and/or management of offending behaviour groupwork and resettlement work with offenders. Probation practitioners based in prisons are also responsible for links with the probation area that offenders will be released to. There are also resettlement teams based in the community. These teams deal with licensees released from prison and ensure that such cases are monitored and managed. In some circumstances they will also ensure that appropriate work is carried out to address and manage any ongoing risks presented by the offender (see chapter 5).

It is important in terms of risk management that offenders have settled and adequate accommodation. This is likely to be crucial in terms of improving the ability of practitioners in the NPS to supervise and manage offenders in the community and also in reducing the risk posed by offenders to the public (Social Exclusion Unit, 2002). In turn this feeds into the central role of the NPS in protecting the public, reducing reoffending and rehabilitating offenders. Accommodation is provided by the NPS in the form of specialist accommodation, often in the form of 'hostels'. Such accommodation is not explicitly for offenders who are homeless in the absence of other problems. Such accommodation is for offenders assessed as needing more intensive support, supervision and monitoring from NPS staff. This may include facilitating improved levels of public protection.

Effective partnership working with the courts was initially the reason for the creation of the probation service and it remains a major role for the NPS. Probation offices are situated at each Crown Court in England and Wales and also provide services to the much larger numbers of Magistrates Courts. The main roles of NPS staff in the courts relate to providing specialist advice and support in relation to bail matters, providing Pre Sentence Reports (PSRs) and other assessment services and offering information on offenders under supervision who reoffend, as well as prosecuting breaches of orders by offenders who fail to comply with court orders.

Partnership working is a critical aspect of NPS work with the courts where effective working with a number of other agencies is required. These would include the judiciary, the Courts Service, the Crown Prosecution Services and Victim Support. In addition the management of community punishments for the courts will often involve partnership working with drug misuse agencies, NHS community mental health teams, social services and the police.

It is evident that NPS pre-sentence services are more than just the formulation of reports and that this work involves accessing the resources of other agencies through formed partnerships using agreed protocols for the sharing of confidential information.

Information sharing between agencies is a process that has developed considerably in line with the importance of public protection issues, and has contributed to the development of effective partnerships. The processes involved in effective and ineffective information sharing have also been studied recently (Home Office, 1998; Nash, 2000, 2003). Nash (2003) examines the significant implications for the rights and freedoms of the individual where Multi-agency Public Protection Arrangements are involved with an individual who may not yet be sentenced. Nash looked at how although a majority of offenders will be the subject of post custody release arrangements or may be undergoing PSR enquiries, there will also be some offenders who do not fall into any of these categories.

The MAPPA began operating in April 2001 (see chapter 9). These arrangements placed a duty upon the NPS and the police to assess and manage offenders who pose a serious risk to the public. The NPS role is to work in partnership with community agencies such as the NHS, local authorities, housing, social services, police services and other statutory and non-statutory organizations as necessary. The benefits of this collaboration of services are that the management and monitoring of the risk of serious offenders is a more effective process in protecting the public. Referrals to the Multi-agency Public Protection Panels (MAPPPs), which form a key part of MAPPA, will generally come from 'risk meetings', which occur, on a regular basis within NPS teams.

The NPS role in working with victims of crime is a recent addition to the work of the NPS. A more 'victim orientated' approach to the management of crime has been instigated as a result of wider changes in the Criminal Justice system and the implementation of the Victims Charter in 1990 and 1996 (Home Office, 1990b, 1996b). The principles underpinning NPS work with victims of crime are to incorporate a perspective of the victim when dealing with offenders in order to reduce crime.

Victim Liaison Workers (VLWs) will become involved post sentence. Victim information may be included prior to this within PSRs but any such information comes from prosecution papers, or from statements made by victims. In many areas though such information is not routinely made available to the probation officer completing the PSR.

The role of the VLW following sentence of the offender is to ensure that the victim is informed of key developments in the offender's progress and has the opportunity to include requirements in a parole licence to enhance the protection of the victim.

Spalek (2003) looked at how NPS work with victims has provided a positive focus, but one that has taken place quickly, with little consideration of the tensions and problems that can arise from having to respond to the needs of both offenders and victims simultaneously. With victim work being a priority for the NPS, it is apparent that caution is needed in implementing a victim perspective as central to its policy and practice. This is likely to be a fertile area for further research and practice development.

The prolific offender project is being undertaken by NPS in partnership with the police service and involves targeting a small number of persistent offenders. This group is placed under the supervision of the NPS. There is considerable potential here for applied psychologists to undertake individual assessment and intervention work in support of supervising officers with this 'high-risk' group of offenders whose behaviour may often be much too chaotic or challenging to engage in groupwork.

The Role of Multi-disciplinary and Multi-agency Team Working

A good working example of the role of multi-agency working in the NPS is that of the function of the Multi-agency Public Protection Arrangements (MAPPA). It is important to look at the contribution of key players in the community to the MAPPA and how they help develop the practice of such professional associations, in the management of high-risk offenders and in protecting the public.

The work of the police service is also involved in the management of high-risk offenders in the community. The Police Service's input into MAPPA is a valuable contribution in terms of police monitoring, intelligence and information sharing. The Sex Offenders Act 1997 has also allowed police to monitor the whereabouts of sex offenders and to manage the risk of sexual reoffending by the requirement that sex offenders register locally with the police.

When considering child protection and vulnerable groups in society, social services take a lead responsibility. They have a major role to play in public protection arrangements, and also have an extensive history of partnership working to protect children. The main areas where social services departments work in the new public protection arrangements are prevention of abuse, the assessment and protection of children who are already deemed 'at risk' and also rehabilitation work with families. Social services departments may also have partnership arrangements with voluntary agencies, such as Barnardo's and the National Society for the Prevention of Cruelty to Children (NSPCC).

The contribution of NHS mental health trusts and private and voluntary healthcare providers to MAPPA varies nationwide, in line with local service provision. There are considerable benefits with the involvement of health practitioners, particularly with those offenders who require mental health services. It has been widely recognized that it has been difficult to engage health authorities in crime and disorder partnerships; this was reflected in a study carried out by the Audit Commission. One of the reasons suggested for this difficulty was that health authorities reported themselves unable to commit to the partnership process due to lack of overall resources and specialist expertise such as forensic psychiatrists and psychologists (Audit Commission, 1999; HM Inspectorate of Constabulary, 2000). Whilst the further development of NHS and social services community-based forensic mental health services would be a welcome development, this does to some extent miss the key point that many offenders have similar health problems to any other citizen but tend to come from more socially excluded groups that are poor at accessing services. The NHS in turn has a duty to try to provide services that meet public needs. It is evident that the NHS has a very important contribution to make towards the assessment and management of risk in a range of offenders. They can also advise other agencies such as the police, probation and others, which may require guidance and support in relation to health assessment and interventions with offenders in the community.

It is likely that the planned reforms to mental health legislation will increase the focus for many NHS practitioners on public protection issues. This legislation may also tackle concerns about interventions in certain types of mental disorder. Alongside this reform is the consideration of arrangements for individuals with 'personality disorders' and the possibility of their being incarcerated if they present a serious risk of significant harm to other people as a result of their mental disorder, even if there is no criminal behaviour, sometimes referred to as 'dangerous and severe personality disorder' (Cook, Harper & Kinderman, 2002; Home Office, 2003d; Morris, 2003).

Close liaison with the prison service also provides a valuable contribution to MAPPA in the identification of offenders who when released may present a risk of serious harm to the public. The existence of a joint psychological service across Correctional Services also presents the opportunity for what might be termed 'seamless' work with offenders. Work completed in custody by applied psychologists can be effectively followed through by community-based colleagues and vice versa.

Housing authorities can also contribute, by being able to monitor the location of 'high-risk' offenders within the community. Although the location of 'high-risk' offenders is a controversial one, the involvement of housing is essential in order to enable offenders to have appropriate accommodation, rather than the offender being left to make inappropriate accommodation arrangements. Close monitoring of the offender is also possible to arrange. In housing such offenders collaboration between local authorities can ensure that use of appropriate accommodation can be optimized. The NPS is also able to provide hostel accommodation to those offenders who may be in crisis, or upon release from custody. NPS accommodation is in great demand and is used as a short-term measure in order to provide some stability for offenders who may have been in custody and are either homeless or require supervision.

Many other agencies involved in the MAPPA nationwide provide important specialist input. The level at which other agencies are involved can often depend upon local availability of such services, and the type of offender and the risk or risks being managed. The main benefits of multi-agency working are that arrangements such as the MAPPA provide a strategic framework to assist in the management of 'high-risk' offenders. Each agency also has a responsibility to be involved in the protection of the public, by reviewing and monitoring the effectiveness of such arrangements. Multi-agency work also assists in building upon existing facilities available locally, by providing a much sharper focus upon the assessment and management of the small percentage of offenders who present an exceptional risk to the public.

Perhaps the most important developments in the area of risk assessment and management is the implementation of a joint prison and probation offender assessment system (OASys) (Home Office, 2001). This is a computer-based system, which has a consistent approach that enables a flow of detailed information relating to risk between organizations. Work is also being carried out on developing a joint police and NPS violent and sex offender register (ViSOR), which will assist the use of OASys.

As noted above, partnership work presents a number of challenges. A number of structural dynamics may be apparent when bringing together a range of diverse agencies whose ideology, mission and interests will vary considerably. Such differences can lead to conflict. It might be suggested that the potential for conflict is greatest in relation to the area of criminal behaviour, since this often involves deciding on which crime and disorder problems need to be prioritized and the proposed solutions (Crawford, 1999).

It is important to acknowledge that the probation service has a long history of working in partnership (Towl, 2000, 2004) and that its rapid growth along with other key agencies is set to continue in order to prevent crime and develop community safety. Despite the necessity for partnership involvement, it has been argued that little attention is paid to equipping practitioners with the skills and knowledge demanded in successful partnership working. In addition successful partnerships working has been found to owe much to being championed by particular individuals and the individual 'good will' of practitioners, rather than structural and organization processes (Rumgay, 2000).

Applied Psychology in Probation and Partnership Working

Applied psychology is broken down into a number of specialist branches: clinical, counselling, educational, forensic, health and occupational psychology. Each of these branches has the potential to contribute significantly to the partnership working of the NPS, either as 'in-house' specialists or as members of partnership agencies (HM Prison Service and National Probation Service, 2003a). In turn such expertise can feed into the effective working of teams within the NPS striving to meet complex public protection and rehabilitation agendas.

Historically the NPS has generally contracted in psychological expertise from the NHS and the private sector. The creation of 'in-house' applied psychology services is a recent development. As such the work of applied psychologists within NPS is best described as being in the developmental stage. Even so it is evident that there are a number of key areas where applied psychologists have been of value in meeting organizational needs. Such areas have included risk assessment and management work with 'high-risk' offenders. Applied psychologists have also been involved in the management and delivery of group-based intervention work.

There are a number of areas of development where it seems likely that applied psychologists may bring an additional contribution to the work of multi-disciplinary and multi-agency working. A striking example of this is the area of resettlement where comparatively little is known about what makes for effective practice. It is also evident that in the initial stages of developing an infrastructure in applied psychology there will be gaps in the delivery of psychological services in the NPS. There is a need to consider the roles of applied psychologists across Correctional Services and how to make the most efficient use of such expertise in relation to service delivery (Towl, 2000, 2004). It is important that this process, which has now begun, continues.

In the delivery of psychological services in an organization such as the NPS, it is essential that psychologists are able to work effectively with senior NPS operational managers as well as heads of applied psychology units. This is in order to ensure that the business priorities of the organization are closely related to the delivery of such services and indeed that new and emergent needs can be addressed quickly and efficiently.

The appointment of a joint head of psychology for prison and probation services in 2001 was a reflection of a clear need for the psychology profession to continue to develop partnership working and shared learning as a process that assists in maximizing effectiveness of the role of applied psychology in Correctional Services. There is also a need for the further development of partnership links with other major organizations that provide applied psychological services such as the NHS. Experience in HM Prison Service has shown that a range of applied psychology specialisms can be used to meet operational needs, and examples of this include the development of counselling psychology services in HMP Holloway and health psychology services in HMP Wandsworth. It seems likely that similar developments tailored to the needs of community-based practice could significantly benefit the NPS.

Conclusions

Working in partnership as part of multi-disciplinary teams is continually developing with the implementation of the restructuring of the major organizations in Correctional Services, along with the introduction of legislation that requires more collaborative approaches to the management of offenders and protection of the public. When focusing on the role of the NPS it is evident that the service has already established a range of effective partnerships working with other agencies and that it is building on existing arrangements, in order to improve practice and shared learning.

Multi-disciplinary teamwork within the NPS is relatively new and the responsibility and accountability for decision-making has tended to be with probation officers. The introduction of applied psychologists into this arena as part of probation teams has initially created some confusion over what psychologists can bring to the NPS, what roles they might best take and levels of professional autonomy. Although the NPS has generally welcomed an 'in-house' applied psychology service, there has also been an air of unease about the rapid changes within the NPS and the transformation into such multi-disciplinary team-based approaches to working with offenders. The introduction of partnership working across Correctional Services has strengthened existing strong professional and practice ties between probation and prisons. It has also allowed the NPS to tap into an existing framework of specialist psychologists, in much the same way that the prison service has, for many years, been able to second a range of skilled probation practitioners into prisons. This seems set to continue with the future development of applied psychological services within the NPS. Further work though is likely to be needed to ensure that such services are more effectively tailored to meet the business needs of operational managers in meeting organizational objectives in a cost effective manner.

It can be argued that applied psychology within multi-agency and multi-disciplinary teams can greatly enrich the quality of service offered, through a range of skills that psychology specialisms can offer. This demonstrates the flexibility of psychology as a science and that its broad range of applied specialisms can be appropriate, and can be applied in working with both staff and offenders across the National Offender Management Service.

NOTE

1 In addition the Commissioner for Corrections holds responsibility for youth justice, within an overall remit of improving 'joined up' working between agencies.

References

Akhurst, M. Brown, I. & Wessely, S. (1994) *Dying for Help: Offenders at Risk of Suicide.* Leeds: West Yorkshire Probation Service, West Yorkshire Health Authority and Association of Chief Officers of Probation.

Andrews, D.A. & Bonta, J.L. (1995) *Level of Service Inventory: Revised Manual.* Toronto: Multi Health Systems.

Andrews, D.A., Zinger, I., Hoge, R.D., Bonta, J., Gendreau, P. & Cullen, F.T. (1990) Does correctional treatment work? A clinically relevant and psychologically informed meta-analysis. *Criminology* 28, 369–404.

Audit Commission (1999) *Safety in Numbers: Promoting Community Safety.* London: Audit Commission.

Bailey, J.E. (1995) The revocation of life licences: An investigation into the reasons for recall. MSc dissertation, University of London.

Barker, M. & Morgan, R. (1993) *Sex Offenders: A Framework for the Evaluation of Community-based Treatment.* London: Stationery Office.

Barr, H. (1966) *A Survey of Groupwork in the Probation Service.* London: HMSO.

BBC Online Network (15 October 1999) Health social upheaval risk for suicide <http://news.bbc.co.uk/1/hi/health/475167.stm>.

Beck, A.T., Brown, G. & Steer, R.A. (1989) Predictions of eventual suicide in psychiatric inpatients by clinical ratings of hopelessness. *Journal of Consulting and Clinical Psychology* 57, 309–10.

Beck, A.T., Kovacs, M. & Weissman, A.S. (1975) Hopelessness and suicidal behaviour. *Journal of the American Medical Association* 234(11), 1146–9.

Beckett, R. (1994) Cognitive-behavioural treatment for sex offenders. In T. Morrison, M. Erooga & R. Beckett (eds), *Sexual Offending against Children: Assessment and Treatment of Male Abusers.* London: Routledge.

Beckett, R. (1998) Community treatment in the United Kingdom. In W.L. Marshall, Y.M. Fernandez, S.M. Hudson & T. Ward (eds), *Sourcebook of Treatment Programs for Sexual Offenders.* New York: Plenum Press.

Beckett, R., Beech, A., Fisher, D. & Fordham, A. (1994) *Community-based Treatment for Sex Offenders: An Evaluation of Seven Treatment Programmes.* London: Home Office.

Beech, A. (1998) Towards a psychometric typology for assessing pre-treatment level of problems in child abusers. *Journal of Sexual Aggression* 3(2), 87–100.

Bell, R. (2001) Focus on . . . forensic psychology in the Hutton Centre MSU. *Forensic Update* 66, 31–5.

Bhui, S.D. (1999) Race, racism and risk assessment: Linking theory to practice with mentally disordered offenders. *Probation Journal* 46(3), 171–81.

Blackburn, R. (1980) Still not working? A look at some recent outcomes in offender rehabilitation. Paper Presented to the Scottish Branch of the British Psychological Society Conference on Deviance, University of Stirling.

Blud, L. (1999) Cognitive skills programmes. In G.J. Towl & C. McDougall (eds), *What Do Forensic Psychologists Do? New Directions in Prison and Probation Services, Issues in Forensic Psychology*. Leicester: BPS.

Blud, L. (2003) Accreditation of offending behaviour programmes and recent developments in what work initiatives in HM Prison Service. *Legal and Criminological Psychology* 8, 65–6.

Blumenthal, S. & Wessely, S. (1992) National survey of current arrangements for diversion from custody in England and Wales. *British Medical Journal* 305, 1322–5.

Bogue, J. & Power, K. (1995) Suicide in Scottish prisons 1976–1979. *British Journal of Forensic Psychiatry* 6, 527–40.

Bor, R. & Watts, M. (eds) (1999) *The Trainee Handbook: A Guide for Counselling and Psychotherapy Trainees*. London: Sage.

Bowen, E., Brown, L. & Gilchrist, E. (2002) Evaluating probation based offender programmes for domestic violence perpetrators: A pro-feminist approach. *Howard Journal* 41, 221–36.

British Psychological Society (1999) *Comments on Review of the Mental Health Act 1983*. Leicester: BPS.

British Psychological Society (2000a) *Code of Conduct, Ethical Principles and Guidelines*. Leicester: BPS.

British Psychological Society (2000b) *Recent Advances in Understanding Mental Illness and Psychotic Experiences*. Leicester: BPS.

British Psychological Society (2001) *Professional Practice Guidelines: Division of Counselling Psychology*. Leicester: BPS.

British Psychological Society (2002) *Ethical Guidelines in Forensic Psychology*. Leicester: BPS.

Brockman, B. & Smith, J. (1990) CAT in the forensic services. In A. Ryle, *Cognitive Analytical Therapy: Active Participation in Change*. Chichester: Wiley.

Brody, S. (1976) The Effectiveness of Sentencing. Home Office Research Study No. 35. London: HMSO.

Brown, A. & Caddick, C. (1993) *Groupwork with Offenders*. London: Whiting & Birch.

Brown, G.C. & Geelan, S.D. (1998) Elliot House: Working with mentally disordered offenders. *Probation Journal* 45(1), 10–14.

Burton, S., Regan, L. & Kelly, L. (1998) *Supporting Women and Challenging Men: Lessons from the Domestic Violence Intervention Project*. Bristol: Policy Press.

Butler-Sloss, E. (1988) *The Report of the Inquiry into Child Abuse in Cleveland, 1987*. London: HMSO.

Cain, S. (1997) An evaluation of brief counselling with inmates at HMP Holloway. MA thesis, City University, London.

Cavadino, P. (1999) Diverting mentally disordered offenders from custody. In *Mentally Disordered Offenders: Managing People Nobody Owns*. London: Routledge.

Chambers (1996) *Chambers English Dictionary*. London: Chambers.

Chapman, L. & Chapman, J. (1967) Genesis of popular but erroneous psychodiagnostic observations. *Journal of Abnormal Psychology* 72, 193–204.

Chapman, T. & Hough, M. (1998) *Evidence Based Practice*. London: HMSO.

Clark, D. (1993) Evaluation of a cognitive skills training programme. Unpublished paper, Prison Service Psychology Conference, Bristol.

Clark, D. (2000a) The use of the Hare Psychopathy Checklist-Revised to predict offending and institutional misconduct in the English prison system. Research and Development Planning Group, HM Prison Service. Unpublished.

Clark, D. (2000b) Theory manual for enhanced thinking skills. Prepared for Joint Accreditation Panel, UK. Unpublished paper.

CMPS (2002) *Navigating Change: A Practitioner's Guide for Delivering Change Successfully within the Public Services*. London: Cabinet Office.

Coker, J.B. & Martin, J.P. (1985) *Licensed to Live*. Oxford: Blackwell.

Cook, A., Harper, D. & Kinderman, P. (2002) Reform of mental health legislation. *Forensic Update* 68, 6–16.

Cooke, D.J. & Michie, C. (1997) An item response theory analysis of the Hare Psychopathy Checklist-Revised. *Psychological Assessment* 9, 3–14.

Copas, J.B. (1982) Statistical analysis for the redevelopment of the Reconviction Prediction Score. Unpublished paper. University of Warwick.

Craig, T.K.J. et al. (1996) *Off to a Bad Start: A Longitudinal Study of Homeless People in London*. London: Mental Health Foundation.

Craissati, J. (1998) *Child Sexual Offenders: A Community Treatment Approach*. London: Psychology Press.

Craissati, J. (2003) Personality disordered offenders in a community context: A mental health perspective. *Issues in Forensic Psychology: Dangerous and Severe Personality disorder (DSPD)* 4, 54–64.

Crawford, A. (1999) *The Local Governance of Crime: Appeals to Community and Partnerships*. Oxford: Oxford University Press.

Crighton, D.A. (1999) Risk assessment in forensic mental health. *British Journal of Forensic Practice* 1(1), 18–26.

Crighton, D.A. (2000) Suicide in prisons in England & Wales. PhD dissertation, Anglia Polytechnic University.

Crighton, D.A. (2003a) Clinical psychology in National Probation and HM Prison Services: A scoping study. Unpublished paper. London: HM Prison & National Probation Services.

Crighton, D.A. (2003b) Working with suicidal prisoners. In G.J. Towl (ed.), *Psychology in Prisons*. Oxford: BPS Blackwell.

Crighton, D.A. (2004a) Risk assessment. In A. Needs & G.J. Towl (eds) *Handbook of Forensic Psychology*. Oxford: BPS Blackwell.

Crighton, D.A. (2004b) Risk assessment and management. In D.A. Crighton & G.J. Towl (eds), *Psychology in Probation Services*. Oxford: BPS Blackwell.

Crighton, D.A. & Towl, G.J. (2002) Intentional self-injury (ISI). In G.J. Towl, L. Snow & M. McHugh (eds), *Suicide in Prisons*. Oxford: BPS Blackwell.

Cullen, E. & Newell, T. (1999) *Murderers and Life Imprisonment*. Winchester: Waterside Press.

Department for Constitutional Affairs (2002) *Review of the Criminal Courts in England and Wales (The Auld Report)*. London: Stationery Office.

Department of Health (1992) *The Reed Report*. London: HMSO.

Department of Health (1998) *Modernising Mental Health Services: Safe, Sound and Supportive*. London: HMSO.

Department of Health (1999a) *National Service Framework for Mental Health*. London: HMSO.

Department of Health (1999b) *Saving Lives: Our Healthier Nation*. London: HMSO.

Department of Health (2000a) *The NHS Plan*. London: HMSO.

Department of Health (2000b) *Framework for the Assessment of Children in Need and their Families*. London: Stationery Office.

Department of Health (2000c) *Reforming the Mental Health Act*. London: Stationery Office.

Department of Health (2001) Major mental health publicity campaign to reduce discrimination. Press release, 24 January. *London: Department of Health.*

Department of Health (2003a) *Every Child Matters: Green Paper*. London: Stationery Office.

Department of Health (2003b) *Keeping Children Safe: Response to the Practice Recommendations Made by Lord Laming in the Report Following his Inquiry into the Death of Victoria Climbié*. London: Stationery Office.

Department of Health, Home Office and Department of Education and Employment (1999) *Working Together to Safeguard Children*. London: Stationery Office.

Department of Health and Home Office (1992) *Review of Mental Health and Social Services for Mentally Disordered Offenders and Others Requiring Similar Services (The Reed Committee)*. London: HMSO.

Department of Health and Home Office (2001) *Changing the Outlook: A Strategy for Developing and Modernising Mental Health Services in Prisons*. London: Stationery Office.

Dexter, P. & Towl, G.J. (1995) An investigation into suicidal behaviours in prison. In N.K. Clarke & G.M. Stephenson (eds), *Criminal Behaviour: Perceptions, Attributions and Rationality*. Leicester: BPS.

DiClemente, C.C. (1993) Changing addictive behaviours: a process perspective. *Current Directions in Psychological Science*, 2, 101–6.

Division of Forensic Psychology (2002) *Ethical Guidelines on Forensic Psychology*. Leicester: BPS.

Dobash, R.E., Dobash, R.P., Cavanagh, K. & Lewis, R. (2000) *Changing Violent Men*. London: Sage.

Dunkley, E., Holland, A., Payne, W., Russell, J., Pinfold, C. et al. (2002) *Research into Deaths of Residents of Approved Premises: An Initial Project*. London: National Probation Service.

Evans, J.St.B. (1989) *Biases in Human Reasoning: Causes and Consequences*. Hove, UK: Erlbaum.

Eyman, J.R. & Eyman, S.K. (1992) Psychological testing for potentially suicidal individuals. In B. Bongar (ed.), *Suicide, Guidelines for Assessment, Management and Treatment*. Oxford: Oxford University Press.

Falshaw, L., Friendship, C. & Bates, A. (2003) Sexual Offenders: Measuring Reconviction, Reoffending and Recidivism. *Home Office Findings*, 183.

Falshaw, L., Friendship, C., Travers, R. & Nugent, F. (2003) *Searching for 'What Works': An Evaluation of Cognitive Skills Programmes*. London: HMSO.

Falshaw, L., Friendship, C., Travers, R. & Nugent, F. (2004) Searching for 'What Works': HM Prison Service Accredited Cognitive Skills Programmes. *British Journal of Forensic Practice* 6(2), 3–13.

Farrington, D.P. (1993) The challenge of teenage anti-social behaviour. Paper prepared for the Martach Castle conference 'Youth in the Year 2000'.

Finkelhor, D. (1984) *Child Sexual Abuse, New Theory and Research*. New York: Free Press.

Fisher, D. & Beech, A. (1999) Current practice in Britain with sex offenders. *Journal of Inter-Personal Violence* 14, 233–49.

Flood-Page, C. & Taylor, J. (2003) *Crime in England and Wales 2001/2002: Supplementary Volume*. London: Home Office.

Freedman, D. (2001) False prediction of future dangerousness: Error rates and Psychopathy Checklist-Revised. *Journal of the Academy of Psychiatry and Law* 29(1), 89–95.

Friendship, C. & Thornton, D. (2001) Sexual reconviction for sexual offenders discharged from prison in England and Wales. *British Journal of Criminology* 41, 285–92.

Gacono, C.B. (ed.) (2000) *The Clinical and Forensic Assessment of Psychopathy: A Practitioner's Guide*. Mahwah, NJ: LEA.

Gardner, W., Lidz, C., Mulvey, E. & Shaw, E. (1996) A comparison of actuarial methods for identifying repetitively violent patients with mental illness. *Law and Human Behaviour* 20, 35–48.

Gendreau, P. & Ross, R.R. (1980) Effective correctional treatment: Bibliography for cynics. In R.R. Ross & P. Gendreau (eds), *Effective Correctional Treatment*. Toronto: Butterworth.

Gendreau, P., Goggin, C. & Smith, P. (1999) Predicting recidivism: LSI – R vs. PCL – R. *Canadian Psychology Abstracts* 40, 2a.

Gondolf, E.W. (2002) *Batterer Intervention Systems: Issues, Outcomes and Recommendations*. London: Sage.

Grant, D. (1999) Multi-agency risk management of mentally disordered sex offenders: A probation case study. In *Mentally Disordered Offenders: Managing People Nobody Owns*. London: Routledge.

Greene, H. & Uganizza, D.N. (1995) The 'stably unstable' Borderline personality disorder: History, theory and nursing intervention. *Journal of Psychological Nursing* 33(12), 26–30.

Grubin, D. & Thornton, D. (1994) A national programme for the assessment and treatment of sex offenders in the English prison system. *Criminal Justice and Behaviour* 21, 55–71.

Gunn, J., Maden, T. & Swinton, M. (1991) *Mentally Disordered Prisoners*. London: Home Office.

Hague, G. (2000) *Reducing Domestic Violence . . . What Works? Multi-Agency Fora. Crime Reduction Research Series*. London: Home Office.

Hankoff, L.D. (1980) Prisoner suicide. *International Journal of Offender Therapy and Comparative Criminology* 24, 461–84.

Hare, R.D. (1991) *Manual for the Revised Psychopathy Checklist*. Toronto: Multi-Health Systems.

Hare, R.D. (2003) *Hare PCL – R Technical Manual* (2nd edn). Toronto: MHS.

Hare, R.D. & Hart, S.D. (1993) Psychopathy, mental disorder and crime. In S. Hodgins (ed.), *Crime and Mental Disorder*. Newbury Park, CA: Sage.

Harris, G.T., Rice, M.E. & Cormier, C.A. (1991) Psychopathy and violent recidivism. *Law and Human Behaviour* 15, 625–37.

Harris, R. (1999) Mental disorder and social order: underlying themes in crime management. In R. Harris (ed.), *Mentally Disordered Offenders: Managing People Nobody Owns*. London: Routledge.

Hart, S.D., Hare, R.D. & Forth, A.E. (1993) Psychopathy as a risk marker for violence: development and validation of a screening version of the revised psychopathy checklist. In J. Monahan & H. Steadman (eds), *Violence and Mental Disorder: Developments in Risk Assessment*. Chicago: Chicago University Press.

Hauser, M. (1987) Special aspects of grief after a suicide. In E.J. Dunne, J. McIntosh & Dunne-Martin (eds), *The Aftermath of Suicide: Understanding and Counselling the Survivors*. New York: W. W. Norton.

Heilbrun, A.B. (1990) The measurement of criminal dangerousness as a personality construct: Further validation of a research index. *Journal of Personality Assessment* 54, 141–8.

Heilbrun, A.B. & Dvoskin, K. (2003) Risk assessment and management. Psychology and Law Conference 2003, University of Edinburgh, UK.

Hemphill, J.F., Hare, R.D. & Wong, S. (1998) Psychopathy and recidivism: A review. *Legal & Criminological Psychology* 3, 139–70.

Hester, M. & Pearson, C. (1998) *From Periphery to Centre: Domestic Violence in Work with Abused Children*. Bristol: Policy Press.

Hester, M. & Radford, J. (1996) *Domestic Violence and Child Contact Arrangements in England and Denmark*. Bristol: Policy Press.

Hills, L. (2002) Working in the courts. In D. Ward, J. Scott & M. Lacey (eds), *Probation: Working for Justice* (2nd edn). Oxford: Oxford University Press.

HM Inspectorate of Constabulary (2000) *Calling Time on Crime: A Thematic Inspection of Crime and Disorder Conducted by HM Inspectorate of Constabulary in Collaboration with the Home Office, Audit Commission, Local Government Association, Office for Standards in Education and the Social Services Inspectorate*. London: Home Office.

HM Inspectorate of Prisons and Probation (1999) *Lifers: A Joint Thematic Review by Her Majesty's Inspectorates of Prisons and Probation*. London: HMSO.

HM Inspectorate of Probation (1997) *The Work of the Probation Service in the Crown and Magistrates Courts: Report of a Thematic Inspection*. London: Home Office.

HM Inspectorate of Probation (1998) *Evidence Based Practice: A Guide to Effective Practice*. London: Home Office.

HM Inspectorate of Probation (2002) *Safeguarding Children: The National Probation Service Role in the Assessment and Management of Child Protection Issues*. London: Stationery Office.

HM Prison Service (1999) *The Lifer Manual*. Prison Service Order No. 4700. London: HM Prison Service.

HM Prison Service (2001a) *The Lifer Manual*. London: HM Prison Service.

HM Prison Service (2001b) *The Life Sentence Plan*. London: HM Prison Service.

HM Prison Service (2003a) *Sentence Management Group: Accredited Offending Behaviour Programmes*. London: Home Office.

HM Prison Service (2003b) *Sentence Management Group: Lifer News*. London: Home Office.

HM Prison Service and National Probation Service (2003a) *Driving Delivery: A Strategic Framework for Psychological Services in Prisons and Probation*. London: HM Prison Service & National Probation Services.

HM Prison Service and National Probation Service (2003b) *Professional Practice Guidelines in Applied Psychology*. London: HM Prison & National Probation Services.

Hollin, C.R. (1995) The meaning and implications of 'Programme Integrity'. In J. Maguire (ed.), *What Works: Reducing Offending*. Chichester: John Wiley.

Hollin, C.R., McGuire, J., Palmer, E., Bilby, C., Hatcher, R. & Holmes, A. (2002) Introducing Pathfinders Programmes into the Probation Service. Unpublished document for National Probation Directorate.

Holtzworth-Munroe, A. & Stuart, G.L. (1994) Typologies of male barterers: Three sub-types and differences among them. *Psychological Bulletin* 116(3), 476–97.

Holtzworth-Munroe, A., Mehan, J.C., Herron, K., Rehman, U. & Stuart, G.L. (2000) Testing the Holtzworth-Munroe and Stuart (1994) Batterer Typology. *Journal of Counselling and Clinical Psychology* 68(6), 1000–19.

Home Office (1990a) *Provision for Mentally Disordered Offenders: Circular 66/90*. London: Home Office.

Home Office (1990b) *Victim's Charter: Statement of the Rights of Victims of Crime*. London: Home Office.

Home Office (1994) *Home Office Statistical Bulletin*. London: HMSO.

Home Office (1995) *Probation Circular 90/1995*. London: Home Office.

Home Office (1996a) *Protecting the Public*. London: HMSO.

Home Office (1996b) *The Victims Charter: A Statement of Service Standards for Victims of Crime*. London: Home Office.

Home Office (1998) *Exercising Constant Vigilance: The Role of the Probation Service in Protecting the Public from Sex Offenders: Report of a Thematic Inspection by HMIP*. London: Home Office.

Home Office (1999) *Punishment and Supervision in the Community*. London: HMSO.

Home Office (2000) *Multi-Agency Guidance for Addressing Domestic Violence*. London: Home Office.

Home Office (2001) *Offender Assessment System (OASys) Manual*. London: Home Office.

Home Office (2002a) *A Better Deal for Victims and Witnesses*. London: Home Office.

Home Office (2002b) *Further Guidance to the Police and Probation Services on the Criminal Justice and Court Services Act 2000*. London: Home Office.

Home Office (2002c) *Management Manual for the Effective Delivery of Accredited Programmes in the Community*. London: Home Office.

Home Office (2002d) *National Standards for the Supervision of Offenders in the Community*. Revised 2002. London: Home Office.

Home Office (2002e) *Probation Offending Behaviour Programmes: Effective Practice Guide No. 2*. London: HMSO.

Home Office (2002f) *Probation Circular, National Probation Directorate PC 33/2002: The New Life Sentence Plan*. London: Home Office.

Home Office (2002g) *Probation Statistics England and Wales 2000*. London: Home Office.

Home Office (2002h) *Protecting Children from Dangerous People*. London: Home Office.

Home Office (2002i) *What Works Strategy for the Probation Service*. London: HMSO.

Home Office (2003a) *At the Heart of the Dance*. London: Home Office.

Home Office (2003b) *Local Probation Boards Standing Orders*. London: Home Office.

Home Office (2003c) *Managing Offenders Reducing Crime (The Carter Report)*. London: Home Office.

Home Office (2003d) *MAPPA Guidance*. London: Home Office.

Home Office (2003e) *National Probation Directorate PC 28/2003: Victim Contact Work: Guidance on Recent Court Judgements*. London: Home Office.

Home Office (2004) *Reducing Crime – Changing Lives: The Government's Plans for Transforming the Management of Offenders*. London: Home Office.

Home Office and Department of Health (1995) *Mentally Disordered Offenders: Inter-Agency Working*. London: Home Office and Department of Health.

Howard League (2002) *Suicide and Self-Harm Prevention Following Release from Prison*. London: Howard League for Penal Reform.

Hudson, B., Hardy, B., Henwodd, M. & Wistow, G. (1999) In pursuit of inter-agency collaboration in the public sector. *Public Management* 1(2), 235–60.

Humphreys, C. (2000) *Social Work, Domestic Violence and Child Protection*. Bristol: Policy Press.

Hunter, J.E. & Schmidt, F.L. (2003) *Methods of Meta-analysis: Correcting Error and Bias in Research Findings*. Thousand Oaks, CA: Sage.

Huxham, C. (1996) *Creating Collaborative Advantage*. London: Sage.

Izzo, R.L. & Ross, R.R. (1990) Meta-analysis of rehabilitation programmes for juvenile delinquents. *Criminal Justice and Behaviour* 17, 134–42.

Inch, H., Rowland, P. & Seliman, A. (1995) Deliberate self-mutilation in a young offender institution. *Journal of Forensic Psychiatry*, 6(1), 161–71.

Jones, R. (2003) *Mental Health Act Manual* (8th edn). London: Sweet & Maxwell.

Kahneman, D. & Tversky, A. (1973) On the psychology of prediction. *Psychological Review* 80, 237–51.

Kahr, B. (1999) The clinical placement in mental health training. In R. Bor & M. Watts (eds), *The Trainee Handbook: A Guide for Counselling and Psychotherapy Trainees*. London: Sage.

Kemshall, H. (2001) *Risk Assessment and Management of Known Sexual and Violent Offenders: A Review of Current Issues*. Police Research Series, Paper 140. London: Home Office.

Kemshall, H. (2002) *Risk Assessment and Management of Known Sexual and Violent Offenders: A Review of Current Issues*. Edinburgh: Scottish Executive.

Kemshall, H. (2003) The community management of high-risk offenders: A consideration of 'best practice' – Multi-Agency Public Protection Arrangements (MAPPA). *Prison Service Journal*, 146.

Kent County Constabulary & National Probation Service Kent Area (2002) *Kent Multi-Agency Public Protection Arrangements: MAPPA Annual Report 2002*. Kent County Constabulary & National Probation Service Kent Area.

Kent Probation Area (2002) *Public Protection Policy*. National Probation Service, Kent Area.

Kershaw, C. et al. (2000) *Home Office Statistical Bulletin 18/00 London*. Home Office.

Kolb, D.A. (1984) *Experiential Learning: Experiences as the Source of Learning Development*. Englewood Cliffs, NJ: Prentice-Hall.

Kosson, D.S., Smith, S.S. & Newman, J.P. (1990) Evaluating the construct validity of psychopathy in black and white male inmates: Three preliminary studies. *Journal of Abnormal Psychology* 99, 250–9.

Kropp, P.R., Hart, S.D., Webster, C.D. & Eaves, D. (1995) *Manual for the Spousal Assault Risk Assessment Guide*. Vancouver: British Columbia Institute Against Family Violence.

Law, K. (1999) *Psychologists Working within the Probation Services*. Issues in Forensic Psychology 1. Leicester: BPS.

Lazarus, A.A. (1989) *The Practice of Multi-Modal Therapy*. New York: McGraw-Hill.

Leiper, R. (2002) Assessing needs for psychological therapies in the context of the national Service framework for mental health. *Counselling Psychology Review* 17(4), 11–19.

Lindsay, J. & Brady, B. (2002) *Nurturing Fragile Relationships: Early Reflections on Working with Victims of Domestic Violence on the National Probation Service's Duluth Pathfinder Research Programme*. Issues in Forensic Psychology 3. Leicester: BPS.

Lindsay, J., Pearce, S. & Reid, A. (2003) Women's safety workers manual draft 7. Unpublished.

Linehan, M.M., Armstrong, H.E., Suareez, A., Allmon, D. & Heard, H.L. (1991) Cognitive-behavioural treatment of chronically parasuicidal borderline patients. *Archives of General Psychiatry* 48, 1060–4.

Lipsey, M.W. (1992) The effect of treatment on juvenile delinquents: Results from meta-analysis. In F. Losel, D. Bender & T. Bliesener (eds), *Psychology and Law: International perspectives*. Berlin: de Gruyter.

Lipsey, M.W. (1995) Juvenile delinquency treatment, a meta-analysis enquiry into the variability of effects. In Cook, T.D., Cooper, H., Cordray, D.S., Hartmann, H., Hedges, L.V., Light, R.J., Louis, T.A. & Mosteller, S. (eds), *Meta-Analysis for Explanation: A Casebook*. New York: Russell Sage Foundation Group.

Lipton, D., Martinson, R. & Wilks, J. (1975) *The Effectiveness of Correctional Treatments*. New York: Praeger.

Loeber, R. & Farrington, D.P. (2001) *Child Delinquents: Development, Intervention and Service Needs*. Thousand Oaks, CA: Sage.

London Probation Area (2003) *The Newsletter of the London Probation Area, Issue 8*. London: LPA.

Low, G. (1998) Treatment of mentally disordered women who self-harm. Paper presented at the Third European Congress on Personality Disorders, University of Sheffield. Sheffield, UK.

Loza, W. & Simourd, D.J. (1994) Psychometric evaluation of the Level of Service Inventory (LSI) among Canadian federal offenders. *Criminal Justice and Behaviour* 21, 468–80.

Maguire, M., Kemshall, H., Noakes, L. & Wincup, E. (2001) *Risk Management of Sexual and Violent Offenders: The work of Public Protection Panels*. Police Research Series, Paper 139. London: Home Office.

Mari, J.J. & Streiner, D. (1996) *Family Intervention for People with Schizophrenia*. Oxford: Cochrane Review; Oxford Update Software.

Marques, J.K., Day, D.M., Nelson, C. & West, M.A. (1994) Effects of cognitive-behavioral treatment on sex offender recidivism: Preliminary results of a longitudinal study. *Criminal Justice and Behavior* 21, 28–54.

Marshall, W.L. & Barbaree, H.E. (1988) The long-term evaluation of a behavioral treatment program for child molesters. *Behavior Research Therapy* 6, 499–511.

Marshall, W.L. & Pithers, W.D. (1994) A reconsideration of treatment outcome with sex offenders. *Criminal Justice and Behaviour* 21(1), 10–27.

Martinson, R. (1974) What works: Questions and answers about prison reform. *Public Interest* 35, 22–54.

McGuire, J. (1995a) Reviewing 'What Works': Past, present and future. In J. McGuire (ed.), *What Works: Reducing Reoffending Guidelines from Research and Practice*. Chichester: Wiley.

McGuire, J. (ed.) (1995b) *What Works: Reducing Offending Guidelines from Research and Practice*. Chichester: Wiley.

McGuire, J. (2000) *Cognitive-Behavioural Approaches*. London: HMSO.

McGuire, J. (2002) Motivation for what? Effective programmes for motivated offenders. In M. McMurran (ed.), *Motivating Offenders to Change: A Guide to Enhancing Engagement in Therapy*. Chichester: Wiley.

McMurran, M. (2002) Motivation to change: Selection criterion or treatment need? In M. McMurran (ed.), *Motivating Offenders to Change: A Guide to Enhancing Engagement in Therapy*. Chichester: Wiley.

Mezey, G. (1997) Domestic violence in pregnancy. *British Journal of Obstetrics and Gynaecology* 104, 523–8.

Miller, W.R. & Rollnick, S. (1991) *Motivational Interviewing: Preparing People to Change Addictive Behaviour.* New York: Guilford Press.

Mills, A. (2002) Mental health in-reach: The way forward for prisons? *Probation Journal* 49(2), 107–19.

Mirrlees-Black, C. (1999) *Findings from a New British Crime Survey Self-completion Questionnaire.* Home Office Research Study 191. London. Home Office.

Monahan, J. (1981) *Predicting Violent Behaviour: An Assessment of Clinical Techniques.* Beverly Hills, CA: Sage.

Monahan, J. (1992) Mental disorder and violent behaviour: Perceptions and evidence. *American Psychologist* 47, 511–21.

Monahan, J. (1997) Actuarial support for the clinical assessment of violence risk. *International Review of Psychiatry,* 9.

Monahan, J. & Steadman, H.J. (1994) *Violence and Mental Disorder: Developments in Risk Assessment.* Chicago: University of Chicago Press.

Monahan, J., Steadman, H.J., Applebaum, P.S., Robbins, P.C., Mulvey, E.P., Roth, L.H., Grisso, T. & Banks, S. (2001) *Rethinking Risk Assessment: The MacArthur Study of Mental Disorder and Violence.* New York: Oxford University Press.

Monahan, J., Steadman, H.J., Applebaum, P.S., Robbins, P.C., Mulvey, E.P., Silva, E., Roth, L.H. & Grisso, T. (2000) Developing a clinically useful actuarial tool for assessing violence risk. *British Journal of Psychiatry* 176, 312–19.

Moos, R.H. (1994) *Group Environment Scale Manual* (3rd edn). California: Consulting Psychologists Press.

Morgan, H.G. (1994) Assessment of risk. In R. Jenkins, S. Griffiths, I. Wytie, K. Hawton, H.G. Morgan & A. Tyle (eds), *The Prevention of Suicide.* London: Department of Health HMSO.

Williams, R. & Morgan, H.G. (eds) (1994) *Suicide Prevention: The Challenge Confronted. A Manual of Guidance for the Purchasers and Providers of Mental Health Care.* London: HMSO.

Morgan, H.G. & Owen, J.H. (1990) *Persons at Risk of Suicide: Guidelines on Good Clinical Practice.* Nottingham: Boots.

Morris, A. & Gelsthorpe, L. (2000) Revisioning men's violence against female partners. *Howard Journal* 39, 412–28.

Morris, M. (2003) *Clinical Pluralism: A Mode of Practice for D&SPD Treatment Teams.* Issues in Forensic Psychology: Dangerous and Severe Personality Disorder (DSPD). Leicester: BPS.

Mullender, A. (1996) *Rethinking Domestic Violence: The Social Work and Probation Response.* London: Routledge.

Mullender, A. & Burton, S. (2001) Dealing with perpetrators. In J. Taylor-Browne (ed.), *What Works in Reducing Domestic Violence? A Comprehensive Guide for Professionals.* London: Whiting & Birch.

Muller-Isberner, R. & Hodgins, S. (2000) Evidence-based treatment for mentally disordered offenders. In S. Hodgins & R. Muller-Isberner (eds), *Violence, Crime and Mentally Disordered Offenders.* Chichester: Wiley.

NACRO (1995) *Mentally Disturbed Prisoners.* London: NACRO.

Nash, M. (2000) Deconstructing the Probation Service: The Trojan Horse of public protection. *International Journal of the Sociology of Law* 28, 201–13.

Nash, M. (2003) Pre trial investigation. In W.H. Chui & M. Nellis (eds), *Moving Probation Forward: Evidence, Arguments and Practice*. London. Pearson.

National Institute for Mental Health in England (2003) *Personality Disorder: No Longer a Diagnosis of Exclusion*. Policy Implementation Guidance for the Development of Services for People with Personality Disorder. London: Department of Health.

National Probation Directorate (2001a) Domestic violence (Duluth) research pathfinder monitoring and evaluation manual. Unpublished draft.

National Probation Directorate (2001b) *National management manual for the domestic violence (Duluth) pathfinder*. Unpublished draft.

National Probation Directorate (2001c) *New Choreography: An Integrated Strategy for the National Probation Service for England and Wales, Strategic Framework 2001–2004*. London: National Probation Directorate.

National Probation Directorate (2002) *What Works: Third Report from the Joint Prison/ Probation Accreditation Panel*. London: NPD.

National Probation Directorate (2003) Probation offending behaviour programmes. Unpublished summary. National Probation Directorate.

National Probation Service (2002) *Approved Premises Handbook*. London: National Probation Service.

National Probation Service (2003a) *Domestic Violence Policy*. London: NPD.

National Probation Service (2003b) *Victim Contact Work-Guidance for Probation Areas*. London: National Probation Service.

Needs, A. & Towl, G.J. (eds) (2004) *Applying Psychology to Forensic Practice*. Oxford: Blackwell.

Nekanda-Trepka, C.J., Bishop, S. & Blackburn, I.M. (1983) Hopelessness and depression. *British Journal of Clinical Psychology* 22, 49–60.

Nichols, H.R. & Molinder, I. (1984) *Multiphasic Sex Inventory Manual*. Available from the authors at 437 Bowes Drive, Tacoma, WA 98466, USA.

Nisbett, R. & Ross, L. (1980) *Human Inference: Strategies and Shortcomings of Social Judgement*. Engelwood Cliffs, NJ: Prentice-Hall.

Norton, K. & McGauley, G. (2000) Forensic psychotherapy in Britain: Its role in assessment, treatment and training. *Criminal Behaviour and Mental Health* 10, S82–S90.

O'Connor, R.C. & Sheehy, N.P. (2000) *Understanding Suicidal Behaviour*. Leicester: BPS.

O'Connor, R.C. & Sheehy, N.P. (2001) Suicidal behaviour. *Psychologist* 14(1), 143.

Palmer, S. (2000) developing an individual therapeutic programme suitable for the use by counselling psychologists in a multi-cultural society: A multi-modal perspective. *Counselling Psychology Review* 15(1), 32–50.

Palmer, T. (1996) Programmatic and non-programmatic aspects of successful intervention. In A.T. Harland (ed.), *Choosing Correctional Options that Work: Defining the Demand and Evaluating the Supply*. Thousand Oaks, CA: Sage Publications.

Parole Board (1982) *Report of the Parole Board for 1981*. London: HMSO.

Paulhus, D.L. (1998) *Paulhus Deception Scales (PDS): The Balanced Inventory of Desirable Responding, User's Manual*. New York: Multi-Health Systems.

182   REFERENCES

Pence, E. & Paymar, M. (1993) *Education Groups for Men Who Batter*. New York: Springer.

Pence, E. & Paymar, M. (2003) *Creating a Process of Change for Men Who Batter*. Duluth: Minnesota Program Development.

Petrie, K., Chamberlain, K. & Clarke, D. (1988) Psychological predictors of future suicidal behaviour in hospitalised suicide attempters. *British Journal of Clinical Psychology* 27, 247–58.

Pettiti, D.B. (1999) *Meta Analysis, Decision Analysis and Cost Effectiveness Analysis*. New York: Oxford University Press.

Platt, S. & Kreitman, N. (1984) Unemployment and parasuicide in Edinburgh 1968–1982. *British Medical Journal* 289, 1029–32.

Plous, S. (2002) *Judgement and Decision Making* (2nd edn). New York: McGraw Hill.

Pollard, S. & Potter, S. (1999) Cognitive Analytic Therapy and the 'hard to help' client. *Probation Journal* 46(1), 3–10.

Pollock, P. (1997) CAT of an offender with borderline personality disorder. In A. Ryle (ed.), *Cognitive Analytical Therapy and Borderline Personality Disorder, the Model and the Method*. Chichester: Wiley.

Prins, H. (1995) *Offenders, Deviants or Patients* (2nd edn). London: Routledge.

Prins, H. (1999) *Will they Do it Again? Risk Assessment and Management*. London: Routledge.

Prins, H. (2002) Risk assessment: Still a risky business. *British Journal of Forensic Practice* 4(1), 3–8.

Pritchard, C., Cox M. & Dawson, D. (1997) Suicide and violent death in a six year cohort of male probationers compared with patterns of mortality in the general population: Evidence of a cumulative socio-psychiatric vulnerability. *Journal of the Royal Society of Health* 117, 180–5.

Prochaska, J. & DiClemente, C. (1984) *The Transtheoretical Approach: Crossing Traditional Boundaries of Therapy*. Homewood: Dow Jones Irwin.

Quinsey, V.L., Harris, G.T., Rice, M.E. & Cormier, C.A. (1998) *Violent Offenders: Appraising and Managing Risk*. Washington, DC: American Psychological Association.

Reason, J. (1997) *Managing the Risk of Organizational Accidents*. Aldershot, UK: Ashgate.

Respect (2000) *Statement of Principles and Minimum Standards of Practice*. Available from DVIP, PO Box 2838 London W8 9ZE.

Rice, M.E., Harris, G.T. & Cormier, C.A. (1992) An evaluation of a maximum security therapeutic community for psychopaths and other mentally disordered offenders. *Law and Human Behaviour* 4, 399–413.

Ridley, C.R. (1995) *Overcoming Unintentional Racism in Counselling and Therapy*. Thousand Oaks, CA: Sage.

Robinson, D. (1995) The impact of cognitive skills training on post-release recidivism among Canadian federal offenders. Internal Research Paper No. R41. Ottawa: Correctional Service of Canada.

Ross, R.R., Fabiano, E.A. & Ewles, C.D. (1988) Reasoning and rehabilitation. *International Journal of Offender Therapy & Comparative Criminology* 32, 29–35.

Ross, R.R. & Fabiano, E.A. (1985) *Time to Think: A Cognitive Model of Delinquency Prevention and Offender Rehabilitation*. Johnson City, TN: Institute of Science and Arts.

Ross, R.R. & Gendreau, P. (1980) *Effective Correctional Treatment*. Toronto: Butterworth.

Rumgay, J. (2000) *The Addicted Offender: Developments in British Policy and Practice*. Basingstoke: Palgrave.

Rumgay, J. (2003) Partnerships in the Probation Service. In W.H. Chui & M. Nellis (eds), *Moving Probation Forward: Evidence, Arguments and Practice*. London: Pearson.

Ryle, A. (1990) *Cognitive Analytical Therapy, Active Participation in Change: A New Integration in Brief Psychotherapy*. Chichester: Wiley.

Ryle, A. (1997) The structure and development of Borderline Personality Disorder: A proposed model. *British Journal of Psychiatry* 170: 82–7.

Salekin, R.T., Rogers, R. & Sewell, K.W. (1996) A review and meta-analysis of the Psychopathy Checklist and Psychopathy Checklist-Revised: Predictive validity of dangerousness. *Clinical Psychology: Science and Practice* 3, 203–15.

Samuels, A. (1996) The Probation Officer in the courthouse. *Probation Manager*, 1.

Scott, P.D. (1977) Assessing dangerousness in criminals. *British Journal of Psychiatry* 131, 127–42.

Shaw, S. (1999) Foreword. In E. Cullen & T. Newell, *Murderers and Life Imprisonment*. Winchester: Waterside Press.

Shepard, M.F. & Pence, E. (eds) (1999) *Co-ordinating Community Responses to Domestic Violence: Lessons from Duluth and Beyond*. London: Sage.

Social Exclusion Unit (2002) *Reducing Re-offending by Ex-prisoners: Report by the Social Exclusion Unit*. London: Office of the Deputy Prime Minister.

Southern, R. (1999) Improving Resettlement for Mentally Disordered Offenders. *Probation Journal* 46(3), 187–91.

Spalek, B. (2003) Victim work in the Probation Service: Perpetuary notions of an 'ideal victim'. In Chui, W.H. & M. Nellis (2003) *Moving Probation Forward: Evidence, Arguments and Practice*. London: Pearson.

Steadman, H.J., Monahan, J. & Robbins, P. et al. (1993) From dangerousness to risk assessment: Implications for appropriate research strategies. In S. Hodgins (ed.), *Crime and Mental Disorder*. Newbury Park, CA: Sage.

Stewart, L., Hill, J., Gorman, T. & Graham, I.J. (1999) *High Intensity Family Violence Prevention Programme*. Correctional Services of Canada.

Stubley, A. (2003) Integrated Domestic Abuse Programme Theory manual draft 1. Unpublished.

Sutton, J. (1999) *Healing the Hurt Within*. London: How To Books.

Svanberg, P.O. et al. (1996) Protocols for the court diversion service for Wearside. Internal NHS Trust paper. Sunderland: Priority Healthcare Wearside.

Taylor, R. (1999) *Predicting Reconvictions for Sexual and Violent Offences Using the Revised Offender Group Reconviction Scale*. Home Office Research Findings, 104. London: Home Office.

Thomas, M. & Jackson, S. (2003) Cognitive skills groupwork. In G.J. Towl (ed.), *Psychology in Prisons*. Oxford: BPS Blackwell.

Thornton, D. (2002) Constructing and testing a framework for dynamic risk assessment. *Sexual Abuse: A Journal of Research and Treatment* 14, 137–51.

Thornton, D., Mann, R.E., Webster, S.D., Blud, L., Travers, R., Friendship, C. & Erikson, M. (2002) Distinguishing and combining risk of sexual and violent recidivism. *Proceedings of the New York Academy of Sciences.*

Towl, G.J. (2000) Forensic psychology in prisons and probation: Working towards an effective partnership. *Prison Service Journal* 131, 32–3.

Towl, G.J. (2002) Working with offenders: The ins and outs. *Psychologist* 15(5), 236–9.

Towl, G.J. (ed.) (2003a) *Psychology in Prisons.* Oxford: BPS Blackwell.

Towl, G. (2003b) Suicide in prisons. *British Journal of Forensic Practice* 5(3), 28–32.

Towl, G.J. (2004) Psychological services in prisons and probation. In A. Needs & G.J. Towl (eds), *Handbook of Forensic Psychology.* Oxford: BPS Blackwell.

Towl, G.J. & Crighton, D.A. (1996) *The Handbook of Psychology for Forensic Practitioners.* Routledge: London.

Towl, G.J. & Crighton, D.A. (1997) Risk assessment with offenders. *International Review of Psychiatry* 9, 187–93.

Towl, G.J. & Crighton, D.A. (1998) Suicide in prisons in England and Wales from 1988–1995. *Criminal Behaviour and Mental Health* 8, 184–92.

Towl, G.J. & Crighton, D.A. (2000) Risk assessment. In G.J. Towl, L. Snow & M. McHugh (eds), *Suicide in Prisons.* Oxford: BPS Blackwell.

Towl, G.J., & Crighton, D.A. (2002) Risk assessment and management. In G.J. Towl, L. Snow & M. McHugh (eds), *Suicide in Prisons.* Oxford: BPS Blackwell.

Towl, G.J. & Hudson, D. (1997) Risk assessment and the management of the suicidal, in Suicide and Self-Injury in Prisons. *Issues in Criminological and Legal Psychology,* 28.

Towl, G.J. & McDougall, C. (1999) *What Do Forensic Psychologists Do? New Directions in Prison and Probation Services, Issues in Forensic Psychology.* Leicester: BPS.

Towl, G.J., McHugh M.J. & Jones, D. (eds) (1999) *Suicide in Prisons: Research Policy and Practice.* Brighton: Pavilion.

Towl, G.J., Snow, L. & McHugh, M.J. (eds) (2000) *Suicide in Prisons.* Oxford: BPS Blackwell.

Vaughan, P.J. & Badger, D. (1995) *Working with the Mentally Disordered Offender in the Community.* London: Chapman & Hall.

Walby, S. & Myhill, A. (2000) *Reducing Domestic Violence . . . What Works? Assessing and Managing the Risk of Domestic Violence. Crime Reduction Research Series.* London: Home Office.

Wald, M.S. & Woolverton, M. (1990) Risk assessment: The Emperor's new clothes? *Child Welfare* 69(6), 483–511.

Waltz, J., Babcock, J.C., Jacobsen, N.S. & Gottman, J.M. (2000) Testing a typology of barterers. *Journal of Consulting and Clinical Psychology* 68(4), 658–99.

Wargent, M. (2002) The New Governance of Probation. *Howard Journal of Criminal Justice* 41, 182–200.

Webster, C.D., Douglas, K.S., Eaves, D. & Hart, S.D. (1997) *The HCR-20: Assessing Risk for Violence: Version 2.* Burnaby, BC: Mental Health, Law and Policy Institute, Simon Fraser University.

Welldon, E.V. (1994) Forensic psychotherapy. In P. Clarkson & A. Pokorny (eds), *The Handbook of Psychotherapy.* London: Tavistock.

Wertheimer, A. (1991) *A Special Scar: The Experience of People Bereaved by Suicide.* London: Routledge.

Whitfield, D. (2001) *Introduction to the Probation Service* (2nd edn). Winchester: Waterside Press.

Wilmott, P. (2002a) Forensic psychology in the National Probation Service. *Forensic Update*, 68, 6–9.

Wilmott, P. (2002b) Life sentence prisoners. In G.J. Towl (ed.), *Psychology in Prisons.* London: Blackwell.

Wilson, C.M. (2003) Circles of support and accountability in the Thames Valley: Questions and answers. *Nota News*, 45.

Wolf, S.C. (1984) A multi-factorial model of deviant sexuality. Paper presented at Third International Conference on Victimology, Lisbon.

Yalom, I.D. (1995) *The Theory and Practice of Group Psychotherapy* (4th edn). New York: Basic Books.

Index

community services, 12
  see also probation services
corporal punishment, as penal sanction,
    vii
corrective training (CT), vii
counselling psychology, xiii, 3, 11,
    23–39
  in HM Prison Service and NPS, 37–8,
    90
  in support of forensic and other staff,
    35, 135, 137, 153–4, 164
  training courses, 38
  see also forensic psychotherapy
Court Duty Officers (CDOs), 15
courts, criminal and civil, 7, 14–22
  bail information, 16–17
  and probation services, 7–8, 14–19,
    159, 162, 163
  sentencing, 8, 16: non-custodial, 8
  and youth, 17
  see also Crown Courts, system of
crime and criminal behaviour
  fear of, 9
  reduction of, 9, 12, 19, 21
  see also criminal justice system;
    reoffending
Crime and Disorder Act 1998, 159
Crime (Sentences) Act 1997, 139, 140
Criminal Justice Acts
  1948, vii
  1991, 53
  2003, 105, 141
Criminal Justice and Court Services Act
    (CJCS Act) 2000, 14, 34, 35, 39n1,
    97, 104, 106
Criminal Justice Boards, 16
Criminal Justice system, 7–8, 8–9, 112,
    138, 139, 163
  government aims for, 8–9
  government reports on, 9
  and mental health provision, 24:
    see also mentally disordered
    offenders
  see also courts, criminal and civil

Crown Courts, system of, vii, 162
Crown Prosecution Service, 121, 162

Derbyshire NPS area, 161
dialectical behavioural therapy, 29
discrimination, 58
  against the mentally ill, 23, 26–7,
    29
  racial, 31, 58
domestic violence, 8, 85, 106, 111,
    112, 115–37
  community approaches to combating,
    120
  as crime, 118–19
  Duluth model/approach, 120–1, 134
  gender breakdown, 117, 121
  interventions, 118, 120
  probation response, 118–19
  research into, 117, 121–2, 135
  victims of, 124, 126, 127, 131
  see also Integrated Domestic Abuse
    Programme (IDAP)
drink driving, 8, 86, 87, 97
  see also substance abuse
'Driving Delivery', 10
drug abuse, 6, 29, 59, 60, 159, 160
Drug Treatment and Testing Orders
    (DTTOs), 15, 18, 160
Duluth, Minnesota (USA), 120
  Domestic Abuse Intervention Project
    (DAIP), 120
  Duluth model/approach, 85, 120–1,
    134
  see also Integrated Domestic Abuse
    Programme (IDAP)

educational psychologists, 12
effective service delivery, 5, 6, 10, 24,
    38, 114, 116, 156, 167
Employment Training and Education
    (ETE) service, 12
Enhanced Community Punishment
    Scheme (ECPS), 95, 101
ethnic minorities, 30, 58, 94